SEASONAL GUIDE TO THE NATURAL YEAR

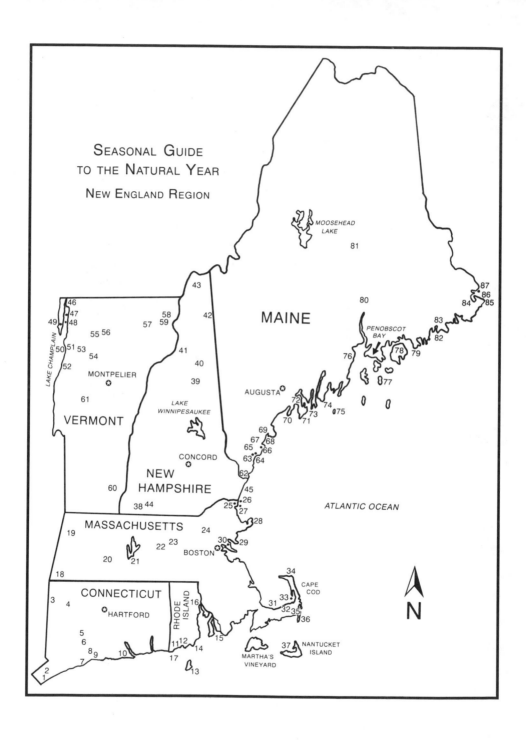

SEASONAL GUIDE
TO THE NATURAL YEAR

NEW ENGLAND REGION

MOOSEHEAD
LAKE

81

MAINE

PENOBSCOT
BAY

LAKE CHAMPLAIN

MONTPELIER

VERMONT

LAKE
WINNIPESAUKEE

AUGUSTA

CONCORD

NEW
HAMPSHIRE

ATLANTIC OCEAN

MASSACHUSETTS

BOSTON

CAPE
COD

CONNECTICUT

RHODE ISLAND

HARTFORD

N

NANTUCKET
ISLAND

MARTHA'S
VINEYARD

LIST OF SITES BY STATE
New England

Abbreviations: NP—National Park; NWR—National Wildlife Refuge; SP—State Park; SR—State Reservation; WMA—Wildlife Management Area; WR—Wildlife Refuge; WS—Wildlife Sanctuary

CONNECTICUT
1. Sherwood Island SP
2. Quaker Ridge
3. Northeast Audubon Center
4. Black Spruce Bog
5. Shepaug Dam
6. Lower Connecticut River
7. Milford Point
8. East Rock Park
9. Lighthouse Point Park
10. Hammonasset Beach SP

RHODE ISLAND
11. Charlestown Beach/ Quonochontaug
12. Trustom Pond NWR
13. Block Island
14. Point Judith
15. Sachuest Point NWR
16. Swan Point Cemetery
17. Napatree Point

MASSACHUSETTS
18. Bartholomew's Cobble
19. Berkshires Foliage Area
20. Mt. Tom SR
21. Quabbin Reservoir
22. Wachusetts Meadow WS
23. Wachusetts Mountain SR
24. Great Meadows NWR
25. Newburyport
26. Salisbury Beach SP
27. Parker River NWR/Plum Island
28. Cape Ann
29. Marblehead Neck WS
30. Mt. Auburn Cemtery
31. Sandy Neck Beach
32. Stony Brook
33. First Encounter Beach
34. Race Point
35. Chatham
36. Monomoy NWR
37. Nantucket Island ferry

NEW HAMPSHIRE
38. Rhododendron SP
39. Kancamagus Highway
40. Mt. Washington
41. Pondicherry WR
42. Lake Umbagog NWR
43. Upper Connecticut River
44. Pack Monadnock Mountain
45. Isles of Shoals

VERMONT
46. Missiquoi NWR
47. Kill Kare SP
48. Popasquash Island
49. Grand Isle/North Hero
50. Shelburne Bay
51. Mt. Philo SP
52. Dead Creek WMA
53. Green Mountain Audubon Center
54. Camel's Hump
55. Smuggler's Notch
56. Mt. Mansfield
57. Mt. Pisgah/Willoughby Cliffs
58. Yellow Bogs
59. Moose Bog/ Wenlock WMA
60. Jamaica SP
61. Robert Frost Nature Trail

MAINE
62. Mt. Agamenticus
63. Wells Harbor
64. Rachel Carson NWR
65. Kennebunk Plains
66. Biddeford Pool
67. Saco Heath Preserve
68. Scarborough Beach SP
69. Scarboro River marshes
70. Bailey Island
71. Popham Beach SP
72. Bald Head Preserve
73. Reid Beach SP
74. Rachel Carson Salt Marsh Preserve
75. Monhegan Island
76. Knight's Pond
77. Isle au Haut
78. Mt. Desert Island/Acadia NP
79. Schoodic Point
80. Caribou Bog
81. Baxter SP
82. Great Wass Island
83. Great Heath
84. Moosehorn NWR
85. Quoddy Head SP
86. South Lubec Flats
87. Eastport

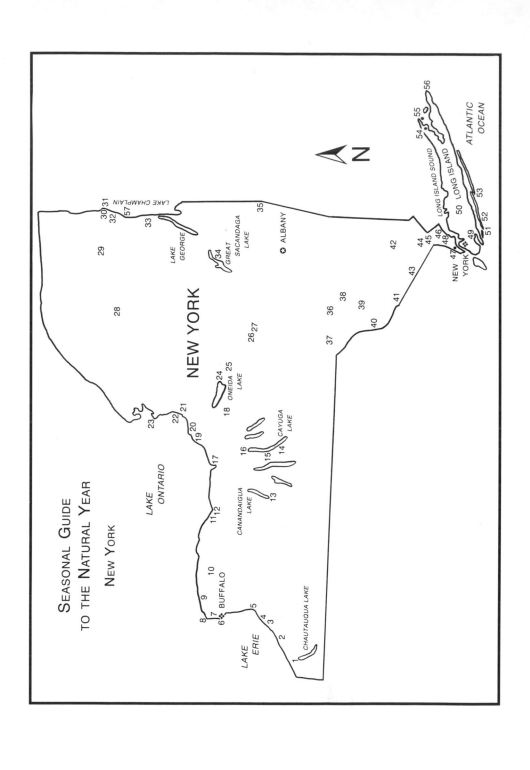

SEASONAL GUIDE
TO THE NATURAL YEAR

NEW YORK

NEW YORK

ALBANY

LAKE ONTARIO

LAKE ERIE

BUFFALO

CHAUTAUQUA LAKE

CANANDAIGUA LAKE

CAYUGA LAKE

ONEIDA LAKE

LAKE GEORGE

LAKE CHAMPLAIN

GREAT SACANDAGA LAKE

LONG ISLAND SOUND

LONG ISLAND

ATLANTIC OCEAN

N

1 2 3 4 5 6 7 8 9 10 11 12 13 14 15 16 17 18 19 20 21 22 23 24 25 26 27 28 29 30 31 32 33 34 35 36 37 38 39 40 41 42 43 44 45 46 47 48 49 50 51 52 53 54 55 56 57

LIST OF SITES
New York

Abbreviations: NWR—Natural Wildlife Refuge; NS—National Seashore; SP—State Park; WR—Wildlife Refuge

1. Chautauqua Lake
2. Dunkirk Harbor
3. Irving hawkwatch
4. Cattaraugus Creek
5. Pinehurst hawkwatch
6. Niagara River
7. Lewiston
8. Old Fort Niagara
9. Keg Creek
10. Iroquois NWR
11. Braddock Bay SP
12. Durand Eastman Park
13. Canandaigua Lake
14. Taughannock Falls SP
15. Cayuga Lake
16. Montezuma NWR
17. Sodus Bay hawkwatch
18. Syracuse cemeteries
19. Oswego Harbor
20. Derby Hill Bird Observatory
21. Salmon River and fish hatchery
22. Sandy Pond
23. Little Galloo Island
24. Sylvan Beach
25. Oneida Hill
26. Franklin Mountain
27. Emmons Bog Preserve
28. Stillwater Reservoir
29. Adirondacks High Peaks region
30. Willsboro Point
31. Four Brothers Islands
32. Whallon Bay
33. Mt. Defiance
34. Great Sacandaga Lake
35. Petersburg Pass Scenic Area
36. Pepacton Reservoir
37. Cannonsville Reservoir
38. Rondout Reservoir
39. Mongaup River reservoirs
40. Upper Delaware River
41. I-84 (Port Jervis) hawkwatch
42. Constitution Island Marsh Sanctuary
43. Mt. Peter
44. Hook Mountain
45. Tappan Zee Bridge
46. Pelham Bay Park
47. Central Park
48. N.Y. Botanical Garden Forest
49. Jamaica Bay WR
50. Oak Brush Plains Preserve
51. Jones Inlet
52. Jones Beach/Short Beach Coast Guard Station/Zach's Bay
53. Fire Island NS/Captree Island SP
54. Cedar Beach Point/Nassau Point
55. Orient Beach SP
56. Montauk Point SP
57. Crown Point

Northern hawk-owls are among the rarest of the Arctic wanderers to the Northeast, showing up in the region only sporadically—and creating a lot of excitement among naturalists when they do.

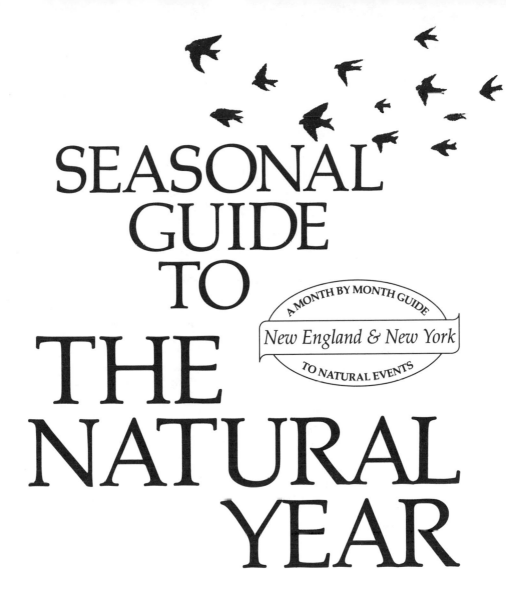

SEASONAL
GUIDE
TO
THE

A MONTH BY MONTH GUIDE

New England & New York

TO NATURAL EVENTS

NATURAL
YEAR

Scott Weidensaul

FULCRUM PUBLISHING
Golden, Colorado

Library of Congress Cataloging-in-Publication Data

Weidensaul, Scott.
    Seasonal guide to the natural year : a month by month guide to natural events, New England and New York / Scott Weidensaul.
        p.   cm.
    Includes bibliographical references (p.   ) and index.
    ISBN 1-55591-135-8
    1. Natural history—New England—Guidebooks. 2. Natural history—New York (State)—Guidebooks. 3. Seasons—New England—Guidebooks. 4. Seasons—New York (State)—Guidebooks. 5. Ecotourism—New England—Guidebooks. 6. Ecotourism—New York (State)—Guidebooks. I. Title.
    QH104.5.N4W44   1993
    508.74--dc20   93-5235
                                                                CIP

Book design and original illustrations
by Paulette Livers Lambert
Photographs and maps by Scott Weidensaul

Printed in the United States of America

0 9 8 7 6 5 4 3 2

Fulcrum Publishing
350 Indiana Street, Suite 350
Golden, Colorado 80401-5093

For the folks.

Bloodroot, named for the crimson juice contained in its rootstock, is among the earliest bloomers in the spring woods.

CONTENTS

List of Maps

ACKNOWLEDGMENTS

Many people contributed their help, ideas, suggestions, guiding services, criticisms and enthusiasm during the production of this book, and it would be impossible to mention all of them. Some, however, merit special consideration.

They include Rick Marsi, sage of the upper Susquehanna; Artie Morris, for much guidance on the New York City-Long Island region; Sheila Buff, a one-woman cheering section; Kyle Stockwell with the Maine chapter of the Nature Conservancy and David Gumbart with the Connecticut chapter; Inez Conner in the U.S. Fish and Wildlife Service's Boston office; Baxter State Park ranger Jonathan Milne; ranger-naturalist Daniel Pettit at Camel's Hump, Vermont; Charlie Conley at DeLorme Mapping Co., whose atlases kept me on track despite myself; Sue Halc and Jeff Schwartz at Antioch New England Graduate School, and Owen D. Winters at the Natural Science for Youth Foundation, for permission to reproduce their nature center listings; Bruce H. Schneck for help on the Salmon River; Ron Milliken and Chris Vredenburg at Franklin Mountain; and the anonymous, bird-watching mail carrier near Canandaigua Lake who told me where to look for ducks. When you're lost, always ask a mail carrier first.

The staffs of the many national wildlife refuges in the region, which figure so prominently in this book, were always helpful, especially Don V. Tiller at Iroquois National Wildlife Refuge; Grady Hocutt at Montezuma; Ed Moses at Great Meadows;

Douglas Mullen at Moosehorn; David Houghton at Rachel Carson; and Steve Haydock at Ninigret.

Thanks, as always, to Bob Baron, Carmel Huestis and the wonderful staff at Fulcrum for their dedication to this series.

Finally, a special thank you to Rick and Sandy Imes and their family. Rick, one of the most skilled naturalists I know, was unfailingly generous in sharing his knowledge of New England, and the Imes' home was a welcome haven on many a journey while researching this book.

INTRODUCTION

Every year in mid-September, when the first hint of autumn is putting a spark in the air and the sky is painted with cumulus clouds, people gather on high hilltops, looking north.

They are watching for hawks traveling south along the ridges of New England and New York. As the sun warms the land and pockets of air begin to billow up invisibly, the rising currents carry the hawks with them, singly at first, then by dozens, sometimes by hundreds or thousands. At times the stream becomes a flood, and the sky spills over with hawks. They swarm in dense flocks, boiling inside the rising thermals, then gliding on locked wings when the lift falters, drifting in sheets across the sky to the next column of warm, buoyant air.

The numbers can be nothing short of breathtaking. In one day, at one place in Connecticut, hawk-watchers have counted more than thirty thousand hawks, a glimpse of the stunning migration that will take these birds all the way to South America.

In nature, timing is everything—the timing of the seasons, of courtship, of migration, of birth. Even though wild animals and plants cannot read the calendar, they respond to the changing length of daylight throughout the year. Coupled with other, subtle clues we do not fully understand, this signal allows nature to progress at a pace, and with a precision, that surprises many people when they first discover it.

Naturalists take great pleasure in knowing and anticipating these predictable changes in the natural year, for they provide benchmarks in our own less-than-predictable lives. It's comforting to know that no matter what else happens in the world, come October the maples will still glow orange in the evening light.

Seasonal Guide to the Natural Year: New England & New York is the second volume in a series of guidebooks with a difference—instead of a listing of natural places, it is a guide to natural events, a when-to-go rather than a where-to-go approach, with the emphasis on timing rather than geography. Built on a seasonal theme, the book is divided into twelve monthly sections, each covering at least four wild spectacles of unusual interest. What's more, each chapter gives detailed directions to hotspots of exceptional quality or easy access, with maps, tips on what to look for and how best to enjoy the experience, and background on the natural history of the spectacle. Breakout chapters in each section provide an in-depth look at one of the month's more unusual features, and a shorttakes section gives quick snapshots of other monthly happenings.

The book covers New York and the six New England states— Connecticut, Rhode Island, Massachusetts, Vermont, New Hampshire and Maine. In many ways these seven states form a cohesive natural unit; although New York is often lumped culturally with the mid-Atlantic states, most of its northern tier has more in common with the forests of New England than with those in Pennsylvania. Taken as a whole, the Northeast is a huge region, covering nearly 116,000 square miles, with an amazing diversity of habitats and topography. The mountains alone make it a fascinating place to explore. The Appalachians snake up its middle, raising the Palisades of New York, the Berkshires of Massachusetts, the lofty Green Mountains in Vermont and the White Mountains in New Hampshire, and gnarled old Mt. Katahdin in Maine. The Adirondacks, scoured by glaciers and protected by law, sit on the western edge of the great Lake Champlain valley, while thousands of lakes, ponds and bogs, most also the work of the ice sheets, pock the region.

Along the coast, the inquisitive naturalist can find oak and pine barrens on Long Island, sand plains grasslands in Maine, life-rich tidal pools along the rocky New England shore—even tidal marshes nearly 100 miles from the sea. Inland, there are lakes that turn golden with wild lotuses, quaking bogs where plants eat insects and visitors walk gingerly on water, and streams that fill with salmon. It is a feast for anyone with a passion for wild things and wild places, and I hope this book encourages you to experience it for yourself.

GENERAL TIPS, SUGGESTIONS AND CAUTIONS

The overwhelming majority of the places listed in this volume are on public land or private property that is routinely opened to public access. In a few instances, auto routes running through private land are given, and in many cases public land and private property abut within the same bog or forest. Obey all "No Trespassing" signs, and treat local landowners with unfailing courtesy and consideration; this is especially important at popular destinations or unusual times of day.

While this book contains maps of some routes and places, it is always a good idea to have several detailed maps of the area you are planning to visit. State highway or travel club maps are fine for major roads, but they leave too much uncovered for back road (or backcountry) travel. The most detailed maps available are the U.S. Geologic Survey (USGS) topographic maps; they come in several scales, the most commonly used being 7.5-minute quadrangles, which cover an area of about 6.5 by 7.5 miles. Their drawbacks are high cost, especially if you need information about a large area, the hassle of handling many big maps in the car or field and a lack of road names. A valuable alternative is the state atlases published by DeLorme Mapping Co; instead of the USGS scale of 1:24,000, the DeLorme atlas maps use a more manageable scale of 1:150,000, and include topographic and forest cover information, all main roads and important dirt roads (often with names for the smaller tracks), as well as many trails. At this writing, atlases are available for Maine, Vermont, New Hampshire and New York. Addresses for the USGS and DeLorme are listed in the Appendix.

You'll do well to remember that, as consistent as these many spectacles are, there is always an inherent unpredictability in nature that must be accepted. Because of weather, a usually lush stand of wildflowers may be paltry; schools of forage fish may shift their offshore summering grounds, taking the great whales and pelagic seabirds with them.

Sometimes changes occur for no apparent reason. During the 1970s and early 1980s, birders in late summer could count on flocks of red-necked phalaropes numbering up to 2 million in Passamaquoddy Bay near Lubec, Maine, but those totals fell dramatically through the late 1980s, so that by 1988 only two hundred phalaropes showed up at their traditional staging grounds. No one is sure if their disappearance is linked to a crash in the local plankton supply, or if it is part of a normal cycle for the phalaropes.

Finally, just as important as courtesy to landowners is respect for the natural spectacles this book celebrates. Wild animals and plants are not a sideshow staged for human benefit; they have their own lives, needs and purposes, an existence quite separate from ours. Human intervention can be damaging, sometimes dangerously so—thoughtless intrusion can keep nesting birds from their chicks, spook flocks from critically needed food or rest, or trample young wildflowers under foot. Stay on trails and obey all signs restricting access at refuges or parks, for such regulations are rarely imposed capriciously. Remember that the best observers have no discernible effect on that which they are watching.

Common sense is even more valuable than a map or guidebook. Be aware that hunting is permitted on almost all wildlife management areas, as well as portions of some state parks and most national wildlife refuges. Before visiting in autumn and winter, find out if hunting is permitted in the area where you plan to be; blaze orange is never a bad idea.

Canoes are invaluable for exploring many of the hotspots. Wear personal flotation devices even if you are a strong swimmer, and learn the basics of canoe handling before setting out on a wild stream or river.

High-altitude hiking: A number of the hotspots listed in this book are peaks well over 4,000 feet in elevation, and while they are within the range of most reasonably fit hikers, a number of special concerns must be addressed.

Weather can change suddenly and with virtually no warn- ing in the mountains, turning what might be a mild summer day into a life-threatening situation. Never hike at high altitudes without being prepared for the worst, and do not hike alone. Be sure to carry extra clothing (preferably wool) and quality rain gear, even if the forecast is for blue skies. Have a good trail map, compass (and practice ahead of time in using it), extra food and water beyond your needs for the day, waterproof matches, a basic first-aid kit and a good flashlight with fresh batteries. Be certain someone knows where you're going and when you'll be back, and if trail registers are provided, do not fail to sign in and out.

A REQUEST FOR HELP

The directions contained in this book are the result of laborious fieldwork. In the time between research and publica- tion, however, things change—roads are switched, bridges are replaced, landmarks removed. Inevitably, readers will find conditions in some places at variance with those described here. To keep future editions as accurate and current as possible, readers are encouraged to send corrections to the author, c/o Fulcrum Publishing, 350 Indiana Street, Suite 350, Golden, CO 80401-5093.

The dozens of wild spectacles that follow are only the tip of the iceberg, because New England and New York are endlessly varied places. If you have suggestions for spectacles that you would like considered for future editions of *Seasonal Guide to the Natural Year*, please send them (with directions and as much background information as possible) to the address listed previously. Bear in mind that the spectacles should be consistent from year to year, be of unusual interest or exceptional quality, and occur on public lands or private land open to the public.

Abbreviations commonly used in the text:

NF   National forest
NP   National park
NRA   National recreation area
NS   National seashore
NWR   National wildlife refuge
SP   State park
SR   State reservation
WMA   Wildlife management area
WS   Wildlife sanctuary

JANUARY

January Observations

1

Snowy Owls

Yellow eyes blinking slowly against the rising sun, a snowy owl surveys the barren sweep of a winter beach from its perch atop a blown-out dune. The January wind carries a skiff of blowing sand along the ground, making the whole dune hiss, but the owl ignores the sound, intently watching for movement.

Dark against the sand, a rat makes a fatal mistake, exposing itself for an instant as its scurries through the dune grass and wind-stunted shrubs. The owl is instantly airborne on huge black-barred wings, skimming just above the ground; the rat realizes its peril a moment too late, as the owl rounds a corner in the low bushes and pounces, feet forward, for the kill.

For many naturalists, the sight of a snowy owl is one of winter's ultimate trophies, and the Northeast region is fortunate to consistently attract a fair number of these Arctic predators each winter. But snowy owls are by no means common, even here, and it takes patient searching—not to mention good luck—to find one.

Snowies are natives of the Arctic coastal plain in both the Western and Eastern hemispheres; in North America they are found from Labrador and the Arctic islands to Alaska, and south to Hudson Bay. They are superbly fitted for life in extreme cold, with thick feathering right down to the toes and nearly concealing the beak.

A snowy owl is all but unmistakable; only the smaller, pale barn owl (rare in the Northeast) looks similar, and barn owls are almost never seen abroad in daylight, perched in the open. Adult snowy owls are nearly 2 feet from head to tail, and at 4.5 pounds are the heaviest owls in North America. The round head, yellow eyes and white plumage are diagnostic, although each bird displays a varying degree of dark barring—heaviest on juveniles and females, and sometimes completely absent on mature males.

Most snowy owls never leave their home ranges, tolerating the perpetual darkness of the Arctic winter and the constant daylight of the brief summers. Each winter, however, a few snowies—mostly immatures—head south in what cannot be described as a migration, but rather an aimless wandering; population pressures and food shortages probably account for the movement. Every few years larger numbers of snowy owls irrupt south, most likely as a result of a bust in the population cycle of lemmings, their major food.

Striking south from the tundra, the owls encounter the vast boreal spruce forest of Canada and the equally inhospitable mixed woodlands of New England and New York. They look instead for landscapes reminiscent of home—open horizons, few trees and lots of rodents. Most often they fetch up for the winter on open farmland, large airports and the Atlantic or Great Lakes beaches.

Snowy owls can seem almost comically tame at times, sitting in broad daylight on top of a television antenna, or perching placidly on a taxiway light as a 747 rumbles past. This lack of fear has, in the past, brought many snowies low from illegal shootings, but a growing concern is the thoughtless behavior of some birders and photographers. Even a "tame" bird can be harassed by too much (or too close) attention, and a snowy owl that spends more time and calories avoiding humans than it does hunting will probably not survive the winter. Keep your distance, and leave the owl in peace.

HOTSPOTS

Snowy owls are found most often in New England and New York along the Atlantic coast, but one inland spot—the flat fields of the **Champlain Valley**—attracts several virtually every winter.

The Champlain Valley is strikingly incongruous, a pancake-flat slice of land wedged between the Adirondacks to the west and the Green Mountains to the east. Unlike in the rest of Vermont, farmers here do not have to work around the capricious contours of the land, but can lay out their fields and pastures in wide stretches neatly stitched with lines of fencing. In winter it is bitterly cold despite the nearby lake, a windswept area of low horizons ideal for snowy owls.

For an owl-seeker, the centerpiece of the Champlain Valley is **Dead Creek WMA** in Vermont, well-known for its waterfowl in spring and fall, but perhaps the best place for snowy owls in all of inland New England. One of them may turn up anywhere— sitting on a wooden fencepost beside Route 17, ignoring the traffic whizzing past, perched stoically on a frozen lump of earth in the middle of a barren, plowed field, or waiting for dusk on the roof of a barn.

A network of paved and dirt roads provides excellent access to Dead Creek and the surrounding farmland. Start at the intersection of Routes 22A and 17 at Addison, proceeding west on 17. Within half a mile, the road begins to pass through large, open fields frequented by snowy owls; watch fences, the tops of utility poles and on the ground for suspicious blobs of white (and remember that some snowies are so heavily barred they appear gray at a distance). Be careful pulling over to look, because the road shoulders here are narrow; it's better to pull into the first small management area parking lot on the right, which provides views of frozen ponds and isolated oaks.

From the lot, continue west on 17 for 1.5 miles, bearing right on Jersey Street North at the "Welcome to West Addison" sign. Go 1.2 miles and turn right at the unmarked T-intersection, then drive another 2.2 miles and turn right into the dirt road leading to Farrell Access Area, a drive of 2.1 miles through excellent owl and hawk habitat.

Return to Jersey Street and turn right; go 2.1 miles, stopping at the intersection with Pease Road, then go straight another .5 mile to Panton Corners; here the road curves right. Follow it 1.1 miles to the bridge across Dead Creek, then turn right onto the small dirt road .3 mile on the other side. Go 1.4 miles, turn right at the T-intersection and drive another .8 mile to the Stone Bridge Access Area, where the road dead-ends at the lake. Retrace your steps to the T-intersection but go straight through this time, driving 1.5 miles to Route 22A.

Turn right onto 22A South, returning to Addison. This time continue south on 22A another 2 miles, then turn right onto Nortontown Road, a dirt lane. Follow this 4.1 miles, twice crossing fingers of Dead Creek Lake before intersecting Jersey Street. Turn left on Jersey, go 2.3 miles and turn right on Town Line Road (unmarked), then drive 1 mile to Route 125. Turn right, go 1.9 miles along the shore of Lake Champlain, then turn right onto Route 17 East to return to Addison.

On the New York side of Lake Champlain, the flat farmland spreading on either side of Route 9N/22 between **Port Henry** and **Willsboro** is also worth searching for snowy owls.

Back in Vermont, the **Champlain lakeshore** in Burlington has a reputation for producing snowies. The area around the ferry dock at the end of Maple Street is the best place to look, although the owls may be almost anywhere along the shore.

Coastal locations for snowy owls are numerous, although none can guarantee a visiting birder the sight of an owl; these huge hunters are too unpredictable for that. Among the most consistent are **Plum Island** and **Parker River NWR** in Massachusetts (see Chapter 2 for directions); and **Sachuest Point NWR** in Rhode Island (Chapter 10).

Most winters a number of snowy owls show up at **Logan International Airport,** although not always in parts of the airport where the general public can see them. Check periodically with the Boston rare bird hotline, listed in the Appendix, for updates on snowy owls.

On Long Island, one or two snowy owls can be found most years by searching the dunes at the west end of Jones Beach on Long Island's south shore; follow the Meadowbrook State Parkway south to **Jones Beach State Park.** An intriguing possibility in the same area are "Ipswich" sparrows, the big, pale subspecies of savannah sparrow that breeds only on Sable Island in Nova Scotia and is a rare wintering bird along the Northeast coast.

Other eastern Long Island snowy owl locations include **Jamaica Bay WR** and the Breezy Point unit of **Gateway NRA** (which forms the southern edge of Rockaway Inlet). See Chapter 43 for directions. On the island's North Fork watch for owls between Little Hog Neck and Orient Point (see Chapter 3) and the area around Montauk Point on the South Fork (also Chapter 3).

Along New York's Lake Ontario coast, snowies show up with regularity at **Braddock Bay State Park** (Chapter 13) and **Oswego Harbor**—the latter is also an excellent place for gulls and winter ducks. To reach **Oswego Harbor** take Route 104 West from I-81 to the city of Oswego. Shortly before crossing the Oswego River, turn off Route 104/East Bridge Street onto East Second Street and follow it to the overlook at Old Fort Ontario.

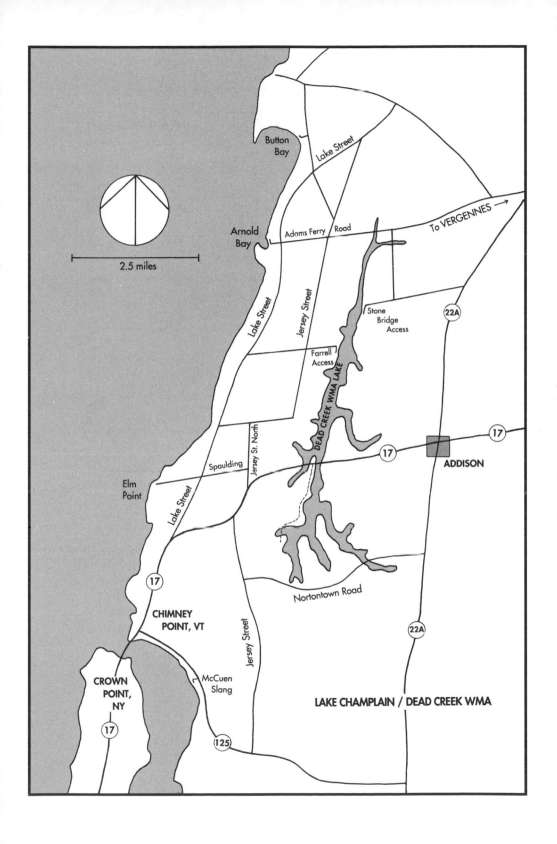

Button
Bay

Lake Street

To VERGENNES →

Arnold
Bay

Adams Ferry Road

Lake Street

Jersey Street

Stone
Bridge
Access

22A

Farrell
Access

DEAD CREEK WMA LAKE

Spaulding

Jersey St. North

17

17

ADDISON

Elm
Point

Lake Street

2.5 miles

17

Nortontown Road

22A

CHIMNEY
POINT, VT

Jersey Street

CROWN
POINT,
NY

McCuen
Slang

LAKE CHAMPLAIN / DEAD CREEK WMA

17

125

2

Rare and Unusual Gulls

It's hard to go far along the Northeast coast without seeing or hearing gulls. They are so common, so ubiquitous, that for most people "seagulls" fade to become part of the background.

Pity. Gulls (there are nearly two dozen species in North America) are among the most fascinating of birds—intelligent, social and easy to observe. Best of all, from a winter-weary naturalist's perspective, they provide interest at a time when little else is moving.

Both along the Atlantic and at such inland points as lakes Champlain, Ontario and Erie, gulls create consistent spectacles each winter. At the mouth of the Niagara River and on Long Island, the attraction is thousands of graceful Bonaparte's gulls; on Cape Ann and near Newburyport in Massachusetts, birders comb through flocks of more common species for rarities that turn up there year after year.

Naturalists in the Northeast may reasonably hope to find as many as ten species of gulls in the winter, with a few others as tantalizing possibilities. The most common are the herring, ring-billed, Bonaparte's and great black-backed gulls, the last largely restricted to salt water.

In large numbers, even the commonest species can be dramatic to watch, but most birders enjoy hunting for rare gulls in the multitudes of ring-bills and Bonaparte's. High on their list are the so-called "white-winged" gulls, a generic term for several large, pale species including the glaucous, Iceland and Thayer's gulls.

The tern-like Bonaparte's gull masses by the thousands at a number of regional locations each winter, including Dunkirk Harbor on Lake Erie, New York.

These three are Arctic nesters, dropping south only in winter. (Thayer's gull normally migrates to the West Coast, but has a penchant for wandering, and is regularly encountered in New England and New York.)

Because gulls are strong fliers, it should be no surprise that several European species have managed to cross the Atlantic, probably by way of Iceland and Greenland, and have colonized eastern Canada and the United States. Perhaps the most widespread of these recent immigrants is the lesser black-backed gull, found coastally (and at a growing number of inland locations) throughout the region. Only two-thirds the size of the native great black-backed, the adult lesser has a paler mantle (as the back and upper wing surface are known) and yellow legs rather than pink; immatures can closely resemble young herring gulls. Other European gulls that can be counted on each winter in the region include the common black-headed gull and little gull, both of which are, like the lesser black-backed, now breeding in small numbers in North America.

HOTSPOTS

The name **Newburyport, Massachusetts,** became branded in the minds of bird enthusiasts in 1975, when a small group of birders looked over a bunch of gulls sitting on the seawall in downtown Newburyport and noticed that one was too pink to be a Bonaparte's gull. The oddity turned out to be a Ross' gull, a delicate little Arctic species never before seen in the Lower 48, and its discovery set off a stampede to Newburyport by thousands of bird-watchers hoping to add it to their North American lists.

While a visitor isn't guaranteed a sighting as earthshaking as a Ross' gull (although a few more have been sighted since 1975 in Massachusetts), the Newburyport area always has something interesting to offer. Take Route 1 North to Newburyport; exit just before crossing the Merrimack River bridge and follow Water Street east (signs for "Downtown Newburyport"). Water Street skirts the south edge of the harbor, and there a number of good pull-offs and parking areas with views of the seawall (where many gulls roost) and the water. In particular try the parking area for shops and restaurants .1 mile from Route 1; the Newburyport Redevelopment Authority lot .2 mile beyond that; and the lot by the seawall another .7 mile down Water Street.

East of town along the Plum Island Turnpike, pull into the Sportsman's Lodge lot, then drive east another 1.8 miles and turn right onto Sunset Drive to **Parker River NWR** and **Plum Island Beach State Reservation**—good for gulls and other winter birds, including waterfowl and northern raptors.

For a weekend trip, combine a visit to Newburyport with a stop on **Cape Ann** just to the south. See Chapter 9 for directions; gull enthusiasts should pay particular attention to Niles Pond on Eastern Point.

Inland, noteworthy flocks of Bonaparte's gulls (along with ring-billed gulls and assorted rarities) can be found along the **Niagara River** linking Lake Erie and Lake Ontario. Hotspots include Horseshoe Rapids just above Niagara Falls, at several points along the Niagara Parkway below the falls, and at Old Fort Niagara, where the river empties into Lake Ontario. The peak at the river mouth usually comes in early December, when as many as forty thousand gulls may be there, but sometimes big flocks linger into January in a mild winter.

The best gull viewing around Niagara Falls is from the Canadian side of the river. From the U.S. side, take I-190 North from the city of Niagara Falls, following signs "To Canada." Just north of the Robert Moses Power Plant, cross the bridge joining Ontario Route 405. Immediately after passing through the customs booth, bear right onto the exit for Niagara Parkway/Queenston, turning right at the stop onto the parkway south.

For the next 4 miles or so the road goes through parkland paralleling the gorge; good overlooks for gulls are the south end of the Beck hydro plant, the Niagara Glen Nature Area, and the lot (opposite the Whirlpool Restaurant) anchoring one end of the aerial tramway. In town, on-street parking is available almost to the base of the falls, but south of there visitors are forced to park in expensive (seven dollars per car) lots.

Since the best gull areas are above the falls, try this instead: Drive on past Horseshoe Falls and the public greenhouse on the right. Go another .8 mile and turn right into the **Dufferin Islands Nature Area,** looping back to the right for .7 mile. Pull into the small lot just before the parkway, cross the main road and scan the rapids near the old barge; note especially the black-crowned night-heron nests in the small island, to which the herons return in early spring. From here down to the falls the air is alive with gulls and the rising mist of the cataracts, and harlequin ducks are not uncommonly seen here.

(After freezing to watch gulls, thaw out in the greenhouse across the parkway, which is free, warm and has a resident population of free-flying Amazon songbirds—quite a pleasant change from the winter species outside.)

Other good areas upstream from Dufferin Islands are the river by the **International Niagara Control Works,** and **Navy Island** at the downstream tip of Grand Island; to reach it, go south on the parkway from Dufferin Island 4.5 miles through town. Eight small picnic areas provide parking, and depending on ice conditions this stretch of the river can be good for gulls and waterfowl. From here one can return north or continue south to the Peace Bridge linking Ontario and Buffalo.

At the mouth of the Niagara River in New York sits **Old Fort Niagara,** which over the years guarded Lake Ontario for the French, English and Americans. Today the fort has been restored to its former glory and provides a good observation point for the vast numbers of gulls, primarily Bonaparte's, which feed at the mouth of the river. From Buffalo take I-190 North to Lewiston, picking up the Robert Moses Parkway North and driving about 7 miles. Follow signs for NY 18, bearing left briefly onto Route 18, then right at the exit for NY 18F/Fort Niagara. Pass through the park toll booths (closed for the winter) and follow the signs for the fort. Although the fort does not open until 9 A.M., the grounds are usually open before then; the best view of the river mouth is at the Rush-Bagot monument at the north bluff. Dress warmly; this is a "hotspot" in the most figurative of senses only, for a late winter day can be brutally cold.

Ice is a limiting factor for gull flocks anywhere away from the ocean, but the warm discharge from the giant Niagara-Mohawk power plant at **Dunkirk Harbor,** on New York's Lake Erie shore, keeps the bay almost ice-free. Consequently, this is one of the best places for concentrations of Bonaparte's gulls, along with white-winged and other rare varieties. Visiting naturalists will also find rafts of diving ducks, wintering loons and grebes.

To reach Dunkirk Harbor, take I-90 to Exit 59 (Route 60 Dunkirk/Fredonia). Coming out of the toll booth turn right at the light onto Route 60, go 2.4 miles and turn left on Route 5 West, and drive another .4 mile to Central Avenue. Turn right and drive out onto the fishing pier, which has excellent views of the harbor. Also worth a try is **Oswego Harbor,** on the Lake Ontario shore; see Chapter 1 for directions.

3

Red-throated Loons

The Northeast is closely associated with loons, conjuring up (to most minds) moonlit summer lakes and the haunting calls of common loons.

But there is more than just one kind of loon in North America, and in winter—when the common loons have abandoned the frozen lakes—the coast holds loons of a different sort. They are red-throated loons from the Arctic, and this region is one of the best places to see them in sizable numbers.

A red-throated loon is a slim, vaguely ducklike bird, but with a needled bill and long, low profile on the water. The species is smaller than a common loon, although at a distance, or by itself, even an experienced birder would be hard put to tell the difference. That is, in fact, a fundamental difficulty in watching winter loons, for these same coastal waters also hold large numbers of common loons. In the summer, the two species look dramatically different, with the common patterned in black and white, including a distinctive all-dark head, while the red-throated has a pale gray head and a chestnut throat patch.

In winter, however, both loons molt into a remarkably similar, drab plumage, pewter gray above and light below. Combine that with the difficulty of peering through a spotting scope or binoculars at a bird that may be rising and falling on the swells, and you have a frustrating mixture.

At one time, birders relied on the relative thinness of the red-throated's bill, compared to the heavy, more angular common loon's, to tell them apart. At fairly close distances that's a good field mark (so is the tendency of a redthroat to hold its bill cocked up at an angle, which accentuates the apparent upturn in the beak), but birders today look at the whole bird before making an identification. Redthroats generally appear somewhat paler than common loons, and the neck shows a smooth, even line between the darker nape feathers and the lighter throat feathers. A common loon in winter plumage, on the other hand, usually has a hint of its summer necklace pattern, making the dividing line between light and gray appear scalloped.

Taking off from the water, a loon looks graceless, flapping madly along the surface with its wings flailing, leaving a trail of foamy footprints in its wake. Airborne, the thin wings pump ceaselessly, for although they are fast, powerful fliers, loons in the air have no margin for effortless sailing.

It is under the water that a loon comes into its own. Loons are built like submarines, streamlined in the extreme; even their tarsus, or leg bone, is flattened from front to back to cut resistance. The legs themselves are hugely muscular, ending in broad, webbed feet. These are the loon's underwater propulsion, for unlike many auks and some ducks, loons do not "fly" underwater with their wings, but use them only for course corrections.

The red-throated loons that winter off the shores of New England and New York breed on tundra lakes and ponds from Newfoundland right around the northern rim of Canada and the United States; the species is also found over the whole rooftop of the globe, including Iceland, Scotland and Arctic Eurasia, making it the most widely distributed loon in the world. It is also unique among the world's five kinds of loons in that it can take off from land (the back-set legs usually preclude a terrestrial takeoff), and take flight from water with considerably less of a run-up.

In winter, the red-throated loons forsake the tundra and fly south along the coast, wintering from New Brunswick all the way to the Gulf of Mexico, where they join common loons, red-necked and horned grebes, diving ducks like goldeneyes and true sea ducks such as eiders for several months spent entirely at sea. Fortunately for naturalists, loons often prefer quiet bays or the zone not far beyond the surf line, making it fairly easy to find and observe them. They'll be patrolling the water, peering every few seconds beneath the surface, then diving strongly in pursuit of such small fish as sand launce. Although they do not appear to be as powerful divers as common loons, redthroats have been known to swim as deep as 90 feet, and stay submerged for a minute and a half—although their typical dives, as an observer will quickly notice, are much shorter than that.

HOTSPOTS

Red-throated loons winter along virtually the entire length of the region's coastline, and it is worth scanning for them wherever there is a somewhat sheltered lee or protected bay. But there are a number of places where concentrations of redthroats (along with common loons, grebes and other waterbirds) can be found year after year.

One of the best is the Kennebec River mouth and surrounding area on Maine's midcoast. There are two especially easy, productive spots—**Popham Beach State Park** on the south side of the river and **Reid State Park** on Georgetown Island to the north. The two sites are less than 5 miles apart as the loon flies, but in this incredibly crenelated section of coastline, you must drive north from Popham nearly 15 miles, cross the river at Bath, then drive south again another 13 miles to Reid.

It's worth the effort, however, if only for the remarkable beauty of the Maine coast in winter, for this is among the state's most scenic stretches. To reach the parks, take Route 1 to Bath. For Popham Beach, turn south on Route 209 and drive 7 miles to the junction with Route 216; bear left, staying on 209. The park entrance is 3.4 miles ahead. Although Popham Beach State Park is open year-round, the entrance gate may be closed; if so, park outside and make the short walk to the beach.

For Reid Beach, return to Bath and take Route 1 North across the Kennebec River; on the far side, turn right onto Route 127 South and drive 10.8 miles. Turn right at the sign for the park and go another 2.2 miles to the park entrance. It, too, is open all year but may be gated. Park outside without blocking the gate or the road, and walk to Outer Head (Griffith Head) about half a mile from the entrance, or Todd's Point about a mile to the southwest. Watch for the unexpected here; a rare western grebe (at least, presumably the same one) recently marked its fifteenth consecutive winter in the Reid Beach/Georgetown area, amazing and delighting local birders.

Elsewhere in Maine, good numbers of wintering loons can be found in the **Wells Harbor** area near Kennebunkport (see Chapter 7 for directions), and at **Scarborough Beach State Park** north of Saco (see Chapter 9).

To the south in Massachusetts, loons can be found regularly near the mouth of the **Merrimack River** near Newburyport. On the north side of the river, try **Salisbury Beach State Park,** also a good place for wintering gulls, hawks and snowy owls. From I-95 take Exit 58 (Amesbury/Salisbury) to Route 110 East. After 2.3 miles the road splits; bear left onto 110/1A, following the sign for the park. Less than .1 mile go straight through the stop on Route 1A North. Drive 2 miles and turn right into the park, then follow the access road to parking lot 4 near the jetty.

On the south side of the Merrimack, **Parker River NWR** holds worthwhile numbers of loons each winter, as do the waters off the northern tip of **Plum Island.** For directions to the refuge see Chapter 2; to check the north end of the island, continue straight on the Plum Island Turnpike past the turn at Sunset for the refuge, then turn left on Northern Boulevard toward the river.

Several of the sea duck hotspots on **Cape Ann** listed in Chapter 9 can also be good for red-throated and common loons, as are the waters off **Martha's Vineyard** and **Nantucket** (see Chapter 4 for ferry information). Other regional loon locales include the sheltered waters from Wellfleet north to Provincetown on **Cape Cod, Sachuest Point NWR** in Rhode Island (directions in Chapter 10), and **Sherwood Island State Park** near Westport, Connecticut; take Exit 18 off I-95 and follow the signs to the park.

Long Island, especially the North Fork enclosing Peconic and Gardiners bays, can be a good area for finding loons. Take I-495 East to Route 58 East, then about 4 miles to Route 25 East; follow Route 25 for approximately 30 miles to its end at the town of Orient Point, then follow the signs to the right for **Orient Beach State Park** 2 miles farther. Two other spots to the west worth checking on the return trip are **Cedar Beach Point** on **Great Hog Neck,** and **Nassau Point** at the end of **Little Hog Neck;** a topographical map or DeLorme New York atlas will help sort out the confusion of small roads on the necks.

Finally on Long Island, dramatic **Montauk Point** is always worth checking for winter seabirds, not only loons but also such rarities as harlequin ducks and several species of alcids. To reach **Montauk Point State Park,** simply take Route 27 (Sunrise Highway/Montauk Highway) East until the land gives up the fight with the Atlantic Ocean and ends in the famous high bluffs. Park and follow the beach path north toward False Point, and enjoy not just the birds but the wonderful sense of isolation and fury that the winter ocean brings to Montauk.

4

Seabirds from Winter Ferries

In summer, it's fairly easy to get offshore from the New England and New York coast, sampling the abundance of birds and marine mammal life that flourishes in the region's rich waters.

But in winter, virtually all of the cruise ships, whale-watches and other pleasure craft are in dock for the season. Even many of the ferry lines that ply the waters to the islands go into mothballs for the winter, while others switch to schedules that are of no help to the naturalist; the famous Bluenose, for instance, linking Maine and Nova Scotia, makes a thrice-weekly run that leaves Bar Harbor at 11 P.M.—hardly prime birding conditions.

There are, however, a few year-round ferries that cross waters holding large numbers of birds. The Hyannis-Nantucket ferry in Massachusetts is a case in point. Its journey across Nantucket Sound in late December and early January can be astoundingly productive for seabirds, especially for the trio of odd marine ducks known as scoters, which may occur here by the tens of thousands.

Scoters are large, heavily built ducks, drab as undertakers. There are three species—the black scoter, with its somber plumage relieved by a lemon-yellow bill; the white-winged scoter, very similar to the black but for its conspicuous wing patches and splash of white around the eye; and the surf scoter, one of the oddest ducks on the winter sea.

Surf scoters have the family's boxy build and sooty plumage, but the male sports white patches on the forehead and back of the neck, and an enlarged bill with swirls of orange, yellow, black and white. As was so often the case with strangely patterned birds, oldtime seamen and hunters came up with a barrage of descriptive names for the surf scoter, among them skunkhead, blossombill coot, plaster-bill, snufftaker, goggle-nose and patch-polled coot. The family name, scoter, is thought to have come from their habit of turning headfirst and "scoting," or scooting, through breaking waves.

Distinguishing between basically black ducks from the deck of a moving ship is not always easy. This is particularly true of female white-winged and surf scoters, which both have a grayish-brown color and pale patches on the cheeks. Remember, there is no dishonor in not identifying everything you see.

All three scoters are shellfish eaters, diving deep to hunt mussels, oysters, clams, scallops and crustaceans like hermit crabs, as well as an assortment of small fish. Underwater, scoters take a middle-of-the-road approach to locomotion. Unlike auks, which "fly" beneath the surface with vigorous wingflaps, or many other species of diving ducks, which use only their feet for propulsion, the scoters power themselves forward with their feet, but use their partially open wings (including the small alulae, or false primaries, at the bend) for steering.

Fascinating as a winter ferry excursion can be, keep in mind that if you stay on deck, where the viewing is best, you'll pay a price in teeth-rattling cold. Damp sea air and biting winds have a way of getting past the best defenses, but you can reduce the misery by dressing in layers, including lots of wool (which insulates even when wet) and topping it off with a layer of Gore-tex or some other waterproof, windproof fabric.

HOTSPOTS

One of the best ferry routes for winter seabirds is the Hyannis-Nantucket ferry, a 23-mile run across **Nantucket Sound;** scoters in particular can be seen in abundance from the ferry boat, with counts as high as fifteen thousand white-winged scoters, and lesser numbers of black and surf scoters. For information on rates and schedules, call the Steamship Authority in Woods Hole at (508) 540-2022; car reservations are required.

Several of the winter-run ferries in the **Gulf of Maine** can provide seabird-watching opportunities, especially the longer trips like the monthly Mantinicus ferry, which covers 23 miles, or the 15-mile Vinalhaven crossing. For information, contact the

Maine State Ferry Service, P.O. Box 645, Rockland, ME 04841, (207) 596-2202.

For those not fond of boat trips, there can also be good seabirding from land points, especially in early January on an east wind. For suggestions, see Chapter 63.

5

January Shorttakes

Frozen Waterfalls

There are hundreds of spectacular waterfalls scattered across the region, many heavily visited by summer tourists. In winter, however, the heaviest crowds are gone, and the waterfalls become intricacies of ice, especially appealing when a silent snow is falling. Among the most accessible is **Taughannock Falls** along Lake Cayuga in New York, at 215 feet the highest falls east of the Rockies, and almost 50 feet higher than Niagara. After a strong cold spell the waterfall is transformed into a wonderland of ice flows and pillars, and the deep gorge leading to the falls is no less dramatic. To get to the falls take Route 89 North/Park Road from Ithaca for 9.7 miles to **Taughannock Falls SP.** The trailhead is on the left.

See also:

Chapter 67, Wintering Bald Eagles. Good numbers continue this month through early March at such notable concentration points as the upper **Delaware River** in New York and the **Shepaug Dam** on the Houstatonic River in Connecticut.

Chapter 70, Christmas Bird Counts (CBC). Many CBCs take place during the first week of January; see the list of regional counts in the Appendix, or write for information to *American Birds* magazine at the address in Chapter 70.

6

Breakout: Arctic Wanderers

Each winter, when the polar cold fronts come whistling down from Canada and blast across the Northeast, they bring more of the Arctic than biting cold and snow. They also bring feathered invaders that forsake their northerly homes for the somewhat balmier climate in New England and New York.

It's hard to believe there's enough of a difference to make the travel worthwhile, especially when a gale is blowing in from the sea or a gnawing wind is blowing skiffs of snow across the frozen farmland of the Champlain Valley. But for the birds—owls, hawks, ducks, finches and seabirds—the difference may spell survival instead of death.

Some of the birds are regular migrants to the region, like the sea ducks on the coast. Others have a less predictable schedule; their wanderings follow no logic, with several years of almost complete absence followed by a major influx. Other species are even less easy to pigeonhole. Goshawks, for instance, are somewhat migratory and are regularly seen in late autumn by hawk-watchers in the Appalachians. But the majority of the goshawks that live in boreal Canada are year-round residents—until their prey species, largely snowshoe hares and grouse, go into a periodic population crash. Then large numbers of goshawks flood south, sometimes traveling as far as Florida.

Biologists use the term *irruption* for mass movements by birds, such as snowy owls and northern hawk-owls, that are ordinarily nonmigratory. Such flights are generally in response to

Goshawks are an irruptive species, spilling south from the northern forests in unpredictable waves whenever their prey supply runs low.

low food supplies on their northern breeding grounds and appear to be made up largely of immature birds. The youngsters, unable to find a territory in the face of competition from older, more established birds, are forced to drift south until they locate a pocket of food or starve.

Many arrive in the south already in poor physical condition, searching for food and a habitat that looks like home. For a snowy owl, that may be coastal dunes or interior farmland, both flat and open like the tundra. Goshawks and forest owls stick to the woods, although they sometimes wind up in wooded neighborhoods, where the goshawk may discover easy pickings at backyard bird feeders.

Such invasions are exciting times for naturalists, giving them an opportunity to see birds they would otherwise have to travel hundreds of miles north to find. The winter of 1991–92 was such a year across New England, New York and the Great Lakes region, when birding hotlines were buzzing with news of unprecedented numbers of northern hawks and owls.

In the Champlain Valley of Vermont that winter, up to seven gyrfalcons, including a spectacular white bird, were found. Researchers banded more than thirty-five snowy owls at Logan airport in Boston, and reports came in of more than 140 seen in

New England, a dozen on Long Island and more than one hundred on the Great Lakes shore of New York from Rochester to Buffalo. As many as eighteen northern hawk-owls showed up in Maine and Vermont, and great gray owls were sighted in Maine and New York. Earlier in the season, a half-dozen boreal owls—another species rarely encountered south of Canada—suddenly appeared near Boston.

Such sojourns south are hazardous for the wanderers, in part because most are likely young, inexperienced birds with little natural caution toward humans or their ways. Their tameness is extraordinary; a hawk-owl or great gray will unhesitatingly swoop down to pluck a live mouse from one's head—if the sight of a bird with a 5-foot wingspan doesn't make you flinch first. This lack of caution works against them, sadly. Snowy owls in particular make inviting targets for unprincipled gunners, although times have changed since the early twentieth century, when ornithologists estimated that the vast majority of wintering snowies were shot.

Today, if an owl can find enough to eat through the winter, it stands an excellent chance of heading north again in the spring. Indeed, the biggest danger a tame northern owl may face is of being loved literally to death. Crowds of birders interfering with its hunting, playing taped calls and getting too close for photographs may keep even the most complacent bird in a state of constant stress, making an already harsh time of year even more difficult.

FEBRUARY

February Observations

7

Harbor Seals

The winter sea is such an alien environment to humans, where the frigid water can kill in mere moments, that the idea of life akin to ours, thriving in the bitter gales and whitecaps, seems likewise unreal.

But when the round head of a seal breaks the sullen gray water and turns shoreward, and you find yourself staring into its liquid eyes, there is a jolt of recognition, warm-blooded mammal to mammal, that for an instant transcends the differences. Then the seal sinks, the link breaks, and you are again a landbound creature.

Of course, the winter ocean is a presumably comforting home to the seal, which is well fitted to this harsh environment. The harbor seal—the most common species by far on the Northeast coast—is built like a torpedo, with powerful hind flippers that propel it through the water at remarkable speeds, and down to depths as great as 200 fathoms. The cold water would be as dangerous to a seal as to a human, were it not for the seal's blubber layer, which provides insulation, a fat reserve and buoyancy all in one thick blanket.

Harbor seals are true, or earless, seals, differing from fur seals and sea lions in their lack of external ear pinnea ("ear lobes") and having flippers that cannot be turned forward when on land; as a result, a true seal must inch forward on its belly like a giant caterpillar whenever it hauls out of the water, as it does regularly to rest.

In summer, harbor seals can be found from New Hampshire and southern Maine north to the edge of the Arctic ice, and they are a common sight among the lobster buoys of the New England coast. In winter they retreat south, however, as far as Long Island (and occasionally much farther than that, to the Carolinas and Florida). Even in summer they are somewhat social, gathering in small groups on offshore ledges exposed by the falling tide, but in winter they may congregate in much greater numbers. One of the largest gatherings of harbor seals in the United States occurs late each winter along North and South Monomoy Island, south of Cape Cod's elbow—up to three thousand, loafing and feeding as they wait for spring.

Harbor seals are rather small, with males less than 6 feet long and females less than 5 feet; the average weight is less than 200 pounds. Dull and blotched as a sea boulder crusted with lichen, the harbor seal's coat (if seen in good light) is an attractive wash of grayish brown, marked with an intricate pattern of spots and mottlings. Individuals vary widely, however, from dark brown to bleached blonde.

Fish make up most of a harbor seal's diet, and that has long brought them into conflict with people. They have been heavily persecuted on the Northeast coast, mostly by fishermen who accuse them of cutting into their catch; bounties were paid in some states until the 1960s, and led to the seals' extermination in many areas. Federal protection has brought an increase in seal numbers, and although they no longer breed in much of their southern range, there is hope that they may recolonize those areas as well. A growing problem is human harassment—much of it unintentional—from recreational boaters like sea-kayakers. This harassment forces breeding seals into marginal calving sites where they are more exposed to storms and predators like sharks.

Although almost all of the seals along the winter coast are harbor seals, there is also a chance of spotting one of the much larger and rarer gray seals, or "horseheads." As the nickname suggests, the shape of the head is the main distinguishing characteristic. Harbor seals have rounded heads with short, doglike muzzles, while gray seals (which may be twice the length and four times the bulk of a harbor seal) have long, drooping muzzles, a sort of Roman nose effect that is very distinctive. Gray seals breed in February in the Canadian Maritimes, and few wanderers will be found south of the breeding colonies at this time of year—although the possibility is always tantalizing.

HOTSPOTS

Harbor seals may be encountered anywhere along the coast in winter, but two areas in particular hold significant numbers, and are worth the trouble of a midwinter visit.

In southern Maine, the area around **Wells Harbor** and **Rachel Carson NWR** just to the north hosts several hundred harbor seals, which haul out of rocky islands and secluded areas of shoreline; their rounded, gray heads are also commonly seen bobbing in the harbor waters before disappearing beneath the surface again.

Despite recent protection, harbor seals remain wary of humans. A good pair of binoculars or—better yet—a spotting scope on a tripod will give you the best views of resting seals. Seals usually choose haul-out spots that cannot be reached by people on foot, but if you should find one resting on the mainland shore, or if you're in a boat, keep a respectful distance so you don't frighten it into leaving.

Harbor seals, a common fixture of the summer ocean along the Northeast coast, congregate in winter at a number of locations, including Monomoy NWR in Massachusetts.

To reach Wells Harbor, take I-95 (Maine Turnpike) to Exit 2, turning left off the exit ramp onto Route 9E/109 South and go 1.5 miles into the town of Wells. Turn right onto Route 9E/1 South, go 1.3 miles and turn left onto Mile Road (unmarked) at the sign for Wells Beach. At the end of the mile-long road you'll find several places to park and scan the sea, then turn left on Atlantic Avenue and drive to the end of the peninsula, where it overlooks the breakwaters at the mouth of the Webhannet River.

For a view of the northern side of the harbor, return to Route 1, turning north through Wells. Go 1 mile and turn right onto Drake's Island Road. Drive to the beach, turn right and follow the road to the overview of the harbor.

To get to Rachel Carson NWR, return once more to Route 9E/1 North and turn right, driving .4 mile to the intersection with Route 9, a right turn (Route 9 is 1.8 miles from Wells). The entrance to the refuge is on the right less than a mile down Route 9.

As previously mentioned, one of the largest concentrations of harbor seals can be found below Cape Cod on **Monomoy NWR,** resting on the beaches and feeding in the fertile waters offshore of North and South Monomoy islands. This is, in part, because the waters around Monomoy are treacherous in winter, and the islands themselves are closed then to most human activity. Each winter, however, guided day-trips are run by private conservation groups to Monomoy to see the seals, as well as the phenomenal numbers of sea ducks, including up to 150,000 common eiders, that also winter here. For information contact Monomoy NWR at the address listed in the Appendix, or contact the Massachusetts Audubon Society at (508) 349-2615, or the Cape Cod Museum of Natural History at (508) 896-3867. In addition to harbor seals, there is the possibility of seeing the rarer gray seal off Monomoy; the species pupped here for the first time in 1989.

8

Maple Sugaring

It looks like water—certainly nothing like the smooth, amber syrup poured out each morning on steaming stacks of pancakes. Yet the spring sap of the sugar maple has just the faintest hint of sweetness and flavor, a promise of better things to come, and a reward for plenty of hard work.

Long before Europeans came to North America, native tribes in the Northeast were tapping what the Algonquins called *sinzibukwud*, treating this gift of the forest with reverence. Their methods were crude, by modern standards; the trees were slashed, and the dripping sap collected in bark boxes to later be boiled down into syrup or (most often) crystallized sugar.

Colonists refined the native techniques and greatly boosted the yield of the "sugarbush," as a stand of maples is known. Instead of gashing the bark, each tree is drilled with one or more holes about half an inch wide and two and a half inches deep, and metal spiles, or spouts, are driven into them; a covered collecting bucket hangs from each.

The sap begins to run as the days warm in late February and March, depending on the location; sugarbush workers know from long experience that mild days and below-freezing nights are the ideal combination, increasing the sap pressure in the layer of living tissue between the outer bark and dead heartwood.

Traditionally, the sap was collected in gathering pails, then emptied into a large tank borne on a horse-drawn sleigh; today tractors are more common than horses, and many sugarbushes sprout networks of pump-driven plastic tubing each spring, connecting the spiles directly to a central collection vat.

Old ways or new, the sap must still be boiled down in the sugarhouse, usually set in a sheltered glen somewhere in or near the sugarbush. Inside, a giant evaporator steams above a wood-burning firebox (or, increasingly, an oil-fired burner), slowly cooking off the excess water, a tedious process given that fresh sap is only 2 or 3 percent sugar; at such concentrations, it takes about 35 gallons of sap to make just one gallon of syrup.

The sugaring season ends in mid-April, except in the highest, coldest areas where the sap may run for a week or two longer. The warmer days not only reduce the flow of sap (which is also changing color and flavor) but make the risk of bacterial growth in the collecting buckets a greater risk.

Any maple can be tapped, although none have as consistently high a concentration of sugar in their sap as the sugar maple (*Acer saccharum*), the queen of Northeast hardwoods; on good, sandy soil with a southern exposure and a not-too-dry winter at its back, a quality sugar maple may produce sap with a sugar content as high as 10 percent. Red maples are also tapped in some sugarbushes, although their sap sugar is rarely greater than 3 or 4 percent.

Unfortunately, in many parts of New England and New York the sugar maples have been in trouble recently. An introduced pest, the pear thrip, has reduced yields in many areas, and a string of bad winters likewise made tapping hard on the maples and sugarbush owners alike. Other experts, noting the dying, scraggly crowns of many sugar maples, believe the problem is a combination of acid precipitation, ozone pollution and poor sugarbush management. A great deal of money and attention has gone into figuring out why maples are suffering in some areas— not surprising, considering the economic importance of the sugar maple in the region.

Given trees, a handful of spiles and a lot of patience, anyone can tap maples and make their own sugar—but it is a long, tedious process, and you'll likely end up with little more than a taste for your trouble. A better idea is to head to the mountains in late February or March and visit any of the sugarbushes, public, private or commercial, that welcome visitors.

HOTSPOTS

Vermont has long enjoyed a reputation as the spiritual home, so to speak, of sugarmaking. The state has registered about fifteen hundred commercial sugaring operations, and an untold number of people tap their family sugarbush each spring for their own use.

One of the best places to see a traditional sugaring operation is the **Green Mountain Audubon Nature Center,** near Huntington, Vermont, owned and operated by the Green Mountain Audubon Society. Each year the center runs about 750 taps, producing 180 gallons of syrup from its picturesque sugarhouse, a process that visitors can experience firsthand. If possible, time your visit with one of the center's "sugar on snow" parties, a celebration of that fine New England treat in which thickened syrup is poured over packed snow to make a chewy dessert.

To get to the nature center, take I-89 to Exit 11 at Richmond, then follow Route 2 East 1.5 miles into town. Turn right at the light onto Bridge Street and drive .3 mile across the Winooski River. Follow the road another .2 mile around a sharp right bend, go .7 mile and bear left with the main road at a fork. The road forks again in .2 mile; again bear left. Drive a final 3.4 miles and watch for the Huntington town sign; the parking lot for the sugarhouse is on the right. Or you can drive .2 mile past the lot and turn right on Sherman Hollow Road, a dirt lane, which leads to the headquarters building in .2 mile.

Another option is to visit one of the large number of commercial sugarhouses in New England and New York that open their doors to visitors during the sugaring season. They run the gamut from ultra-modern facilities with vacuum pipelines to collect the sap, to old-fashioned farms that still use horses and buckets. You'll have a chance to see the operation and, if you wish, you can usually purchase some of the finished product. Because there are so many (Vermont alone has more than one hundred), a comprehensive rundown here is impossible, but most states offer a listing of such sugarhouses. See the Appendix for the numbers of the various state agricultural or tourism departments that handle these requests.

9

Winter Waterfowl

Spring and autumn, when the wheel of seasons is shifting and continental bird populations are on the move, are the most exciting times to watch waterfowl. Huge flocks string the sky with movement, and the constant arrival of new birds makes the chance of discovery even greater.

Winter would, on the face of it, seem to be a disappointingly barren season for the waterfowl enthusiast, but nothing could be further from the truth. Although there are fewer birds, measured in sheer numbers, what's here are some of the most intriguing species of the year, passing the winter in some of the most dramatic settings.

On the Massachusetts coast, for example, you can bundle yourself to the nose and brave the fearsome gales on Halibut Point, at the northern tip of scenic Cape Ann; there you'll see eiders, oldsquaws and other northern ducks, as well as winter seabirds like black guillemots and gannets.

Or you can travel to New York's Finger Lakes region, where large flocks of diving ducks seek out ice-free water; the stellar attractions include some of the biggest numbers of redheads and canvasbacks at any inland site in the region.

Weather obviously plays a major role in determining how successful your excursion will be, not only in terms of physical comfort, but in how many birds will be around. A prolonged or unusually severe cold spell may freeze even those large lakes that generally retain expanses of open water—and once the ducks are chased south, they may be reluctant to retrace their travels north until spring.

On the coast, strong winds are a fact of life all winter, but the direction changes with the shifting of atmospheric highs and lows. Look for the biggest numbers of birds in the lee of the shore, where they can avoid the heaviest buffeting.

HOTSPOTS

The **Finger Lakes** region of central New York has a number of consistently outstanding waterfowl hotspots, among them Cayuga and Canandaigua lakes.

The western shore of **Cayuga Lake**, north of Ithaca, annually hosts large flocks of diving ducks, especially lesser scaup, redheads and canvasbacks, rafting in flocks of more than one hundred at a time; the canvasbacks and redheads are especially unusual in such numbers at an inland location.

From Ithaca take Route 89 North/Park Road, which hugs the western lakeshore. About 18 miles north of town pass an intersecting left with a sign for Interlaken and note your odometer; go another .9 mile and turn right onto County Road 141. Bear left at the lake, stopping frequently over the next 4 miles in the villages of Kidders and Sheldrake to scan the lake. At Wyers Point bear left and return to Route 89.

Although the Kidders/Sheldrake area is the best on the lake, good numbers of ducks may also be found farther north. Turn right onto 89 North and go 5.5 miles to the jetty at Dean's Cove; other overlooks can be found near East Varick, although this is a busy road and pull-offs are few. **Cayuga Lake State Park,** 17 miles north of Sheldrake, is another reliable area for waterfowl, depending on ice conditions.

Although the numbers vary from year to year, the south end of **Canandaigua Lake** may hold as many as four thousand redheads in February and March, one of the largest inland concentrations of this species in the region.

From I-390 take Exit 2 to Route 415 South, go half a mile and turn left onto Route 371 North. At North Cohocton continue straight on Route 21 North to Naples. Note the intersection with Route 245, but continue north on 21 for another 3.2 miles to the fishing access area. Scan the lake here, but ice may have forced the birds farther north on the water. Return to 245, turn left and drive to the town of Middlesex. Turn left onto Route 364, drive about a mile and turn left onto South Vine Valley Road. Follow this west to the lake, then take Route 11 north along the shore, stopping wherever possible to scan.

In extreme southwestern New York, **Chautauqua Lake** may have sizable numbers of diving ducks and mergansers, although its real claim to fame are the hundreds of tundra swans that stop off here in mid-March on their way north. For directions, see Chapter 18.

Between New York and Vermont, **Lake Champlain** is a magnet for open-water species like goldeneyes, but the limited amount of public access along its shoreline makes it a frustrating place to bird; many apparently promising roads end in private drives, and places combining a parking spot and a good view are rare. Still, there are several points near the Lake Champlain Bridge worth a visit during the winter, depending on ice conditions (generally, the lake freezes south of the bridge first).

From the Lake Champlain Bridge linking Crown Point and Chimney Point, take Route 17 East 2.2 miles to Lake Street, a left fork. Go .7 mile and turn left opposite Spaulding Road at the sign for the Tritown Water Treatment Plant; drive back down this road, bearing right at the fork, to the plant, which has a view of the lake at Elm Point. Return to Lake Street and turn left, drive 5.4 miles and turn left again, this time at the sign for the Vergennes-Panton Water District Plant, a distance of .2 mile. The tiny lot by the plant has a view of Arnold Bay, which may freeze even when the main lake is ice-free.

Return to Lake Street, turning left, and drive 1.7 miles, bear left at the fork with the "State Park" sign, and go another 1.9 miles to the Button Bay Boat Access Road, a left. The dirt parking area provides a spectacular vista of Button Bay, the sweep of Champlain to the south and Adirondacks to the west. It is also likely to have good numbers of common goldeneyes, common and red-breasted mergansers, black ducks, mallards and several other species of waterfowl.

Return, via Lake Street and Route 17, to the Champlain bridge. From here south the lake narrows dramatically, and this area usually freezes first. If it is not frozen, however, take Route 125 East 1.2 miles and watch for a small pull-off on the right. Then continue another half-mile to the entrance to **McCuen Slang Waterfowl Area** on the right, with its ponds and backwaters.

On the Massachusetts coast, the north wind cuts with a cruel edge on **Cape Ann,** but the abundance of winter ducks takes some of the bite out of the weather. Take Route 128 to Route 133 southeast toward Gloucester. Turn right onto Route 127 South; on the left a few hundred yards later is **Stage Fort Park,** which you can drive through, pulling over periodically to scan the waters of Gloucester Harbor. The road through the park rejoins Route 127, and you again turn left (south). Go .8 mile and turn left at the sign for "Hammond Castle Museum." This is Hesperus Avenue, but may not be marked as such. On the left 1.3 miles farther is a chain-link fence with a gate in the middle, the entrance to a trail leading to Rafe's Chasm, a reliable spot for sea ducks including harlequins.

As you approach the village of Magnolia the road becomes Northern Avenue. Turn left onto Shore Road and follow it around **Magnolia Point,** with the sheltered bay on the right and then views of the open ocean; this is a good place for buffleheads, eiders, oldsquaws, goldeneyes and horned grebes, while the islands offshore support huge flocks of gulls.

Return, via Northern/Hesperus Avenue, to Route 127 and turn north toward Gloucester. Follow 127/Rogers Street until it joins Main Street, turning right on Main. Follow East Main Street and signs for East Gloucester for 1.6 miles to Niles Beach on the right, where you can look out over the harbor (early in the morning you'll have the sun at your back here). You can continue straight ahead to **Eastern Point** and the **Dog Bar Breakwater,** with **Niles Pond** (a gull hotspot) along the way.

The final stop on this Cape Ann tour is **Halibut Point** at the cape's northern tip, one of the most scenic parts of this coast, but also the most brutally exposed to the winter winds. From Gloucester take Route 127 North through Rockport and Pigeon Cove. Once through Pigeon Cove you'll cross a quarry bridge; exactly 1 mile farther turn right onto Phillip's Avenue, which leads to Long Branch Avenue on **Andrews Point,** an excellent overlook for **Hoop Pole Cove.** Because this is a residential area with extremely limited parking, exercise the utmost in courtesy.

Retrace your route to Route 127 and head north again, watching for Gott Avenue on the right, marked by a sign for "State Park." The entrance for **Halibut Point State Reservation** is on the right, with the entrance trail to the point across the road. It ends at the ocean and a lookout on a high jetty—a fine place to see sea ducks, pelagics (if the wind is strong from the sea) and black guillemots. It is not, however, a place to underdress for the weather.

In southern Maine, **Scarborough Beach State Park** is known for its concentrations of common eiders, as well as rarities

Flocks of waterfowl, like these mallards and black ducks, can be found each winter on ice-free portions of the Finger Lakes, Lake Champlain and along the coast.

like king eiders. Take I-95 (Maine Turnpike) to Exit 5, then Route 195 to Route 1 North. Go 8.8 miles to Route 207 (Black Point Road, becoming Spurwink Road), a right, then 4.1 miles on 207 to the park entrance on the left. About 20 miles north (although considerably more by road) are **Popham Beach State Park** and **Reid State Park,** both of which can afford good winter duck watching, in addition to loons, grebes and other interesting waterbirds. See Chapter 3 for directions.

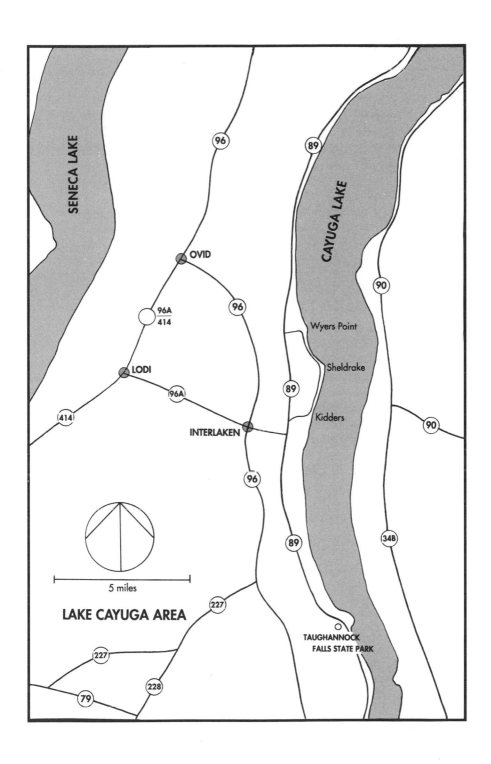

SENECA LAKE

CAYUGA LAKE

96

89

OVID

96

96A / 414

90

Wyers Point

LODI

Sheldrake

96A

89

414

Kidders

90

INTERLAKEN

96

89

34B

5 miles

227

LAKE CAYUGA AREA

TAUGHANNOCK
FALLS STATE PARK

227

227

228

79

10

Harlequin Ducks

North America may hold no more arrestingly (many would say bizarrely) patterned bird than the harlequin duck. The female is ordinary enough—brown, with a small spot of white at the ear, and a larger patch at the base of the bill.

The male, though, is something else altogether, a flamboyance of gun-metal blue and chestnut, with black-edged stripes and blotches of white. The combination is utterly unlike any other North American waterbird's plumage. One drake harlequin duck is remarkable; several dozen are astonishing.

Many naturalists never see one harlequin, however, much less a flock of them, for this species of sea duck is exceedingly scarce in New England and New York; one recent estimate puts the wintering eastern U.S. population at just seven hundred. During the summer, the species breeds well to the north, on rapids-strewn rivers in Labrador, Quebec and the Maritimes, and in winter retreats only slightly south, as if giving only the barest notice to the cold weather.

Even stranger from a human perspective, the harlequin prefers to pass the coldest months in a hard environment—the pounding surf zone along the coast, where it dives nonchalantly for mollusks and small crustaceans while breakers crash all around it. A person falling in this frigid water would die within minutes, but the harlequins, along with such other sea ducks as common eiders, goldeneyes and oldsquaws, are so thoroughly insulated by their oily feathers that they can spend months at sea with impunity.

Come summer, the harlequins head north and inland, returning to wooded streams and fast-moving rivers, often choosing territories at the outflow of lakes, where food—crayfish, insects and occasional small fish—is plentiful.

For harlequin ducks, the faster the water, the better; this is North America's only true "torrent duck," a species adapted for life in rapids and wrenching currents, where it can exploit food resources out of the reach of other birds. The female nests near the feeding grounds, sometimes picking a hollow tree but more often than not making a shallow, grass- and feather-lined nest under the low-hanging branches of a spruce or shrub.

Harlequins are far more common along the northern Pacific coast, with counts of a million or more recorded in the Aleutians; they are also found around the northeastern rim of Asia but are absent from Europe, suggesting that the much smaller populations in eastern North America, Greenland and Iceland are the result of a relatively recent expansion.

While observers have, in recent years, noted an increase in harlequin duck numbers in the region, there is still a tremendous amount of empty winter habitat—rocky, ice-free shoreline—along the Northeast coast. If, as some people suspect, the harlequin duck is still just recovering from nineteenth century abuses like egg collecting, naturalists may see a steady growth in the flocks of this most unusual bird in the years to come.

HOTSPOTS

While harlequin ducks may be found in very small numbers along the entire coastline of the region (including even rarer appearances on the Great Lakes), there are two stellar concentrations worth any naturalist's visit—**Sachuest Point NWR** in Rhode Island, and **Isle au Haut** on the Maine coast.

Sachuest Point NWR is tiny, a mere 242 acres covering the roughly T-shaped finger that separates Sachuest Bay from the mouth of the Sakonnet River east of Newport. Its rough waters, however, support the largest concentration of harlequin ducks south of Maine, with as many as one hundred counted here in recent years. It also offers unmatched opportunities to easily see harlequins at relatively close range, since they frequently feed close to the eastern shore of the refuge; on my first visit, I crouched quietly along the rocky bluff while a flock dove and rose just a stone's toss away, filling my scope with their strange colors. For optimal viewing, try to arrive in early afternoon at low tide, when the ducks will be resting on offshore rocks and the angle of the sun is ideal.

To reach Sachuest Point from the north, take I-195 to Exit 8A (Route 24 South, Tiverton-Newport) at Fall River. Go 9.5 miles on 24S/138S, then take the Turnpike Avenue Exit to Route 138 South, bearing right off the ramp and following the sign for the beaches. Go .8 mile and turn right at the light onto 138, then drive 6.2 miles and turn left at the light. Drive another 2 miles to a T-intersection, turn left again, go .5 mile and make still another left onto Purgatory Road. Bear right at the fork .9 mile later by the beaches; the refuge parking lot is 1.5 miles farther.

Coming from the east, take Route 1A to the Providence-Westerly Exit (Route 138W), crossing the Newport and Jamestown bridges on 138 West. Once through Newport, cross a third, street-level bridge and turn right at the light onto Purgatory Road.

Although the refuge is open every day, its office hours are highly variable, and if you arrive to find the road leading to the visitors' center gated, park in the small lot below the gate and walk up, past the office to the start of the footpath. Go east toward the ocean, scanning Island Rocks offshore. From here you can walk left (north) toward Flint Point, or south toward Sachuest Point. Either trail will loop back to the visitors' center, and each circuit covers about a mile.

In addition to harlequin ducks, visitors are likely to see common eiders, common goldeneyes, red-breasted mergansers, buffleheads and a smattering of other species of waterfowl.

The East's biggest harlequin show takes place each winter along the Maine coast, in the waters off **Isle au Haut,** in part a unit of Acadia NP. Although not nearly as accessible as Sachuest Point, Isle au Haut offers highly dedicated naturalists a chance to see as many as three hundred harlequins. Because the mailboat running from Stonington makes only a single trip each day, the only way to see the ducks (short of hiring a local fisherman or arranging to board overnight with an island resident) is to make the 45-minute ride out, then turn around and come straight back to the mainland. For more information on the mailboat, call the Isle au Haut Co. in Stonington at (207) 367-5193.

11

February Shorttakes

Bonaparte's Gulls and Other Winter Goodies

Each winter the waters of **Jones Inlet** on Long Island's south shore are filled with thousands of birds, including brant, oldsquaw, occasional harlequin ducks and lots of Bonaparte's gulls—up to five thousand of them in some years. The best observation spot is **Point Lookout** at the east end of Long Beach, just off the Loop State Parkway; an outgoing tide is best, and may also produce winter shorebirds like dunlin, sanderlings and turnstones, and rare gulls like little and black-headed gulls.

See also:

Chapter 67, Wintering Bald Eagles. Large numbers can be found this month and in early March in places like the **upper Delaware River** in New York and the **lower Houstatonic River** in Connecticut.

12

Breakout: Winter by the Sea

With a furious, leaden sky spilling its guts overhead and curtains of rain making the air a thing of liquid, an epic gale was raking the Maine coast. Ferocious winds were coming in from the ocean and raising enormous breakers, which crashed into foam that was flung to shore in a bitter mist. It was dead low tide, but the long, low boulders offshore disappeared beneath frenzied walls of dishpan-gray water and dreary foam that surged and fell and rose again.

In the midst of this maelstrom there was life. Small flocks of sea ducks—chunky eiders, slimmer goldeneyes, oldsquaws all white against the pewter sea—were riding out the storm just beyond the surf line. Every few seconds their world tilted violently as another great wave rose beneath them and the water became nearly vertical; then it slid past to its roaring death, and the ducks calmly slipped down its back side. Once, when an especially big wave rose and crested early, breaking over their heads, they all turned bill-first into it, as though by command, and vanished beneath the boil, only to roll to the surface again on the other side. It was, I suppose, just another day on the winter sea for them.

For me as an observer standing on shore, leaning hard into the gale and soaked to the skin despite the best efforts of modern synthetics, it was a humbling realization of the gulf that separates humans from the inhabitants of the winter ocean. This is no idyllic place of sailboats and puffy clouds, but a bitter, harsh place where life treads the thin edge.

So why, then, should any creature capable of fleeing before winter—and certainly that includes birds—elect to stick it out in so uncompromising an environment? The reason, of course, is that the winter sea is brutal by human standards, but not by those of, say, an eider. The sea provides shelter and food, and the bird's physical and behavioral adaptations provide the cushion of comfort and safety that allow it to thrive in the face of winter's worst challenges.

In fact, the seacoast in winter is one of the most exciting places for a naturalist. Ocean birds are the most visible attraction; sea ducks from the Arctic, pelagics blown inshore by strong winds, hardy shorebirds and blizzards of gulls.

Where the tide exposes mud flats, or the shore is gentle enough for a beach, one is likely to find sanderlings skittering in synchronization with the waves; farther north on the rock-bound coast, or on jetties in the south, look for purple sandpipers the color of the sea, and ruddy turnstones whose orange legs are the only reminder of their springtime elegance.

On the beach itself, and in the shifting dunes just beyond, another community of birds endures the cold weather. Flashing their black and white wings like tiny explosions, snow buntings cascade along with the wind, having traveled south from the islands of the Arctic Ocean. With them come a handful of other rarities, including a few Lapland longspurs, which have traded their dramatic breeding plumage of black and russet for a camouflaging mix of ocher, brown and rust that merges seamlessly with the withered vegetation of the back dunes. Most common of all are the horned larks, their frugal brown relieved by the faintest hint of yellow on the throat and belly, tiny feather "horns" tickled by the sea breeze.

There are mammals here, too, most notably meadow voles and shrews where the ground cover is thickest. And with the prey come the predators; the winter coast is the hunting ground of harriers and rough-legged hawks, northern shrikes and short-eared owls. In an invasion year, any piece of wide-open coastline is liable to have a snowy owl, starkly white and yellow-eyed, perching on old pilings or jetty walls or the lightpoles of beachside parking lots, waiting for a rodent to make the mistake of showing itself. For the exceptionally lucky, the winter shore may also hold a glimpse of a huge gyrfalcon, white or gray or charcoal-black, bringing a piece of the Far North south on its powerful wings, like an embodiment of the wind.

MARCH

March Observations

13

Spring Hawk Flights

They come from as near as the open farmlands of the Finger Lakes valleys, and as far as the jungles of South America—birds of prey, drawn north to breed. Some will go little farther north than New York, while others will not stop until they reach the Canadian Arctic or Greenland.

Each spring, from late February through the first week of June, a changing stream of hawks, eagles and falcons flows north through the region, borne on warm southerly breezes with their hint of better weather in the offing. Their passage is one of the benchmarks of the season, and their numbers can be incredible.

For the most part, the raptors migrate north across a fairly broad front, using such landscape features as mountains and river valleys—what biologists call "leading lines"—to guide them. But the hawks, for all their skill in the air, seem to have an aversion to crossing large bodies of open water—and the Great Lakes lie directly in their path.

Rather than cross the 50 or 60 miles of Lake Ontario, for instance, the birds turn east, following the lakeshore hundreds of miles out of their way until they can loop around the lake and resume their northward track. As they follow the edge of the lake they may move in tremendous numbers, half a continent's worth of hawks funneled into a narrow corridor. While there are some interior spring hawk-watches, they cannot compare to the sights found along the lakeshore.

Naturalists have known for years about the spring hawk migration along the Great Lakes, and in recent years more and more locations for observing the flights have been found; two, at Derby Hill and Braddock Bay, now boast formal bird observatories that are manned throughout the season. In the process, we've come to understand the effects of timing and weather on the birds' movements.

As in the fall, the composition of the flights changes through the spring. Bald eagles, rough-legged, red-tailed and red-shouldered hawks start the parade in late February, but the bulk of the flight waits until March, when about nine species, including northern harriers, Cooper's hawks, goshawks and American kestrels, start flying in sizable numbers. Most of these species also carry over into April, when the staggering flocks of broad-winged hawks, sometimes numbering more than fifteen thousand in a day, capture the spotlight (for more on the broadwing flight, see Chapter 20).

The best weather conditions at most of the lake sites are southerly winds of about 10 miles per hour and a low pressure system approaching from the west; this gives the hawks a tail wind and an incentive to move. North winds (or from the east or west, depending on the location) usually keep the hawks away from the lake, and rain or snow produce poor flights. The peak numbers each day usually pass between about 9 A.M. and 3 P.M.

One unique opportunity to see raptors at close range is available just outside Rochester, where Braddock Bay Raptor Research (BBRR) operates a banding station from March through the middle of May. Each spring about seven hundred hawks are captured alive, fitted with numbered metal leg bands issued by the U.S. Fish and Wildlife Service, and released; this research tells scientists volumes about the movements and life histories of the migrants. Visitors are welcome at the banding station, located on Manitou Beach Road just east of the Lake Ontario Parkway, along the northwest edge of the bay. Complete directions to Braddock Bay follow, and the address of BBRR can be found in the Appendix.

HOTSPOTS

The premiere spring hawk-watch sites in New England and New York are all on the Lake Erie or Ontario shoreline, where the northbound migrants concentrate rather than crossing the open water, although several lesser sites are found much farther east in New York and Massachusetts.

Perhaps the best is **Derby Hill Bird Observatory** near Texas, New York. Owned by the Onondaga Audubon Society, Derby Hill is a bluff high above Lake Ontario, where on good days in March and April visitors can see a marvelous parade of raptors, waterfowl and landbirds. In March, goshawks, red-tailed, red-shouldered and rough-legged hawks are the main attractions, with bald eagles, harriers, golden eagles, kestrels and Cooper's hawks passing in appreciable numbers. The best flight conditions are a south wind prior to the passage of a low pressure system.

To reach Derby Hill from the south, take I-81 to Route 104 East near Mexico; follow 104 to Route 3 North, then turn left onto Route 104B. Go .6 mile and turn right onto Sage Creek Road. After 1.2 miles either bear right up the hill through the cottages, or—if signs to that effect are up—park at the Sage Creek Marsh and walk the .3 mile up the road to the observatory. Because this is a residential area, be careful not to block driveways or road access.

Visitors coming from the west should take Route 104 for 7 miles from Oswego, then bear left onto Route 104B. A mile east of Texas turn left onto Sage Creek Road.

About 12 miles southwest of Oswego is **Sodus Bay,** site of an informal hawk-watch each spring on a hill on the west edge of the bay. From I-90 take Route 14 North for 19 miles to the intersection with Route 104; go straight on 14 for .4 mile, turn left at the stop sign and almost immediately right again, still on Route 14. Drive 1.8 miles and turn right on Red Mill Road, then go another 1.8 miles (Red Mill joins Shaker Road half a mile along). At the crest of the hill Shaker makes a sharp right curve along the bluff of the bay; pull off here and watch for hawks coming from the west.

Next to Derby Hill, Braddock Bay is New York's best-known spring hawk-watch. Redtails, harriers and roughlegs start the migration off with a bang in early March, joined by turkey vultures, Cooper's hawks, kestrels and red-shouldered hawks, among other species, in a stream that continues through May and the first weeks of June. A modern visitors' center at **Braddock Bay State Park** has interpretive displays, and the nearby hawk-watch platform is manned daily through the migration by staff from **Braddock Bay Raptor Research**.

To reach Braddock Bay take I-309 to Rochester, skirting the western edge of the city to its junction with the Lake Ontario Parkway. Go 3.2 miles on the parkway to the exit for Braddock Bay Park/East Manitou, turn right at the stop sign and left into the park,

*All eyes scan the distant horizon on the hawk-watch platform at
Braddock Bay State Park, New York, one of the best locations for
spring hawkwatching.*

following signs for the picnic area. The hawk-watch platform is on
the left, and the visitors' center beyond.

Two areas along New York's Lake Erie shore have gained
reputations for their spring hawk flights—the bluffs in **Pinehurst**
and two locations near Irving, at the mouth of **Cattaraugus Creek.**
Unfortunately, all roads near the Pinehurst bluffs have been posted
against parking, but dedicated naturalists may want to park
elsewhere and walk in. To reach the Pinehurst bluffs, take I-90 to
Exit 57 (Route 75 Hamburg), bearing right out of the tolls onto
Route 75 North. Go 2.1 miles to a light where 75 veers right; instead
go straight on Camp Road, then turn left on Route 5 West. Drive
3.6 miles to the intersection with Old Lakeshore Drive and turn
right; you might want to look for parking near Route 5. The bluff
is straight ahead on Old Lakeshore less than a mile.

CAUTION: *The bluff is severely undercut by
lake erosion and extremely dangerous near the
edge. Stay well back from the concrete and metal
barricades that have been erected.*

About 25 miles southwest of Pinehurst is the village of Irving, site of two unmanned hawk-watches—one at the mouth of Cattaraugus Creek, the other on a hill a mile or so out of town. To reach the creek site, take I-90 to Exit 58 (Silver Creek-Irving), then follow Route 20/5 East for 1.1 miles across the creek. The road splits; bear left on Route 5E for .7 mile, going under two railroad trestles. At the far side turn left and immediately left again onto an unmarked road. After 1.3 miles the macadam road bends right; turn instead onto the dirt road to the left. Go .3 mile, bear right at the fork, and right again at the next fork. The road dead-ends at the beach another half-mile along. Beware of potholes and getting stuck in loose sand at the beach.

If the hawks are not following the shoreline, try the hill location. Return to Routes 20/5 West, going .7 mile past the exit for I-90. Turn left onto Allegany Road at the light and drive uphill .3 mile, pulling over by the large, flat fields. The shoulder is narrow and ground soft, so be careful to get far enough off the road—but not too far.

Spring hawk-watches are less common (and less productive) away from the Great Lakes, but there are two worth exploring in eastern New York and southern New England.

Northbound hawks, for example, follow the gash of the Lake Champlain valley in good numbers, along the way passing **Mount Defiance,** where in 1777 British cannon forced the surrender of the Americans manning Fort Ticonderoga far below. From the village of Ticonderoga take the main street, Montcalm, to the intersection of Champlain Avenue and turn south on Champlain. At the triangular green the road splits; take the left fork, Portage, for .2 mile and bear left again onto Mount Defiance Street. This ends .4 mile later at the gated summit road. If the gate is closed you'll have to climb the last mile to the top, where wonderful views of the lake valley—and the hawks—are your reward.

Hawk-watchers in central Massachusetts have had good luck in spring from the Bray Tower at **Mt. Tom State Reservation** north of Holyoke. For directions see Chapter 50; from park headquarters Bray Tower is just 100 yards to the left up a short road.

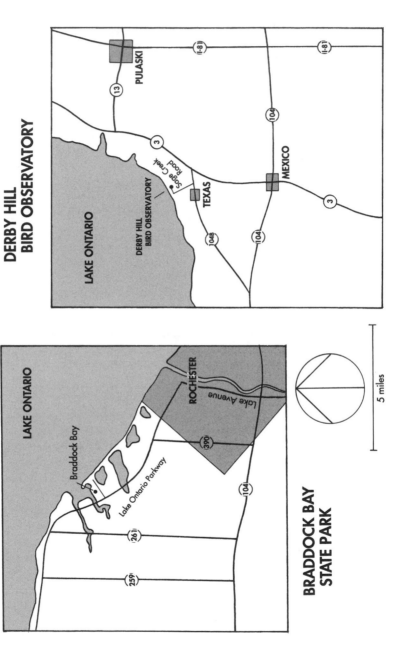

DERBY HILL
BIRD OBSERVATORY

LAKE ONTARIO

DERBY HILL
BIRD OBSERVATORY

Sage Creek Road

PULASKI

TEXAS

MEXICO

13

3

3

104

104

104B

104B

I-81

I-81

BRADDOCK BAY
STATE PARK

LAKE ONTARIO

Braddock Bay

Lake Ontario Parkway

Lake Avenue

ROCHESTER

259

261

390

104

5 miles

14

Right Whales from Shore

There are few mammals in the world as rare as the northern right whale which, after more than four centuries of constant pursuit, was virtually annihilated in the North Atlantic. Even today, after nearly sixty years of complete protection from whalers, northern rights number only a few hundred individuals, making the sight of one an experience to be treasured for a lifetime.

Spotting a right whale usually entails a long string of summer whale-watching trips off the Northeast or Canadian coast, but during March the whales are migrating north from their wintering grounds off the Southeast, and—if you are exceedingly lucky—you may chance upon one from shore.

Right whales, unlike many of the great baleen species, are by nature near-shore animals, migrating and feeding fairly close to land. This, combined with their relatively slow speed and the fact that they float when dead, made them the "right" quarry for early whalers; shore-based whaling stations quickly sprang up at Cape Cod and south in New Jersey soon after colonization; hunters intercepted traveling whales with rowboats. Basque whalers traveled to Newfoundland to hunt them as early as 1530. By the 1750s, right whales were already considered quite rare along the New England coast, one of the first large North American mammals to suffer severe declines at the hands of Europeans.

Right whales are not acrobatic, and the best a shore-based watcher can hope for is a clear view of the billowing spout, the low, dark back of the whale cruising at the surface, and a quick glimpse of the raised tail when the whale dives. As whalers knew, the shape and size of a whale's spout can be a distinguishing characteristic, and a right whale's is low and bulbous, similar to a humpback whale's from the side but making a distinct V-shape when seen from the front or rear. Unlike any other baleen whale in the area, right whales have no dorsal fin, a field mark that can be seen under good conditions, and the tail flukes lack the scalloped trailing edge of a humpback.

HOTSPOTS

Right whales may be encountered anywhere along the Northeast coast where the land pokes out into the whales' travel route, but one of the most consistent locations is Fire Island off the south shore of Long Island, New York. There are a number of good locations along the 32-mile-long barrier island; try **Seashore Trail** in the national seashore area to the east, and **Jones Beach State Park** at the western end. To reach Seashore Trail, from Route 27 (Sunrise Highway) take Route 46 (William Floyd Parkway) South to the Smith Point Bridge on Narrow Bay. The Seashore Trail, which runs 8 miles west from the parking area, provides good views of the water.

Reach Jones Beach State Park by taking the Meadowbrook State Parkway south from the Southern or Northern State Parkways. In either area, your best bet is to pick a place with some elevation, set up a spotting scope and scan for a spout. Even here, you'll need an inordinate amount of luck to see a right whale—but while you're looking you should see an interesting assortment of seabirds to pass the time.

15

Steelhead Runs

A native of the West Coast, the steelhead is a superb example of fish evolution—long and bullet-shaped, with a subtle grace and explosive power. Introduced years ago to the Great Lakes, it has in the past twenty-five years established itself as one of the dominant game fish in the Northeast, famous for its slashing runs and dramatic leaps.

Most of the year the steelhead travel freely in the deep waters of the lakes, feeding on alewives and other forage fish, but in fall and again in spring, they make spawning runs up a number of tributary rivers. This provides excellent fishing for anglers, as well as a wonderful spectacle for non-anglers.

Steelhead are big fish, ranging from 5 to more than 20 pounds. Actually a sea-run strain of the rainbow trout, the steelhead has (along with the rainbow) recently been reclassified with the Pacific salmon like the coho and chinook, rather than with the true trout.

Using an incredibly keen sense of smell, the fish home in on the unique odor of their natal streams (which, because of the limited natural reproduction on Great Lakes streams, means the place in which they were stocked as fingerlings). As they move into the spawning rivers their color changes from its normal silver-green to dark, steely black, with a deep maroon stripe running down the side.

Although steelhead may be found in the spawning streams anytime from November through early May, the spring peak occurs from the middle of March through the end of April. Be aware that this is also the peak time for fishermen, and if you are planning an overnight stay near a good steelhead river, it's a smart move to call ahead for motel reservations.

HOTSPOTS

Although steelhead runs occur in a number of Lake Erie and Lake Ontario tributary streams, visitors are more likely to see hordes of fishermen than hordes of fish on most of them. The exception is the Salmon River near Pulaski, New York, which has the state's main salmon and trout hatchery on its headwaters.

The **Salmon River Fish Hatchery** at Altmar produces about 4.5 million trout, salmon and steelhead fingerlings each year; most are the product of eggs stripped from adults that migrate up the river to Beaverdam Brook and are diverted through a fish ladder to the hatchery's holding areas. Here the fish are stripped of their eggs and milt. Each spring about two thousand steelhead are captured for spawning, yielding about 1.5 million eggs.

Visitors can see the whole process, including a self-guiding tour of the hatchery, but the real attraction are the steelhead jamming the fish ladder, stacked like proverbial cordwood in the pools and lunging through the low falls. When the gate to the holding area is down, frustrated steelhead may leap constantly out of the water, trying to get as far upstream as possible.

To reach the hatchery, take I-81 to Exit 36 (NY13/Pulaski). Turn right onto Route 13 South toward Altmar, a drive of about 7 miles. At Altmar turn left at the hatchery sign onto Cemetery Street, go straight at the stop sign for a total of .7 mile. The hatchery, which is on the left, is open every day from 9 A.M. to 4 P.M., but the fish ladder area is open from dawn to dark. Obviously, no fishing is allowed in this area.

On your return from Altmar, turn off at the Route 2A bridge or, space permitting, stop at the Fishermen's or Trestle pool parking areas to watch the fishing. Bridges also cross the river in Pulaski and on Route 3 west of town, and if the river isn't too high or turbid (and with a pair of polarized sunglasses) you may be able to see the torpedo shapes of steelhead lancing upstream, drawn by instinct toward their home waters. For other areas on the Salmon River where fish-watching is possible see Chapter 55.

16

Nesting Bald Eagles

With its 7-foot wingspan, white head and tail and chocolate-brown body, the bald eagle may be the most instantly recognizable bird in North America. Seeing one wheeling against a brilliant spring sky, huge against the blue, can be the highlight of any naturalist's day.

And fortunately for residents and visitors in the Northeast, the region has one of the largest populations of bald eagles in the Lower 48, with the number of nesting pairs increasing every year as the eagles continue to recover from the disastrous effects of pesticide poisoning in the thirty years following World War II.

Bald eagles are waterbirds, for the most part, feeding heavily on fish and nesting near the ocean, large rivers and lakes. In the Northeastern United States the species is most common along the Maine coast, with smaller numbers scattered across New York and southern New England. The inland population in particular has benefited from reintroduction projects like New York's, in which large numbers of eagle chicks from Alaska were released in the state, and later returned to breed.

Most large birds have prolonged reproductive schedules, and bald eagles are no exception. Their courtship season begins in late winter, with egg-laying occurring in March or early April, depending on latitude. The eggs are incubated for about 35 days, and the chicks may spend more than 12 weeks in the nest before fledging. Even then they are still dependent on their parents for weeks more.

Eagle nests are used year after year, and presumably generation after generation; one was known to be used for more than thirty-five years. Generally, the eagles choose a huge tree near water with a commanding view of the surrounding area, and most often pick a site far from humans (this isn't always the case, however). Because eagles add to the nest each season, it may eventually grow so big and heavy that the tree breaks beneath its weight; one famous nest in Ohio was 12 feet thick and more than 8 feet in diameter when it finally came down. By February, in many areas, the eagles will be active near the nest, carrying in sticks and branches to build a fresh layer on which to raise the latest generation.

This is also the time to watch for courtship flights, which include pursuits, a rising and falling "skydance," and—most spectacular of all—a display in which both eagles lock talons and somersault or spin toward the ground.

By March (early April in the north) the pair will settle down to incubation, which the male and female share; observers from a distance can see the white head of the incubating adult, and the periodic trade of responsibilities when the mate comes in from hunting and changes places. There are usually two eggs, although as many as five have been recorded—and because the adults begin incubation as soon as the first is laid, there can be a substantial difference in age (and size) between the oldest and youngest chick. If food is abundant this might not pose a problem, but if not, the oldest will hog the lion's share of the prey, either starving or actively killing its younger siblings. Cruel as this seems, it is an insurance policy that at least one chick will survive; if the food were shared equally, there is a good chance none of the chicks would get enough to live.

By early summer the eaglets, clad in dark brown from head to tail, are using the nest as a practice platform for flying, exercising their wings by flapping endlessly. Eventually, and with so little fanfare that it looks accidental, one will launch itself from the nest and take to the sky—another generation in a wildlife success story.

HOTSPOTS

While eagles now nest in many parts of New England and New York, the pairs tend to choose inaccessible areas—and if they don't, wildlife managers often close the land around the nests to give the great birds security. Fortunately, there are a few places where naturalists can enjoy the sight of nesting eagles without disturbing the birds.

Nesting eagles are easy to see, for example, at **Iroquois NWR** in western New York; visitors can set up their scopes on the back patio of refuge headquarters and look out through the treetops at the giant nest in the distance. Even with binoculars, it is easy to see the white heads of the adults as they refurbish the nest and incubate the eggs. To reach Iroquois from I-90, take Route 77 North to the village of Alabama, then north on Route 63 for .9 mile to Casey Road. Turn left and drive .8 mile to the headquarters building. Walk around back and look to the north, just along the tops of the trees, for the mass of the nest.

Maine has one of the largest bald eagle populations in the region, but most of the nests are remote, often on islands kept closed to the public for that very reason. Fortunately for naturalists, however, a pair of eagles set up housekeeping in the early 1990s in a uniquely observable location at **Moosehorn NWR** near Calais, Maine—on an artificial nesting platform a short distance from busy Route 1.

Maine eagles usually wait until April to lay their eggs, but this month the adults should be active in the vicinity, sprucing up the shaggy stick nest and taking part in courtship flights. If you're lucky, you may even see the pair (or one of the others that nest in the area) locking talons and spinning through the air.

To get to Moosehorn, take I-95 North to Bangor, then follow Route 9 to Route 1 South. Go 3.7 miles, watching for Charlotte Road on the right, marked by a sign for Moosehorn. The nest is just beyond the intersection, on the right. While the area beyond the road is obviously kept closed to protect the birds from disturbance, binoculars or a spotting scope will give you an unmatched look at the nesting pair. A second platform, about .2 mile down Charlotte Road, is occupied by a pair of ospreys later in the spring.

17

March Shorttakes

Clouds of Blackbirds

From the second week of March until early April, tremendous numbers of blackbirds of several species migrate along the shores of Lake Ontario. **Derby Hill Bird Observatory** in New York, one of the best places to see the migration, has recorded hundreds of thousands in a single day. For directions to Derby Hill, see Chapter 13.

Black Ducks

The black duck, once one of the most abundant species of puddle ducks along the coast, has suffered significant population declines in recent decades—making the sight of hundreds of these handsome ducks each March at **Rachel Carson NWR** in southeastern Maine all the more exciting. For directions to the refuge, see Chapter 7; take the Carson Trail and boardwalk that overlooks the small ponds known as salt pannes for the best observation points.

Tundra Swans

On their way from the Chesapeake Bay and Outer Banks to their breeding grounds in the Arctic, tundra swans pass through the region each spring, although few locations produce consistently large numbers. One spot is the northern end of **Chautauqua Lake** in southwestern New York, where each March as many as one thousand swans stop for a time. From the east take Route 17 across the lake, then turn north on Route 394 for about 9 miles to Mayville. (From the north or west take I 90 to Exit 60, then follow Route 394 East through Mayville)

Stop beside the Chautauqua Historical Society's depot museum to scan the lake, depending on ice cover, then turn right on the north side of the museum onto Lakeview Avenue; the next half-mile has good views of the upper end of the lake. Make a right on Sea Lion Drive and go 1 mile (the road becomes Whallon Street) to Mill Road. Turn left, go .4 mile to Route 430 and turn right. Cross a small bridge and make an immediate right onto Elmwood, which leads .3 mile to a boat launch. Return via Galloway to Route 430.

Snow Geese

This month the spring waterfowl migration carries with it tens of thousands of snow geese, most of which stop—as in the fall—in the **Champlain Valley** to feed and rest. As many as three thousand per day may pass through this area; Chapter 62 has more details. Flocks totaling five thousand or more may also be present at **Montezuma NWR** in New York; see Chapter 19 for directions.

See also:

Chapter 8, Maple Sugaring. The sugaring season, which began last month, hits its peak during March across most of the Northeast.

18

Breakout: The Remarkable Comeback of the Bald Eagle

For a national symbol, the bald eagle has had a rough time of it. National recognition in the eighteenth century did not bring legal protection, and for almost two hundred years this great bird was shot, trapped and poisoned by the thoughtless and ignorant.

Nor did the pervasive changes of colonization sit well with the eagles. The Adirondacks, for example, are thought to have originally held as many as two hundred pairs, which nested in the branches of the giant white pines that dominated the mountains. Timbering in the 1800s destroyed the pineries, however, and the eagles, robbed of their nest sites, rapidly declined. By the turn of the century only a few dozen pairs remained, and they were gone completely fifty years later.

Elsewhere in the eagle's range, habitat destruction and human disturbance also took a toll, but along the coast, where eagles were once common, the greatest threat may have been the indiscriminate use of powerful pesticides like DDT, which became popular after World War II. DDT is a persistent chemical, not easily broken down but very easily stored in the fat tissues of the creatures that ingest it. Even worse, it is subject to a phenomenon known as "biological magnification," in which the concentration increases dramatically at each step in the food chain. Eagles (as well as ospreys, peregrine falcons and several other predatory birds) are at the end of long food chains and suffered the toxic effects of the pesticides.

The worst was DDT's interference with reproduction,

causing destruction of hormones like estrogen, which in turn caused the birds to lay eggs with abnormally thin shells; the eggs often broke, and those that didn't frequently couldn't supply enough calcium for the bones of the growing embryo inside.

The eagle population, already reduced by long association with humans, crashed. By 1960, New York had only one pair, and the situation was little better elsewhere. The plight of glamorous birds like falcons and bald eagles galvanized opposition to DDT and related pesticides, and their use was largely banned (although the chemicals remained in the bodies of the adult eagles, interfering with breeding for the rest of their lives).

Eventually, however, biologists began to see an improvement, greatly aided by a reintroduction technique known as hacking. Chicks from Alaska and Canada, where eagles remained common, were placed in huge flight cages built on towers in remote spots like Montezuma NWR in New York and Quabbin Reservoir in Massachusetts; when they were ready to fledge the doors were opened, and food was provided as long as the youngsters needed it.

Mortality in a hacking project is high, and the eagles do not always return (after four or five years of wandering) to breed in the same place from which they were released. But over the years enough eagles were hacked out in enough places that a new breeding population has been established within the region. New York, for example, had fourteen nesting pairs in 1990, producing sixteen chicks, and the following year Massachusetts had five eagle pairs on territory.

But the bald eagle isn't out of the woods yet. Populations in Maine, for instance, while substantial, remain below recovery targets set by the U.S. Fish and Wildlife Service, and there is growing concern that the eagles may run into trouble from habitat loss. While some eagles seem remarkably tolerant of people, most require solitude during the breeding season, and increasing human disturbance, especially by boaters, may force eagles from otherwise suitable nesting sites. Only time will tell if we have saved the eagle from one disaster just in time to saddle it with another.

APRIL

April Observations

19

Hordes of Geese

No other sound is so evocative of spring as the gabbled honk of a flock of Canada geese, rowing north by the hundreds on balmy south breezes. This is one natural event that almost everyone looks forward to, and when the geese fill the sky with their calls, none but the dullest souls ignore them.

Situated on the Atlantic Flyway, New England and New York are perfectly positioned to host large numbers of waterfowl, and in early April the Arctic population of Canada geese, which winter from Pennsylvania south to the Outer Banks, begin to trek north again to the wide swath of boggy tundra that stretches hundreds of miles across Newfoundland, Quebec and Ontario.

In centuries past these birds would have found abundant natural marshes in which to rest and feed along the way, but modern humans have a deep-seated aversion to wetlands, and in the past two hundred years many of those traditional staging areas have vanished. Those that remain, often protected as state or federal wildlife areas, have become crucial to the survival of geese and other migratory waterbirds.

In presettlement days, for instance, the north end of Cayuga Lake in New York was covered with a vast marsh that stretched across more than 100 square miles, making it one of the largest and richest on the continent. Around the turn of the century, however, the lake's outlet was dammed, changing water levels, and dredging for the New York State Barge Canal was begun. The marsh shrank drastically, and draining accelerated the losses, so that by the 1930s all but a pitiful remnant had been destroyed or degraded.

With the establishment of Montezuma NWR in 1937, though, the tide began to change. Today about 6,500 acres of former marsh have been restored and are managed for wildlife, particularly waterfowl. While the sun-blocking multitudes of the past are a memory, visitors here can still see remarkable concentrations of geese.

HOTSPOTS

In western New York, **Montezuma** and **Iroquois NWR** are the focus of the Canada goose migration, funneling a large percentage of the northbound birds through their marshes and impoundments.

At the peak in the first half of April, more than 120,000 Canada geese may be found in Iroquois and the adjoining **Tonawanda** and **Oak Orchard WMAs,** a complex of wetlands, forests and agricultural lands sprawling across 20,000 acres northwest of Batavia. Almost any of the refuge's large impoundments will hold birds. The last hour before dark is the ultimate show, as geese that had fanned out across the countryside to feed return for the night in gabbling, honking droves. Year to year, the best spots for observing the spectacle, refuge staffers say, are Cayuga Pool, Ringneck Marsh and the marshes along Route 63.

To reach Iroquois from I-90, take Route 77 North to the village of Alabama, then north on Route 63 for .9 mile to Casey Road. Turn left and drive .8 mile to the headquarters building, which is open on weekends in the spring. To reach the best goose-viewing areas, leave headquarters and turn right onto Casey Road, go a mile and turn right onto Route 77. Drive 1.8 miles and park at the lot for the Kanyoo Nature Trail, which runs for nearly 2 miles along dikes separating the main pools, including Cayuga (note that, like all refuge lands, the trail closes at dark).

Return by car past headquarters to Route 63, turn left and immediately right onto Roberts Road. Drive 1 mile and turn left onto Sour Spring Road; this dirt lane runs for several miles through a wooded swamp and past several large lakes where geese and a wide assortment of ducks can be found. The Mallard Overlook on Ringneck Marsh is especially good for geese at dusk. Continue north on Sour Spring past Tibbets Road, turn left onto the Macadam Road and proceed to two more overlooks before intersecting Route 63 about 2 miles north of the headquarters turnoff.

Each April, vast numbers of Canada geese pour through the Northeast on their way to their Arctic breeding grounds, stopping along the way at places like Montezuma and Iroquois NWRs in New York.

At the head of Cayuga Lake near Seneca Falls, New York, **Montezuma NWR** attracts eighty thousand to one hundred thousand Canada geese and twelve thousand snow geese each spring, as well as ducks, swans and other waterbirds on migration.

To get to Montezuma, take I-90 to Exit 41 (Waterloo). Turn right onto Route 414 South and drive .4 mile, then turn left onto Route 318 and go 4.3 miles to the intersection with Routes 20/5 East, a left turn. Refuge headquarters is on the left 1.7 miles down the road.

The 3.5-mile auto route, which runs along two sides of the huge Main Pool, is the best place on the refuge for waterfowl observation. From headquarters follow the one-way dirt road north around the pool to its end on Route 89, where you can turn right, crossing over I-90 to the Tschache Pool observation tower. More waterfowl are visible here, as well as more than two hundred great blue heron nests in the far trees, and there's an excellent chance of spotting bald eagles in the area, since Montezuma was the first release site for captive eaglets in the state, starting in 1976.

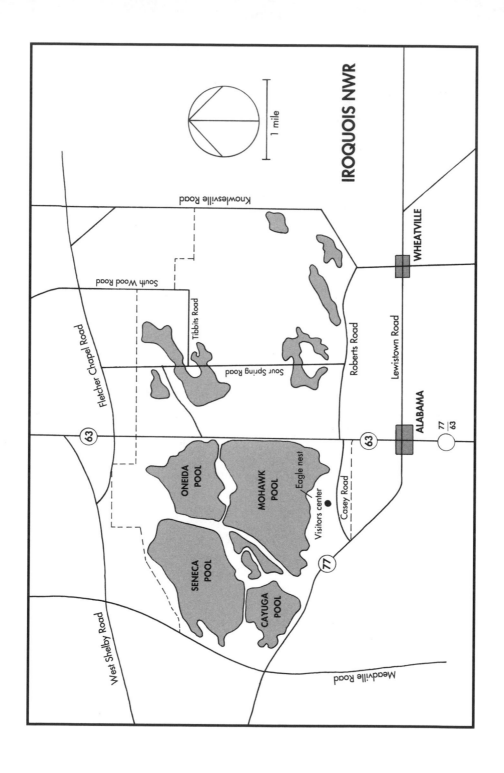

IROQUOIS NWR

1 mile

Knowlesville Road

South Wood Road

Tibbits Road

Sour Spring Road

Fletcher Chapel Road

Roberts Road

Lewistown Road

WHEATVILLE

ALABAMA

77/63

63

63

ONEIDA POOL

MOHAWK POOL

SENECA POOL

CAYUGA POOL

Eagle nest

Visitors center

Casey Road

77

West Shelby Road

Meadville Road

20

Broad-winged Hawk Multitudes

The broad-winged hawk is something of an anomaly among raptors, a clan known for its solitary behavior. Even in migration most hawks keep their distance from one another, moving at most in small groups, and most often alone.

Not so with the broadwing. This smallish soaring hawk, or buteo, common across forested New England and New York, is exceptionally social during the spring and fall migration, forming huge flocks known as kettles as they move from one air thermal to another.

Being so common and so gregarious, it is no wonder that the late April migration of the broad-winged hawk is one of the highlights of the spring for many naturalists, capping a hawk flight that began in the coldest days of February.

Broadwings are smaller than the more familiar red-tailed hawk—about the size of a crow, with a chunky body, broadly fanned tail and wide wings that taper to a sharp point. Adults are barred with rust across the breast, but in flight their most distinctive features are their white, black-tipped wings and boldly barred black-and-white tails.

Their breeding range stretches from Newfoundland to Alberta and south to the Gulf coast; in deciduous woodlands of the Northeast it is one of the most common raptors, often seen perched along forested interstates, unconcernedly watching for snakes, frogs or small mammals while the semis roar past. This innate tameness is typical of broadwings, which may also sit quietly along well-traveled trails, all but ignoring passersby.

Broad-winged hawks have one of the longest migratory paths of any North American raptor, flying south in fall along the Appalachians to the Gulf Coast, down through eastern Mexico and Central America to the rain forests of Peru and Brazil—a one-way journey of as much as 6,000 miles that takes the birds up to 2 months.

Come spring they turn back again, retracing their route. The vanguard reaches the Northeast around the beginning of April. The bulk of the flight arrives about 2 weeks later, and the peak usually hits the last week of the month.

And although broadwings, passing through in the tens of thousands, may steal the show, they are by no means the only species aloft; thirteen other species of raptors routinely migrate this month, along with often massive numbers of swallows, blackbirds and songbirds. It's a wonderful time to be at a hawk-watch, looking skyward.

HOTSPOTS

By far the best place to watch the broadwing flight is the southeast shore of Lake Ontario, particularly at **Derby Hill Bird Observatory** near Texas, New York, and **Braddock Bay State Park** just west of Rochester.

The numbers at either observatory can be nothing short of astonishing; one-day counts at Derby Hill have exceeded eighteen thousand, while at Braddock Bay on April 27, 1987, counters tallied forty-one thousand hawks, thirty-four thousand of them broadwings. During the 1992 spring flight at Braddock Bay, fifteen thousand broadwings were seen April 20, and another fourteen thousand two days later—and ironically, no broadwings at all had been sighted up to that point in the season.

Directions for both hawk-watches can be found in Chapter 13.

Weather and timing are both critical for catching the peak of the flight. The greatest numbers usually pass between April 20 and May 1, with many hawk-watchers staking out the entire last week of April in hopes of hitting it lucky. South winds of 10–25 mph, accompanied by warming temperatures and a low pressure system to the west, consistently produce the best flights at both lookouts. North, east or west winds may stop the flight or move it inland at Derby Hill, while north and east winds are bad news at Braddock Bay.

Each year, Braddock Bay Raptor Research hosts a Bird of Prey Week, usually the third week of April, to coincide with the biggest broadwing flights. The celebration includes hawk identification workshops, crafts sessions for kids, banding demonstrations and displays of live raptors. For more information, contact the association; the address is listed in the Appendix.

21

Alewife and Smelt Runs

In April, as the Earth tilts and the Northern Hemisphere once more angles toward the sun, the strengthening sunlight and warming temperatures affect not only the land, but the waters as well. In the newly ice-free lakes, and off the coast, the change in season means the start of the spawning period for several intriguing fish.

Alewives and rainbow smelt, although unrelated, are joined each spring by the urge to head for shallow water and breed, and their sudden presence signals a rush by fishermen, birds and naturalists, each with their own interest in the spectacle.

Alewives are members of the herring family, ranging from 6 to 15 inches in length, with the classic herring physique: a deeply compressed body, forked tail, silvery scales and a large head, with a jutting, underslung jaw. The row of serrated scales along the stomach gave the alewife one of its colloquial names, sawbelly.

The rainbow smelt is a tiny javelin, usually less than 9 inches long, with a slender body built for speed, and a surprisingly predatory mouth studded with pronounced canine teeth, used to capture small crustaceans. In many ways, in fact, a smelt resembles its close cousins, the salmon and trout, but is brilliantly silver, fading to greenish on the back and with a marvelous hint of pink and purple iridescence on its sides.

Both alewives and rainbow smelt can be found in salt water along the Northeast coast, and in landlocked populations in the Great Lakes, several river systems and a number of large lakes. For both species, April marks the spawning season, although the smelt may begin breeding in March and continue until May, while the alewife begins spawning in mid-April in most areas and may continue breeding through early summer.

An alewife run can be an experience not just of sight, but sound and smell as well. This species is prone to wild swings in abundance in the Great Lakes, and in a peak year when the schools come flooding into shallow water near beaches, harbors and stream mouths, they may attract large numbers of fish-eating birds like gulls, terns and cormorants. Many of the alewives are so exhausted by the stress of spawning (and by the pressures of overpopulation) that the water may be filled with dead or feebly swimming fish, washing up in windrows on the beach.

In lakes and ponds, spawning occurs in shallow water offshore, but along the coast the alewives are anadromous, migrating from salt water to fresh water up rivers and streams, sometimes in amazing numbers. The eggs are scattered across the bottom, usually over gravel or clean sand; once they hatch, the alewife fry feed on planktonic animals, a diet (augmented by small insects and fish) that the alewife will stick to for the rest of its life.

Unlike the alewife, which was never an important food species, the rainbow smelt has attracted a faithful following of commercial and sport fishermen. During winter, smelt fishing on ice-bound lakes is a popular pastime, with the delicately flavored, oily fish as ample reward for frozen fingers and toes.

By early spring, however, the smelt have moved to the shore, gathering near tributary streams and rivers for the spawning run, which is in full swing this month. The schools are pursued by diving birds, as well as by trout and salmon in fresh water—for, like the alewife, smelt are a critical link in the Great Lakes food chain.

For anglers, the method switches from baited lines to long-handled dip nets wielded from docks and piers along the fish's upstream routes. Those smelt that evade the obstacle course of hungry fish, birds and humans will spawn over gravel beds, dropping their sticky eggs at random.

Also in April, American shad—much larger and better known than their near-relatives the alewives—make their own spawning run from the ocean. As long as 20 inches and as heavy as 8 pounds, the shad is a justly famous game fish, known for its tenacious runs and repeated leaps. Shad spawn in regional rivers from the Hudson and upper Delaware north through Maine, with the bulk of the run in the southern rivers coming this month and next.

HOTSPOTS

Alewives and smelt can be found at a number of locations both on the coast and inland lakeshores.

Coastally, one of the most easily viewed alewife runs is in **Stony Brook** on Cape Cod's lower arm, where each spring untold tens of thousands of "herrings" (as they are locally known) choke the creek. Take Route 6 onto Cape Cod and drive 20 miles to Route 134 North; go 4 miles and turn right onto Route 6A East. Drive 1 mile, turning right onto Stony Brook Road, and go another 1.8 miles to the historic grist mill to park. The creek in this area has old fishways, fish ladders and netting pools that date from the days when alewives were harvested for fertilizer.

Alewives also make heavy runs on **Mount Desert Island,** although here the run comes somewhat later, peaking in May and June. One of the easiest areas to observe the fish is the upper end of Somes Sound, the spectacular fjord that nearly bisects the island; small streams in and around Somesville are good bets.

On the Great Lakes, alewives are usually very much in evidence by late April in **Dunkirk Harbor** on Lake Erie in New York, where they attract big flocks of birds; see Chapter 2 for directions. Alewives are particularly abundant in Lake Ontario, although their population is subject to boom-and-bust cycles.

The Great Lakes are also home to millions of smelt, and while they don't *all* spawn in the Niagara River, enough do that Lewiston, New York, claims the title of "Smelt Capitol of the World." Using long-handled dips at night, fishermen may dip more than a bushel each of these wriggling delicacies. In Lewiston the most popular fishing points (and thus the best places to watch) are the fishing docks at **Earl W. Brydges Artpark,** a big recreational facility along the Niagara gorge off Fourth Street, and **Sand Dock** (Guard Park) at the end of Center Street. Another good smelt run can be found to the northeast, where Route 18 crosses **Keg Run** 3 miles east of Olcott.

22

Woodcock Skydances

To the untrained ear it is the squeak of a frog, perhaps, or maybe the distant beep of machinery. There is a mechanical quality to the sound, certainly, a flat, nasal peent repeated with precision every five or six seconds.

Listen closely, though, for eventually the beeps are replaced by a frenetic twitter, and against the horizon where the last of the sunset shows red, you'll see a dumpy bird on buzzing wings, spiraling higher and higher in the air. Binoculars show a fat body, round head and an absurdly long bill before the bird is lost against the indigo sky overhead, leaving only the whistle of its wings.

Again now the sound changes; the twitter stops, and a lovely gurgle floats down from above, and as you crane your head back, looking, the limp body of the bird tumbles toward you as if dead. Only a few yards above the ground—and doom—the wings flare open, the bird rights itself and lands near its original position. A few heartbeats later the *peents* begin once again.

This, strange as it appears, is how a woodcock gets a mate.

Actually, almost everything about the woodcock is strange. This is a shorebird that has forsaken the shore, a nocturnal member of a diurnal family, a creature that dances to catch earthworms and can see behind it better than it can in front. It looks like a bird assembled by committee, with too-short legs, too-long bill, too-big eyes and a ridiculous little tail. No wonder the pioneers thought up so many odd names for it: bogsucker, timberdoodle, Labrador twister.

The woodcock is an easterner, found during the breeding season from the southern Appalachians to the Canadian Maritimes, and west to the edge of the plains—wherever there are damp woods and bogs where it can probe with its long bill for earthworms, its preferred food. When hunting, a woodcock may do a little stamping dance on the ground, much as old-time fishermen would "fiddle" for worms by driving a notched stick in the ground and rapidly running another stick along it; the vibrations may drive worms close to the surface.

Although woodcock may be found anywhere in the region, their center of abundance is the woods of Maine. They arrive here at the end of March, and as long as the temperature is above freezing the males will continue their courtship flights until the first week of June. The flights start around sunset and last for about 45 minutes, and for an equal period in the morning before sunrise.

Although it is possible to closely approach a performing male, stay at least 35 or 40 yards away, since your presence will deter females from coming into the lek, as the dancing grounds are known. A pair of binoculars will help you pick out the flying bird as twilight deepens, and give you a front-row seat to one of the strangest and loveliest shows of the natural year.

HOTSPOTS

Far and away the best place in New England and New York to see the woodcock's skydance is **Moosehorn NWR** near Calais, Maine, only a stone's throw from the New Brunswick border. Moosehorn, in fact, is the only one of the nearly 450 national wildlife refuges whose primary purpose is the management of woodcock, which nest—and skydance—here in abundance.

Moosehorn is comprised of two units: Baring, covering 16,000 acres just west of Calais, and Edmunds, another 6,665 acres to the south along Cobscook Bay near Dennysville. Both units have good numbers of woodcock, but visitors would do well to stop at headquarters at the Baring unit and check on current hotspots. It is also possible, by advance arrangement, to accompany biologists in the field banding woodcock as part of their research work.

To reach headquarters take I-95 to Bangor, then Route 9 East to the junction of Route 1 South just west of Calais. Go 3.7 miles and turn right at the refuge sign onto Charlotte Road; the turn into the refuge is another 2.6 miles. Where you turn into the refuge you'll see the Woodcock Trail, a short loop that serves as something of a demonstration area for woodcock land management practices, and can be a good place to watch the skydancing; there are other footpaths in the Baring unit that pass through prime woodcock habitat.

To get to the Edmunds unit return to Charlotte and turn right. Drive 8.7 miles to Route 214 East, turn left and and go 6.4 miles to Route 1 South at Pembroke. Drive another 9 miles on Route 1; the entrance to the North Trail, an auto-accessible loop, is on the right, but you'll see more woodcock (and other wildlife) if you park and walk in. A map sign of the route is posted at the entrance.

23

April
Shorttakes

Wealth of Hepatica

On warm days in mid-April, the limestone outcropping known as **Bartholomew's Cobble** in southwestern Massachusetts turns bright with the flowers of round-leaved hepatica, one of the earliest spring wildflowers. This is one of the largest hepatica colonies in the region, and is known for the variety of color displays, from pure white to deep cobalt. The flowers need mild temperatures and bright sun to open fully, so a visitor on a cloudy day is apt to be disappointed. The best displays are along the Ledges Trail; see Chapter 44 for directions.

Songbird Migrations

Although May is the peak month for migrant warblers, vireos and other songbirds, some species start north in April, and their numbers can be remarkable. Swallows, in particular, are in evidence in late April, especially following the coasts of lakes Erie and Ontario; good observation points include **Derby Hill** and **Braddock Bay**, New York (Chapter 13). For such early songbirds as yellow-rumped, palm and pine warblers, see the listing of songbird "traps" in Chapter 25.

Gulls and Terns

The alewife run in Lake Erie, bringing as it does an abundance of dead and dying fish, is a bonanza for fish-eating birds. At **Dunkirk Harbor** in western New York, several thousand Bonaparte's gulls linger on their wintering grounds through late April, most of them now in their natty, black-headed breeding plumage. They are joined by large numbers of common terns, as well as herring and ring-billed gulls and double-crested cormorants. For more on the alewives, see Chapter 21; for directions to Dunkirk, see Chapter 2.

See also:

Chapter 15, Steelhead Runs. Good but declining numbers of fish can be seen through the end of the month; consider combining a trip to the **Salmon River Fish Hatchery** at Altmar, New York, with a stop at **Derby Hill** for hawk-watching (see Chapters 13 and 20 for directions to hawk-watching sites).

Chapter 16, Nesting Bald Eagles. While the view of the nest in New York becomes obscured by tree leaves later in the month, the **Moosehorn NWR** nest is in the open just a short distance from Route 1 near Calais, Maine.

Chapter 37, Heronries. The great blue heron colonies at **Iroquois** and **Montezuma NWRs** are becoming active this month; watch especially for the graceful "neck-stretch" display and other ritualized movements among the courting herons. Also worth visiting is the large black-crowned night-heron colony on the **Dufferin Islands** on the Niagara River on the Canadian side, just above Horseshoe Falls; see Chapter 2 for directions. Be sure to read the cautionary note on disturbance in Chapter 37.

24

Breakout: Amphibian Choruses

Admittedly, it is not everyone's idea of a fun evening to be standing knee-deep in chilly water, at night, in the middle of a marsh or mountain bog. But those that take the time and trouble, this month and next, will experience something the stay-at-homes never hear—the amphibian chorus in full voice, ringing in the return of spring.

Frogs and toads are the singers of spring as much as any warbler or wood thrush; their voices fill the night as the birds' do the day. On a mild spring night across much of New England and New York, a naturalist may hear the songs of as many as a dozen amphibian species. Some, like the western chorus frog, are found only in a few locations in the region, while others, like the wood frog and spring peeper, are common almost everywhere there's a damp patch in the forest or fields.

Wood frogs, in fact, are among the earliest, sometimes appearing by late February or early March in southern New York, should the weather turn unusually warm; wood frogs do not always even wait for the ice to completely thaw before commencing with the business of courtship. Unlike most spring amphibians (and probably because they breed so early in the year) wood frogs are most active at warm midday, when their quacking calls are often mistaken for ducks.

While wood frogs will breed in marshes surrounded by forest, they frequently pick much less permanent locations, including temporary woodland ponds of meltwater, and even

A male gray treefrog, his vocal sac inflated like a balloon, trills on a warm spring evening—just one singer in the many-voiced amphibian chorus.

deep roadside ditches. Slip up quietly, and you'll see dozens, sometimes hundreds of males, each brown with a black robber's mask, floating on the surface, legs extended and the vocal sacs in front of the forelegs inflated, giving them the appearance of wearing water wings.

A receptive female will swim toward a calling male, who grasps her just behind the front legs and fertilizes the mass of gelatinous eggs she extrudes around a branch, forming an orange-sized mass containing several hundred embryos. The males are not particular, and will grab for any frog (or piece of floating debris) that comes their way. If one should mistakenly grab another male, the interloper gives a distinctive chirping call that signals the mistake.

As the weather warms, more and more amphibians leave their underground hibernacula and head to the breeding ponds. Soon after the wood frogs finish their explosive breeding cycle, which ends within a week or two, the spring peepers take up the refrain. These tiny chorus frogs are scarcely an inch long, but their voices can rattle your bones, especially if there are several hundred frogs, all belting out piercing preeeeeps! to the night air. Unlike wood frogs, spring peeper males call from hidden positions among dead marsh grass and cattails, and finding one takes patience (having someone along so you triangulate the frog's position helps, too). Look for a small, gray-brown frog with a dark X across its back. Males have dark throats, while females' are white or cream.

Still later in the season—usually by May in the southern half of the region—the marshes fill with a choir. American toads give their musical trills, while green frogs plunk like out-of-tune banjos. Across the northern half of the region, mink frogs pound like hammers on soft wood, and leopard frogs snore and snort. Bullfrogs, which wait until the spring is assured before making an appearance, jug-o-rum through the night, and from the shrubs surrounding forest ponds, gray treefrogs chur like red-bellied woodpeckers. Spring is back, and the amphibians don't care who knows it.

MAY

May Observations

25

Spring Songbird "Traps"

May is the month that many naturalists live for, and a big reason is the return of migrant songbirds. After a winter of staring at the same chickadees and siskins at the feeder, naturalists can see waves of brilliantly plumaged warblers, elegant thrushes, vireos, tanagers and orioles, up from the south, sweeping the last of the doldrums away.

Almost any woodlot or park this month will have its share of migrants, stopping off after a night of flying to rest and feed; summer residents will also be returning, to immediately begin the task of defending territories and attracting mates. But what a naturalist hopes for is a migrant "wave," when the treetops are alive with hordes of birds.

Hitting a songbird wave is largely a matter of luck, simply being in the right place at the right time (especially nowadays, given the rather alarming declines in many Neotropical migrants). But you can stack the odds in your favor if, instead of birding in just any old woodland, you head for one of the many songbird "traps" in the region.

A songbird trap is an accident of geography and prevailing weather patterns, a place where the land, water and wind conspire to force migrating birds into a small area. It may be a peninsula jutting into the Great Lakes, a coastal island that provides a convenient resting place for weary travelers, or a park surrounded by a sea of concrete.

One such place is Monhegan Island, 10 miles off Maine's central coast. Songbirds trying to take a shortcut across the Gulf of Maine often find this small speck of land a convenient rest stop, while to those blown out to sea by strong northwest winds, it can be a lifesaver. Regardless, Monhegan—and the other migrant traps listed here—are ideal places for a naturalist to spend a morning in late May.

HOTSPOTS

Monhegan Island, Maine, has a reputation as one of the best migrant traps in New England, but access is by ferry only, and since there are no cars allowed on the island, once there you'll have to rely on shanks' mare to get you around. Yet the island is so small (only a mile and a half long) that nowhere is more than a short walk away. For the best birding, try the western edge of the island from the village south to Lobster Cove and Burnt Head; around the village itself, check the swimming beach, where insect-eating migrants often feed on the ground.

NOTE: *Before traveling to Monhegan, make firm lodging reservations on the island, since accommodations are limited in the off-season, and there is no camping.*

For ferry information and rates, contact Capt. James Barstow, P.O. Box 238, Port Clyde, ME 04855, (207) 372-8848.

Accessible by car, **Bailey Island** south of Brunswick is another coastal Maine bird trap, although not as consistently good as Monhegan. From Brunswick take Route 24 South 16 miles to the island, which is laced with small roads—the only access, as most of the ground is private.

To the south, off New Hampshire's limited coastline, lie the **Isles of Shoals,** another outstanding songbird trap. Here, however, private property makes it very difficult to bird on one's own, so it is better to join an organized trip; contact the Audubon Society of New Hampshire, whose address is listed in the Appendix, for details on scheduled excursions.

Other good regional locations for migrant songbirds include **Parker River NWR** in Massachusetts, especially the boardwalk through Hellcat Swamp; see Chapter 2 for directions to the refuge. Also in Massachusetts, Marblehead Neck north of Boston is productive for spring songbirds, particularly **Marblehead Neck**

Wildlife Sanctuary. From Salem take Route 114 through the town of Marblehead, then right onto Ocean Avenue. After crossing onto Marblehead Neck, watch on the left for Risley Road, which leads to the refuge parking lot.

Part of Connecticut's **Hammonasset Beach State Park,** Willard "Island" (actually a woodland surrounded by tidal marsh) east of New Haven provides forest songbirds with a convenient stop-off point in otherwise unsuitable habitat, especially if strong north winds are forcing the birds to the coast. To reach Hammonasset, take I-95 to Exit 62, then follow the connector road south two miles across Route 1 to the park entrance. Go through the traffic circle and drive toward Meig's Point; there is a left turn just before the point onto a loop road. Park at the far end and follow the footpath back to Willard Island.

Moving down the coast about 25 miles, try **Milford Point,** south of the town of Milford; the area is also good for marsh and seabirds, but the thickets and woodland of the point often attract good numbers of flycatchers, warblers and vireos. For directions, see Chapter 43.

On the western shore of Lake Champlain, **Crown Point,** New York, sticks like a finger north into the lake, providing a natural cul-de-sac for northbound migrants forced against the lake by strong winds. Bird from the fort ruins on the western side of Route 903 down through the woodlands along Bulwagga Bay to the old lime kiln. To get to Crown Point, take I-87 to Exit 28, following Route 74 East for 18 miles to Routes 9N/22; turn left and go north for 11.6 miles. Turn right on Route 17 and go 4 miles to the park. During midday you can park in the lot near the fort, although visitors arriving early in the morning will have to park along the berm of Route 17, since the access road will be gated.

The Great Lakes are a formidable barrier to migrating songbirds, many of which detour around the lakes rather than risk an over-water crossing. On the Lake Ontario shoreline, **Braddock Bay** west of Rochester, New York (directions in Chapter 13) is an excellent place to watch for migrant songbirds, especially in the woods near the hawk-watch, West Spit and the woods near Island Cottage Road, all in Braddock Bay State Park.

For city-dwellers, urban parks offer the most convenient springtime birding of all, and many, like **New York City's Central Park**, are justly famous for the caliber of their spring migration; a morning spent wandering the stands of hardwoods on **The Ramble** may turn up more species than in more truly wild settings.

The best birding in Central Park usually occurs the first 2 weeks of May, when there is a southwest wind and rising temperatures.

Indeed, almost any wooded city park has the potential as a migrant magnet, although some, like **Forest Park** in Queens, **East Rock Park** in New Haven, Connecticut, and **Durand Eastman Park** in Rochester, New York, have long-standing reputations as such.

> CAUTION: *Security is a growing problem in many urban parks, and birders, tramping around at odd hours, may be at especially great risk. Make it a habit to never travel alone, and keep at least part of your attention off the birds and on your surroundings. There is safety in numbers; after about 7:30 A.M. in spring, there are usually large numbers of birders on The Ramble in Central Park, for instance, if you haven't a partner. Some parks, like* **Prospect Park** *in Brooklyn and* **Alley Pond Park** *in Queens, are considered simply too dangerous by even some local birders, although they are excellent for birds.*

While it may seem a trifle morbid to non-birders, naturalists know that urban cemeteries are often among the best places to watch migrant songbirds, which find old tree-lined burial grounds a perfect place to feed and rest (temporarily, not eternally). In New England and New York, some of the most reliable are **Swan Point Cemetery** on Blackstone Boulevard in Providence, Rhode Island; **Mount Auburn Cemetery** on Mount Auburn Street in Cambridge, Massachusetts (known as "the Central Park of New England" for its excellent birding); **Evergreen Cemetery** on Steven's Avenue in Portland, Maine; and **Oakwood, Morningside** and **St. Mary's** cemeteries in Syracuse, New York.

26

Shorebirds

For many of North America's shorebirds, the year is a constant race against distance and time. They shuttle back and forth between continents, trading hemispheres in an endless quest for long days and abundant food. As spring spreads across the Northern Hemisphere, they again head toward the Arctic, many having been (just a few weeks before) on a lazy lagoon in South America. Once on their tundra breeding grounds they will court, mate and try to raise their chicks before the snows of autumn return in August.

Because there is so little time to waste on the northbound leg of their yearly trip, shorebirds do not linger in New England and New York; many overfly it completely on their way back to the Arctic. In autumn, by contrast, the flocks work their way south more slowly, feeding heavily in preparation for the long flights ahead.

Yet even if the numbers aren't as impressive in spring as in fall, the sheer elegance of the birds themselves makes up for any shortfall. Chasing the seasons north to breed, the birds have molted into their summer finery—in many cases a dramatic change from the drab plumages of winter.

Black-bellied plovers, for instance, that had been flecked with battleship-gray all winter, develop a trademark black face, throat and belly, set off by a white band and a boldly checkered back of black and white. Ruddy turnstones, too, have blossomed with the spring, a harlequin mix of black, white and rusty orange. Even the ubiquitous sanderling, that gray wraith that chases the waves endlessly, becomes (for the brief nesting season) as bright as a robin's breast.

Even though spring shorebirding in New England and New York is, generally speaking, not quite as good as the fall migration (which actually hits its peak in August), there are nevertheless some very productive areas worth a visit during May.

Maine, with its dramatic tidal rise and fall, has some of the best shorebirding in the East. In southern Maine, the **Scarboro River marshes,** the **Wells area** and **Biddeford Pool** are considered the best by local birders.

General directions to Wells are found in Chapter 7. At the light at the junction of Route 9/109 and Route 1, turn left onto Route 1 North, then just .1 mile later turn right at the sign for "Wells Harbor and Boat." This is lower Landing Road, and it leads for a mile through fine salt marsh. Also worth exploring is Mile Road, which leads to Wells Beach; directions are also given in Chapter 7.

Migrant shorebirds—some passing through on their way north, others like these willets staying for the nesting season—enliven the coast and regional wetlands this month.

Biddeford Pool is a huge tidal pond near the mouth of the Saco River, and on a falling tide its invertebrate-rich mud flats are a feast for northbound shorebirds. To get there from the town of Biddeford, take Route 9/208 (Pool Road) South about 4.5 miles, then follow Route 208 when it splits to the left; the pool is the large body of water to the left of the road.

The Scarboro River marshes are the largest tidal marsh in Maine, stretching from Route 1 southeast to the Pine Point Narrows. The best starting point is the **Scarborough Marsh Nature Center,** a Maine Audubon Society facility. From Portland take Route 1/9 South about 5 miles to West Scarborough, where Route 9 bears left; follow 9 (Pine Point Road) less than a mile to the center. From the south take I-95 to Exit 5, then I-195 to Route 1 North to West Scarborough and Route 9, a right turn.

Shorebirds can also be found on the huge flats at Lubec, Maine, near the New Brunswick border—although here again, not in the riveting concentrations seen in fall. For directions to the **South Lubec Flats,** see Chapter 43.

In Massachusetts, shorebird enthusiasts should make a point of checking out the salt pannes and flats of **Parker River NWR** east of Newburyport, where good numbers of spring shorebirds may be found. For directions to Parker River, see Chapter 2.

Rhode Island, for all its famous lack of size, has an impressive 400 miles of shoreline, making it a terrific place for shorebird watching. Two of the best spots in spring are **Charlestown Beach** and **Quonochontaug,** tidal zones with a rich assortment of sandpipers, plovers and other migrants. For directions, see Chapter 43; be prepared to get wet and muddy, since you must do some hiking through muck to reach the best birding sites.

In Connecticut, **Hammonasset Beach State Park** is worth a visit, especially the Willard Island and Cedar Island trails and the pond area west of the traffic circle. For directions to the park, see Chapter 25.

Pink lady's-slipper orchids are one of the jewels of the May woods, growing best in forests of oak and pine.

27

Spring Wildflowers

It's hard to find a naturalist who doesn't love May. By now, spring is no longer a tentative hint, but a fulfilled promise, and even in the highest elevations winter is a memory by this month's final days. There are the returning flocks of songbirds to look forward to, waterfowl in their breeding finery, choruses of frogs and toads—and, of course, wildflowers.

May is a botanist's delight, when many of the most lovely and delicate native flowers come into their glory. In woodlands, trilliums are among the most distinctive hallmarks of the season, with their characteristic three-fold build: three leaves, three petals, three sepals. Earliest, and most common in rich, alkaline forests, are the red trilliums (*Trillium erectum*), with deep maroon petals. Preferring cooler, more acidic forests, the unmistakable painted trillium (*T. undulatum*) has gorgeous white flowers stained with purple at the throat—a striking combination, and one that is a common sight over much of northern New England and New York.

Another standard-bearer of May is the jack-in-the-pulpit, a member of the arum family and one of the most instantly recognizable of eastern wildflowers. Oddly, the distinctive green and purple structure we think of as the flower is not; rather, it is a sheath designed to protect the flower-covered spike ("Jack") within. This sheath, known as a spathe, is one of the defining features of the arums, which include skunk cabbage and the tropical peace lily sold in greenhouses.

The spring woods are full of flowers whose shape, like the jack-in-the-pulpit's, or colors seem inexplicable at first notice, but make good natural history sense. The reddish throat of the painted trillium, for instance, serves as a landing indicator for pollinating insects, directing them to the nectar. The wild columbine's red, long-spurred petals, curving up and in like claws, are perfectly suited to long-tongued bumblebees (and to the probing bills of ruby-throated hummingbirds, which frequently visit them for nectar, but do not pollinate the plant).

One of the strangest of spring flowers is the pink lady's-slipper or moccasin-flower, with its bulbous, pouched blossom, a shape that is also designed for reproduction. The pouch is slit down the front, but the opening is tightly shut, and small insects are excluded. A bumblebee, on the other hand, is strong enough to pry open the pouch and squeeze in, but when it does it discovers that the only exit is up through the throat of the flower. As the bee struggles out the narrow opening it is painted with pollen, to be deposited in the throat of the next lady's-slipper it visits.

Nor do a flower's machinations end with pollination. Many spring-blooming species, including violets and trilliums, bear seeds coated with a thin, nutritious coat that attracts ants, which carry them off and eat the jacket. Discarded by the ants, the tough seeds eventually sprout, usually some distance from the parent plant.

The flowers of the May woodlands may seem serene, but they are actually in a battle against the clock—and against their vastly bigger neighbors, the trees. Early spring is the one time of the growing season when the forest floor is bathed in bright sunshine, before the canopy of trees' leaves cuts off most of the vital energy; it is the best time for woodland wildflowers to bloom and set fruit. So the flowers run the risk of late frosts for their own moment in the sun, and thus ensure another generation of blossoms.

Timing is always a tricky thing in the outdoors, what with the vagaries of weather and altitude; a flower blooming in late April in the lowlands of Connecticut might not bloom until early June in the Adirondacks. So May is a smorgasbord of spring, both a look back and a peek forward, depending on where and when you go. If you discover that, for instance, you've missed the trailing arbutus in one area, try a spot farther north or at a higher altitude. Even the difference in bloom time between a sunny south slope and a shady north slope may be as much as a week. By playing latitude and altitude against the calendar, you should be able to catch the season's best show, in one of the year's best seasons. What more could a naturalist ask for?

HOTSPOTS

The spring bloom of wildflowers is a regionwide event, and almost every forest hollow, woodlot or marsh edge south of Maine and the Adirondacks will have blossoms this month. But for unusually diverse or abundant flowers, try one of the following locations.

On Long Island, the unusual **Oak Brush Plains Preserve,** a remnant of a once-widespread habitat, holds a number of unusual flowers for curious visitors; until recently, most of the land was part of the now-defunct Edgewood State Hospital in Brentwood. The land protected by the reserve was once part of a much larger prairie/pine barrens community that covered portions of central Long Island with natural grasslands surrounding pockets of stunted oak and pine. Among the spring wildflowers here are birdsfoot violet, wild lupine, trailing arbutus and pink lady's-slipper.

The Oak Brush Plains Reserve is managed by the New York Department of Environmental Conservation (DEC). To reach it, take the Long Island Expressway (I-495) east from New York City. Shortly before the Sagtikos State Parkway, take Exit 52 onto Route 4 (Commack Road) South. Go about 3 miles; the preserve is on the left, and should be posted as a DEC property, although vandals often tear the signs down.

Even closer to city-dwellers is the remarkable **New York Botanical Garden Forest,** a 40-acre tract of original hemlocks and northern hardwoods, miraculously untouched in the middle of the Bronx; in May it is a wonderful place for hunting up typical woodland wildflowers, not to mention listening to migrant song-birds. The forest is often called the Hemlock Grove, and is only part of the 250-acre botanical garden off Fordham Road, opposite the zoo. Admission is charged.

Perhaps the best wildflower site in the region is **Bartholomew's Cobble,** south of Great Barrington in western Massachusetts. Limestone outcroppings have enriched the soil, and a mosaic of habitats from forest to river edge and old meadow account for the stunning diversity of plant life here—among the richest plant communities in New England, with 450 species of wildflowers.

From late April through May, visitors can expect to find spring beauty, Dutchman's breeches, fringed polygala, columbine, red trillium, jack-in-the-pulpit, cut-leaved toothwort and much, much more, including the finest collection of ferns in the United States (covered in more detail in Chapter 44, along with directions). Plan to spend at least a day exploring the trails that wind through this state-owned reserve's 278 acres, and be sure to bring a good field guide.

In central Massachusetts, the **Wachusett Meadow Wildlife Sanctuary,** more than 1,000 acres owned by the Massachusetts Audubon Society, provides a wonderful mix of meadows, maple swamps, hardwood and conifer forests—with the abundance of wildflowers that such a diversity of habitats brings. To reach the sanctuary, take Route 62 West from Princeton Center .8 mile, then turn right on Goodnow Road; the sanctuary is 1.1 miles ahead. Admission is charged to nonmembers.

Nearby, the hiking trails of **Wachusett Mountain State Reservation** beckon, with good numbers of spring wildflowers (including arbutus) on the Bicentennial, Pine Hill, Semuhenna and Old Indian trails, which vary greatly in length and degree of difficulty. For directions to Wachusett Mountain see Chapter 50; ask at the visitors' center for a summary of hiking trails and a map.

In northwestern Connecticut, wildflower buffs can spend a lazy late-May morning wandering the miles of trails that wind through the **Northeast Audubon Center.** The sanctuary's rich woods produce an impressive bloom each spring, augmented by marsh and field species. To reach the center, take Route 7 North from I-84 35 miles to Route 4 at Cornwall Bridge; turn left on Route 4 West and go about 7 miles toward Sharon. The center is on the left.

In southern Vermont, spring wildflowers put on a fine show at **Jamaica SP** near the town of Jamaica. The prime time is from mid-May to mid-June, when wild sarsaparilla, Indian cucumber root, painted and red trillium and a host of other species typical of mixed and northern hardwood forests bloom. To reach the park, take Route 100 to Jamaica, then follow the signs across the West River to the park.

28

Nesting Peregrine Falcons

The peregrine falcon has been called the ultimate expression of avian evolution, and watching one sailing high on scimitar wings, then folding into a blistering, 175-mph dive that simply overwhelms whatever smaller bird it is chasing, few people would think to dispute the claim.

Every nuance of a peregrine's form is shaped by the wind, streamlined to slide through the air like a bolt. The head is bullet-shaped, the chest heavy and powerful, the wings and tail long and tapered; the contour feathers of the body lay flat and smooth, like plating. Even the nostrils are built for the race, with internal baffles so the falcon can breathe at literally breathtaking speeds.

Once, peregrine falcons were widespread across the region—never common, perhaps, but found in every corner of New England and New York, nesting on high, inaccessible cliffs. It is thought that their major prey may once have been the passenger pigeon, and that with the demise of that super-abundant bird, the peregrine may have suffered a decline. But through the early days of the twentieth century the species was a fixture, breeding on the Palisades bluffs above the Hudson, beside scenic Taughannock Falls in New York, on high ledges in the Adirondacks and Green Mountains, and even on city sky-scrapers in Boston and New York.

Then came World War II, and the recognition that a new class of chemical pesticides, the organochlorines, were amazingly effective against a variety of insect pests. This family of chemicals, especially DDT, came into wide use after the war—and the consequences for many birds, especially peregrines, were devastating.

As they did with bald eagles, ospreys, brown pelicans and several other predatory birds, the chemicals interfered with the reproductive system of the peregrines, rendering their eggshells so thin that the eggs broke. With no young being produced, peregrine populations went into free-fall. The damage was so swift and complete, in fact, that in the early 1960s, when biologists began to suspect something was terribly wrong, a survey of historic eyries (or nest sites) in New England and New York produced the shocking find that not a single one was occupied.

In the course of less than fifteen years, the peregrine had become virtually extinct as a breeding species east of the Mississippi, and populations elsewhere in subarctic North America were declining rapidly.

The use of DDT and a wide variety of related pesticides was banned in the United States starting in 1972, a first step toward cleaning the environment for the falcons. Meanwhile, a small group of ornithologists and falconers, like Cornell University's Tom Cade, were breeding peregrines in captivity. In 1974, Cade formed the Peregrine Fund, based at Cornell and designed to place captive-reared falcon chicks back in the wild.

The technique they used is known as hacking; the young chicks are placed in a high, remote cage on a cliff, tower or skyscraper. Caretakers hide when they feed the chicks (so the chicks do not associate people with food), and when they can fly the cage door is opened. Food is provided as long as they need it, but eventually instinct takes over, and the young falcons learn to hunt on their own.

Over the next ten years more than 750 chicks were released in the East, many of them in New England and New York. With no adults for protection and guidance, juvenile mortality was high, but enough survived their first few years to return to breed, often picking the same cliffs and ledges where peregrines had historically nested. There are now several dozen nesting pairs in the region, and each year the number of breeding falcons increases.

The peregrine reintroduction has not been without controversy. The original subspecies in the east was *Falco peregrinus anatum,* while the captive birds were a genetic mishmash—many *anatum* birds, but also *tundrius* peregrines from the Arctic, the very dark Peale's peregrine of the Pacific Northwest, even falcon subspecies from Spain, Scotland and Chile. The released birds are essentially nonmigratory, while the original *anatum* birds from New England and New York traveled to the Gulf coast and Mexico for the winter.

Some biologists now question whether the reintroduction should have been attempted at all, arguing that the native *anatum* birds would have repopulated the region on their own, given time. Others, however, hold a different view. The differences between the subspecies are slight, they say, and natural selection will weed out the genetic lines unsuited to the region. In the meantime, one of nature's masterpieces has been restored to the sky—no small feat, and no small thing.

HOTSPOTS

Peregrine numbers are still fairly low in the region, but there are several locations where naturalists can easily watch courtship, nesting and chick-care behavior without disturbing the rare birds.

Vermont, with about ten nesting pairs, is second only to New York in resident peregrine numbers. Hacking began in the Green Mountains in 1977, and in 1985 the first wild pair in twenty-seven years nested in the state, on Mount Pisgah. In 1987 peregrines reclaimed a historic eyrie site among the soaring, scenic cliffs of **Smugglers Notch** on the flanks of Mount Mansfield, and began nesting there in 1989.

The Smugglers Notch pair are the most easily viewed falcons in Vermont; although the actual nest ledge varies from year to year, it is usually around Elephant Head, a rock face on the eastern side of the narrow gorge. From I-89 take Exit 10 to Route 100 North; at Stowe turn left onto Route 108 North past the base of Mount Mansfield into Smugglers Notch. There is parking in the middle of the notch near Smugglers Cave, but once the trees leaf out, the best view is from a small pull-off on the left, at the south end of the gorge.

Perhaps the finest opportunities for watching a peregrine nest are on the cliffs of **Champlain Mountain** at Acadia National Park in Maine. Starting in 1988 a male falcon, hacked out on the nearby Jordan Cliffs, set up territory and, with the mate he later attracted, began nesting in 1991; this site, too, is a historical eyrie. To prevent disturbance the park has been closing the popular Precipice Trail, which climbs the face of the cliff, through late August.

Follow Route 3 from Ellsworth onto Mount Desert Island, then south from Bar Harbor to the Sieur de Monts entrance of the park loop road. The Precipice trailhead lot is 2.7 miles from the entrance, right below the flat wall of the cliff. Morning is best, since by afternoon the sun drops low over the cliff and viewing is extremely difficult. During the summer a park ranger is often stationed here with a spotting scope trained on the nest, which can be remarkably hard to pick out among the hundreds of ledges and nooks. With patience, however, you should see one of the adults fly in with prey, and may even see an aerial transfer from the male to the female—and hear the spirited kek-kek-kek-kek of the peregrine, so long absent from these skies.

Although there's a special thrill in seeing falcons reoccupying their traditional haunts, urban peregrines have their own charm, providing a breath of wilderness in the busiest downtown. In New England and New York, most urban falcons have taken to bridges as nest sites, but some habitually return to the same skyscraper ledges year after year. In Springfield, Massachusetts, for instance, a pair of peregrines has been nesting since 1989 on the **Monarch Place** building, the city's highest.

With fourteen pairs of peregrines, New York has the largest breeding population in the Northeast—and one of the most urbanized. While a few pairs have returned to historical eyries in the Adirondacks, the bulk of the Empire State's peregrines nest in or near New York City, where bored commuters are often startled to see a peregrine hurtling past the bridge deck in pursuit of a pigeon or gull.

The **Verrazano-Narrows** and **Throgs Neck** bridges, where the first post-restoration falcons nested in 1983, continue to support nesting peregrines. Other pairs can be found on the **Riverside Church,** on Riverside Drive between 120th and 122nd streets in upper Manhattan, and **New York Hospital-Cornell Medical Center,** along the East River in midtown Manhattan. There are other nesting falcons in the city, including a pair on the **Pan Am Building,** but perhaps due to the problems imposed by an urban environment they often fail to raise young.

Outside of the city, a pair has taken up residence under the **Tappan Zee Bridge,** linking Tarrytown and Nyack, and another at the **Rockaways** south of Jamaica Bay. Bridge falcons usually nest under the decking supports, out of sight of all but maintenance workers, so you'll have to be content with views of flying adults—certainly no hardship.

29

May
Shorttakes

Gull Colonies

This month the raucous breeding season at regional colonies hits its full stride (and volume), providing remarkable spectacles. One of the most accessible is the huge colony of herring and great black-backed gulls on **Captree Island,** part of the barrier island complex along Long Island's south shore. This month the gulls are involved with nest-building and egg-laying; take the Robert Moses State Parkway to the Moses Causeway, following signs for Fire Island. The gulls are easy to observe, but do not enter the gullery itself, which is posted against disturbance.

Other gulleries in the region that are active this month include **Little Galloo Island** in Lake Ontario west of Watertown, New York; **Four Brothers Islands** in Lake Champlain northeast of Willsboro, New York; and **Popasquash Island** on the Vermont side of Champlain, northwest of St. Albans. Viewing is by boat only, and landing on the islands is prohibited; in fact, close approaches, which disturb the birds, are discouraged. Popasquash can be viewed from the road with a scope, however. From St. Albans take Route 36 North 8.3 miles and watch for the low island just offshore; there is no real place to park, however, and the lakeshore is all privately owned.

See also:

Chapter 16, Nesting Bald Eagles. Any chicks in the **Moosehorn NWR** nest in Maine should be active and visible all month.

30

Breakout:
The Flies of Spring

If, instead of hunched backs and dingy gray bodies, black flies had the colors of, say, swallowtail butterflies, people would come from around the world to see their emergence in May.

Sadly, black flies not only lack pretty colors, they have a nasty bite and a big appetite—and this month uncounted billions of them take to the air, looking for a warm-blooded meal. It is a natural spectacle as remarkable as any in this book, but it is difficult to keep that fact in mind when you're flailing blindly at a buzzing horde. Black flies can make an otherwise wonderful time of the year a hellish experience for anyone caught unprepared.

Black flies are found throughout North America, but they are most closely associated with the boreal forests of northern New England and New York, where an abundance of mountain streams and rivers provide a perfect breeding ground. There may be as many as two dozen species of these small, biting gnats in a single creek. They are actually indicators of good stream health, for in general their larvae require extremely pure water during the weeks or months it takes them to reach maturity.

Once they pupate and take to the air, however (starting soon after ice-out in spring) the females begin looking for a blood meal, necessary if she is to produce a batch of eggs. Most species will take whatever comes their way, be it a moose or a hiker, but some specialize in particular hosts, including one that appears to feed only on the blood of loons. They leave behind a ferociously itching, bloody welt, made worse by the fact that you almost never get just one black fly bite.

Knowing that maternity is the driving force behind a black fly is slim consolation when you find yourself surrounded by hundreds of them, crawling in your ears, up your sleeves and through your hair, biting all the while. But by taking a few common-sense precautions, you can reduce the nuisance level considerably and have an enjoyable day outdoors.

Most important, keep the bugs away from your skin. Wear loose-fitting, long-sleeved shirts and pants, with elastic bands at the cuffs to prevent the flies from crawling inside; athletic sweat bands work nicely. Tuck your pant legs inside heavy socks (the black flies will bite through thin pairs), and wear a hat. Odd as it seems, a pair of latex surgical gloves will keep them from biting your hands, and you can use masking tape to seal the connection with your sleeves, as well as to close off the open flap above the cuff.

A good insect repellent, one containing a high level of the chemical DEET, is probably the most effective control, although many people find the acrid smell almost as bad as the bugs—DEET also has a damaging effect on clothing and plastics if it rubs off your skin, and may pose possible health problems. Soak the brim of an old, expendable hat in insect repellent to keep black flies away from your head. Some people have luck with a dilute solution of Avon's Skin So Soft lotion, while others (perhaps because of a quirk of body chemistry) find it completely ineffective.

Northwoods veterans swear that black flies are attracted to the color blue, even in small amounts; avoid light colors. Regardless of what you wear, any kind of scented shampoo or soap—to say nothing of perfume or cologne—is an invitation to be bitten.

And if all else fails, wear a head net and have patience. By the end of June the worst of the black fly season will pass, and the forests will become a little less blood-thirsty.

JUNE

June Observations

31

Alpine Tundra Wildflowers

Standing on the summit of a high mountain, with the clouds looking closer than the valleys so far below, it is easy to think yourself on an island, floating somewhere between earth and sky.

But beyond any metaphysical sense, the highest peaks in the Northeast really are islands—islands of place and time. Even more so than the bogs that dot the flatlands, they are remnants of the Ice Age, preserving a snapshot of a time when all of the region lay in the grip of the continental glaciers.

When the ice sheets retreated north, they in effect pulled successive plant communities along in their wake: first the arctic tundra, with its dwarfed, cold-tolerant plants, then the boreal conifer forest, then the mixed transition woodland, then the belt of solid hardwoods and so on, like the banded train of some great skirt dragging across the land. The high mountains of the Adirondacks and northern Appalachians, however, provided a refuge for the more northerly species, which were eventually cut off in a sea of more southerly plants.

Today the tundra community is found hundreds of miles to the north, in Canada—except on a few of the tallest mountains, where the altitude, lingering cold and wind have preserved Arctic-like conditions, and allow unique alpine tundra plants to survive.

Camel's Hump, in Vermont's Green Mountains, is typical of the wind-scoured peaks that support alpine tundra. Climbing up the 3.5-mile trail to the summit, the visitor passes through several distinct life zones, as ecologists term the plant and animal communities that change with altitude. At the trailhead the forest is typical New England hardwood, dominated by sugar maples and American beeches, but soon large numbers of yellow and white birches appear, until the forest is almost solid birch.

Around 3,000 feet, patches of conifers begin to mix with the birch, and, by 3,200 feet, the birches have been almost completely replaced by red spruce and balsam fir. The higher you climb the shorter the spruces become, until just below the summit you eventually find yourself walking through a dwarf forest of waist-high trees; such stunted alpine forests are known by the German name *krummholz.*

Camel's Hump's distinctive, rounded top is only a few minutes' climb above the krummholz. Here the trees are finally defeated by the incessant wind, growing only in a few small pockets where a boulder offers some protection, and sheared off just inches above the ground; a spruce only a foot high, sprawled along a rock crevice, may be seventy-five years old. Yet the very conditions so harsh for trees are ideal for the mountain's tundra plants, which carpet the open ground between the rock slabs.

The most obvious are the green swaths of what look, at first glance, to be turf. This is Bigelow's sedge, one of the most abundant alpine specialists on Camel's Hump. A grass relative, the sedge does not look nearly as exotic and unusual as many of the alpine plants, and suffers badly in consequence; uninformed hikers tend to want to stretch out in what seems like a handy lawn. Unfortunately, such abuse can quickly kill the delicate sedges.

The alpine plants thrive by keeping their heads down, so to speak. Growing low to the ground has several advantages—the rocks collect and retain a measure of warmth, and the wind, which can both dry out a plant and snap it off, is somewhat deflected. Because the alpine species are retiring by nature, you'll have to look closely to appreciate them.

In the cracks between boulders, look for small mats of thin-leaved foliage, topped by delicate, five-petaled white flowers. This is mountain sandwort, a member of the pink family, to which domestic carnations belong. No more than two or three inches high, it is an Arctic Canadian species found on mountaintops as far south as the Adirondacks.

With the sandwort, one of the prettiest flowers in the alpine environment is *Diapensia,* which forms dense cushions crowned by short stalks, each with a single white flower. (You can tell *Diapensia* from mountain sandwort by looking at the tips of the petals, which are slightly notched in the sandwort. The sandwort also has small, paired leaves on the flower stalk.)

The most spectacular of this dwarfed community, though, may well be Lapland rosebay, a diminutive rhododendron with purple flowers less than an inch across. The rosebays bloom in early to mid-June, along with the *Diapensia*, making this the perfect time to discover the alpine environment.

Many of the plants that are high-altitude species in the Northeast mountains are lowlanders much farther north. One of these is Labrador tea, a common bog plant in northern New England and Canada. In June its white flower clusters are among the prettiest sights on Camel's Hump, where it grows just off the edges of the barest summit, where there is a bit more protection. A heath that is related to mountain laurel and rhododendron, Labrador tea has thick, leathery leaves with a slightly rolled edge and a fuzz of rusty wool on the underside, in part as protection against drying. The flowers form small globes of white, weaving and bobbing in the ever-present breeze.

Careful observation will show many other tundra species blooming or getting ready to. The tiny pink Japanese-lantern flowers of the alpine blueberry are common mid-June, and it takes a close examination to tell them apart from those of the alpine bilberry, which also bears a tiny purple-black fruit later in the summer. Berries, in fact, are common alpine species, and most summits have a number of species. Watch for a creeping plant with thin, glossy oval leaves and a cluster of minute pink flowers at the end of a short stalk, this is mountain cranberry, whose berries (many of which will still be left from the previous year) are unimaginably tart. Black crowberry grows in many of the same places, and can be identified by its narrow, waxy leaves and very small purple flowers; the clusters of small berries ripen to black.

A good field guide to Northeastern wildflowers will help you sort out what's what, but the most important things you can bring to the tundra are care and respect. A single footstep can compact the soil around the roots of these delicate plants, killing them; this is a particular problem for the miniature meadows of Bigelow's sedge. Be absolutely sure to stay on marked trails and, if you go exploring, carefully hop from bare rock to bare rock. On many summits, especially on weekends, you'll meet ranger-naturalists who guard the fragile tundra communities against thoughtless humans while sharing their knowledge of this unique environment.

HOTSPOTS

There are three areas within the region that support alpine tundra communities—the **Green Mountains** in Vermont, the **Presidential Range** in New Hampshire, and the **High Peaks of the Adirondacks**. The blooming period begins in June for *Diapensia,* many of the berries and Labrador tea, and lasts through late summer for other species of wildflowers.

> NOTE: *For all their tolerance of extremes in climate, alpine plant communities are extraordinarily fragile. A single footstep can compact the soil around their roots and kill them, so always stay on the marked trail or areas of bare rock. Having survived tens of thousands of years since the glaciers, the greatest threat facing this rare habitat is careless foot traffic.*

Before planning any alpine trip, read the general cautions on high-altitude hiking in the Introduction.

In the Green Mountains only **Mount Mansfield** and **Camel's Hump** have significant areas of tundra. Because of easy access, Mansfield's tundra has been severely degraded, but Camel's Hump's 10 acres, accessible only by foot, remains in fairly good condition.

The hike up Camel's Hump, while not technically difficult, is quite steep in places, rising more than 2,600 feet in less than 3.5 miles, and takes about three hours for the average hiker; good boots or hiking shoes are a must.

Take I-89 to Exit 10 (Routes 2 and 100, Waterbury/Stowe), turning onto Route 100 South. Go all the way through Waterbury to the bridge at the far end (currently a one-lane span with a traffic light, but due to be replaced). Across the bridge turn right, still on 100 South, then right again almost immediately at a small sign for Duxbury Elementary School. Three-tenths of a mile farther the road bends sharply left; instead go straight on an unmarked dirt road. Drive 5.1 miles to the tiny hamlet of North Duxbury and, at the intersection, turn left onto another dirt road. Go 2.3 miles, turn right across the bridge, and go another 1.4 miles to the Couching Lion Farm trailhead.

The summit is 3.4 miles from here; the easiest route is to follow the blue-blazed Forestry Trail to its intersection with the red/white-blazed Long Trail, which leads the final .3 mile to the

Hikers scramble up the steep summit of Camel's Hump in Vermont's Green Mountains, where one of the finest alpine tundra communities can be found.

top. On the way back you may want to continue south on the Long Trail a short distance to the yellow-blazed Alpine Trail, a steep descent past the remains of an old airliner crash. The Alpine Trail rejoins the Forestry path in half a mile.

One could argue that **Mount Mansfield** is too accessible for its own good, with both an auto toll road and gondola service too near the summit. The constant foot traffic has seriously damaged the tundra, despite the efforts of ranger-naturalists on duty through the summer to educate the crowds, but for someone physically unable to climb a tall mountain, this is the best bet for alpine tundra. To reach the Mansfield area take Exit 10 (Waterbury/Stowe) off I-89 onto Route 100 North, turning left after 9.5 miles onto Route 108 N in Stowe. The entrance to the toll road is another 5.9 miles on the left, at the Toll House Ski Area. It is open from 10 A.M. to 5 P.M., weather permitting, and the 1992 fee was ten dollars per car. Bicycles are not allowed.

In New Hampshire, **Mount Washington,** the highest of the northern Appalachians at more than 6,200 feet, has a large area of alpine tundra, but suffers from the same overuse as Mount Mansfield. The climb to the summit is difficult and (if the weather turns sour) potentially dangerous. Most visitors come either by car, taking a toll road from Glen House on Route 16, or the famous cog railway up the Bretton Woods side of the massif off Route 302. Both routes have their disadvantages. The toll road is quite hard on vehicles, and costs about eleven dollars per car and driver and four dollars for each passenger, while the cog railway charges thirty-two dollars per rider (less for senior citizens and children), takes three hours round trip and only allows 20 minutes on the summit; the route is also frighteningly precipitous and the clouds of coal smoke and soot from the engine boiler can be choking.

In the Adirondacks, ten peaks that reach 4,900 feet or higher support alpine tundra communities. Among them is **Mount Marcy,** which, at 5,344 feet, is the tallest of the High Peaks. Others include **Algonquin Peak** and its neighbors in the **MacIntyre Range.** These peaks lay in true wilderness, some accessible only after long, hard hiking, and it is beyond the scope of this book to provide detailed trail directions for them. Highly recommended is *Discover the Adirondack High Peaks* by Barbara McMartin, which covers routes and trail maps for this wild area.

32

Loon Laughter

There is no other sound quite like it, the tremulous wail that floats across a northern lake at dawn, rising and falling, carrying in its haunting notes a summation of wilderness.

Few people can listen to the call of a common loon without being moved. This is the signature sound of the North Woods, and for many visitors to the region hearing one laughing through the night is a high point of the trip.

The common loon, with its necklace of white and checkerboard pattern on the back, is the species that comes to most people's minds when they think of loons. There are four other species—the yellow-billed, the arctic, the Pacific and the red-throated—but only the common loon is found south of Canada in summer, with the southern edge of its breeding range stretching from the Adirondacks through northern Vermont and New Hampshire to Maine. It is strictly a warm-weather resident in the region's inland, migrating in late fall to the sea from the Maritimes to Florida.

Taxonomically, loons are ranked as among the most primitive of birds, yet there is nothing unsophisticated about them, from their elegant plumage to their many physical adaptations for an aquatic lifestyle. The legs, which are powerfully muscular, are set far back on the body; this provides maximum strength for swimming, but forces them to push along on their bellies when they are on land. The wings are kept folded underwater, and the loon propels itself with sweeps of its webbed feet; on the forward stroke, the flattened tarsi, or leg bones, cut resistance by the water.

In fact, almost everything about a loon's body helps it dive and swim. It has the ability to store unusually large amounts of oxygen in its muscle tissue just before plunging underwater. Many bones are solid, rather than hollow as in most birds, resulting in a specific gravity close to that of water, so the loon can slip under without a ripple when it needs to escape quietly.

Loons have been caught in fishing nets more than 200 feet deep, but most of their time is spent in shallow water, where they dive for small fish, their primary prey. Cruising slowly along the surface, the loon will repeatedly stick its head underwater, watching for fish. When it sees a school it dives with a quick thrust of both legs, arcing down like a dolphin. Although loons will catch gamefish like brook trout, they tend to capture slower prey, like small catfish and suckers, more often.

Soon after they return from their wintering grounds, loon pairs pick a nest site, usually returning to the same secluded cove or backcountry pond they used in years past. The nest—a low, flattened bowl of sedges and grasses built right along the water— is finished, and the eggs (normally two) are laid around Memorial Day. Incubation takes about a month, and the chicks can swim

The wild, laughing call of the common loon can be heard throughout the northern half of the region in summer, including the Adirondacks and central Massachusetts.

almost from birth. For the rest of the summer they stay close to their parents, eventually learning to dive and hunt on their own.

Vocalizations play an important role during the breeding season, keeping loon pairs together and delineating their territory. Ornithologists recognize four or five different calls, including the famous "laugh" and a longer, more complex version known as a yodel; loons also wail, and have a number of low, short calls that they use to communicate when they are near each other.

Although you may hear loons call at anytime of the day during June, they will be most vocal at dawn and again at dusk; if there is a bright moon the loons may well call straight through the night. Some people can imitate a loon call well enough to draw a bird close, but this (or the use of tape-recorded calls) should be avoided, since it disrupts the loon's routine and may leave its nests or chicks vulnerable to predators.

Loons have, in fact, suffered some serious setbacks in New England and New York in recent decades, largely from increased human use of the lakes they need for breeding. Motorboat wakes are especially disastrous, swamping the shoreline nests and drowning the eggs, while too much disturbance of any kind may cause the loons to desert the nest entirely. Sometimes the harassment is more direct; ignorant boaters may chase loons, forcing them to dive repeatedly. Loons pressed this hard may die from exhaustion and a buildup of toxins as a result of holding their breath for long periods.

Other problems plague loons. One study of dead loons on New England lakes found that more than half had died from lead poisoning after swallowing fishing sinkers, probably in mistake for gizzard stones picked from the lake bottoms. Loons also suffer mercury contamination on the wintering grounds, and from acid precipitation, which can render their breeding lakes sterile.

Loon-lovers have not been idle, however. Anglers are being urged to avoid lead weights in lakes that support loons, and floating artificial nest platforms, anchored just offshore so they rise and fall with a boat wake, have shown promise. Public awareness of loons has also made boaters more aware of the dangers of disturbance, and in some areas the long decline in loon numbers appears to have reversed itself.

HOTSPOTS

Common loons breed throughout the northern half of the region, often picking remote backcountry lakes. What follows, however, are suggestions for fairly accessible areas with healthy populations of loons. Remember that this is the height of the breeding season, and you should never approach an area you suspect of harboring a loon nest.

In New York, loons are restricted to the Adirondacks, where **Stillwater Reservoir** in Herkimer County has between five and sixteen pairs, the highest concentration in the state. Researchers have found that the construction of artificial dams in the Adirondacks, like Stillwater, has greatly benefited nesting loons, even at a time when loon populations have declined significantly in most of the rest of the region.

Stillwater is a popular (perhaps overly popular) recreational lake, especially on weekends when lines of motorboats wait to launch at the west edge. But a system of lakeside campsites around the giant impoundment allows a visitor to escape to a quiet cove where the evening is alive with loonsong. To reach Stillwater from the west, take Route 12/26 North to Lowville; from the light at the 12/26 juncture, go .4 mile and make a right onto River Street, then drive 4.4 miles and turn left at the sign for Stillwater. This is Number Four Road, which leads 14 miles to the hamlet of Number Four; make a right onto Stillwater Road and go another 9 miles to the boat launch area. Half a mile before the launch is a road leading to the right, which skirts the southern edge of the reservoir for about 4 miles.

Coming to Stillwater from the central Adirondacks, take Route 28 to the town of Eagle Lake and turn west onto Big Moose Road. Go 6 miles and turn left at the T-intersection, then go another 2 miles to Big Moose Station. The road becomes dirt for the next 10.5 miles, ending at the junction with Stillwater Road a half-mile from the boat launch.

Northern New Hampshire has a number of lovely, accessible lakes with nesting loons. Cherry Pond in **Pondicherry Wildlife Refuge,** an Audubon Society of New Hampshire property outside Whitefield, is especially easy to reach, requiring an easy 45-minute walk over old railroad beds. From the Franconia Notch Parkway (I-93) take Route 3 North about 11 miles to the junction of Route 115. Continue on Route 3 another 5.9 miles toward Whitefield, then turn right onto Colby Road, following signs for the airport. Go 1.6 miles, turn right onto Airport Road and park near the office by the airstrip.

The railbed begins to the right of Hanger A and sweeps east, skirting the end of the runway and a high-tension line before

*The placid waters of Cherry Pond, part of Pondicherry Wildlife Refuge
in northern New Hampshire, are home to common loons, which make
the air ring each summer with their calls.*

joining another rail line; bear right at the juncture. After another
15 minutes' walk the line splits and you'll see signs for Pondicherry,
with Cherry Pond dead ahead.

In the northern panhandle of New Hampshire, the upper
Connecticut River system supports a number of loon pairs on the
chain of lakes stretching from Pittsburg to the Quebec border.
Second and Third Connecticut Lakes are especially good bets;
for more complete directions see Chapter 49. Other New Hampshire lakes with breeding loons include **Lake Winnipesaukee**
and smaller, nearby **Squam Lake**.

Lake Umbagog, on the New Hampshire-Maine border, has
a healthy population of loons—in fact, it represents New
Hampshire's largest concentration. Those loons, along with a
diverse mix of other wildlife, will be protected by the newly
created **Lake Umbagog NWR,** which when fully purchased will
cover more than 15,800 acres near the junction of the Androscoggin
and Magallaway rivers, close to Errol, New Hampshire.

Maine has the largest population of loons in the Northeast,
with breeding pairs on many of the larger interior lakes; loons are
much less common along the coast, although a pair may occasionally
set up territory in such heavily used areas as Acadia National Park.

Knight's Pond, on the western shore of Penobscot Bay, is on the Maine Register of Critical Areas and is part of the Maine Nature Conservancy's St. Clair Preserve; it is close to Route 1, the tourist artery, is easily reached by canoe, and has nesting loons. From Northport go west on Beech Hill Road to Knight's Road, a left turn; the jump-off point is the boat launch at the east end of Knight's Pond. Because the pond is so accessible, it is critically important that people not approach the loons, particularly if visitors suspect a nest is nearby.

Loons are especially easy to hear (and see) in **Baxter State Park,** the 201,000-acre wilderness north of Millinocket. Baxter is primarily a foot park, with an encompassing 175-mile network of trails linking many of the backcountry lakes and ponds where loons nest, but less energetic visitors have several options as well.

Togue Pond, on the park border by the southern (Millinocket) gate, hosts several pairs of loons on both sides of the lake, and has the advantage of being outside the park gatehouse, so visitors needn't pay the entrance fee of eight dollars. Within the park, **South Branch Pond**, about ten miles from the Matagamon gatehouse, is usually popular with loons; rangers here often see as many as ten on the lake, most having flown in from smaller ponds to fish, then returning to feed their young. There is a campground at South Branch Pond (reservations are required; see the Appendix for more information about Baxter State Park), and campers are often treated to dawn and dusk choruses. A trail leads to **Upper South Branch Pond** about 2 miles away, another good place to see and hear loons.

Just outside the park to the northeast, **Grand Lake Matagamon** and **Scraggly Lake** are also hotspots for loons, as well as being especially productive for moose. See Chapter 49 for more details.

Massachusetts would not, at first thought, seem to be likely loon country, but the giant **Quabbin Reservoir** annually supports between five and eight breeding pairs. For general directions to Quabbin see Chapter 67; the loons normally breed among the islands in the northeastern arm of the lake, and the areas near gates 27, 33, 35 and 37 are usually the best bets. Unlike the southern half of the lake this area is open to both shore access and boats, but watch any loons you see from a discreet distance so you don't disturb them.

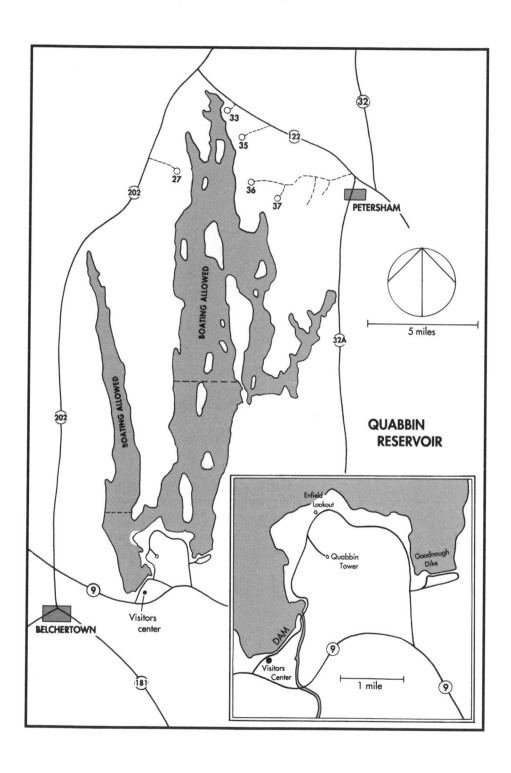

QUABBIN RESERVOIR

BOATING ALLOWED

BOATING ALLOWED

PETERSHAM

BELCHERTOWN

Visitors center

5 miles

Enfield Lookout

Quabbin Tower

Goodnough Dike

DAM

Visitors Center

1 mile

33

Exploring Bogs for Plants and Birds

A bog is an otherworldly place, like something out of a fairy tale—a place of meat-eating plants, quivering ground and stunted trees.

But a bog is also an endlessly fascinating habitat for the naturalist to explore, and New England and New York have more than just about any region of the Lower 48.

At its simplest, a bog is an acidic, chronically wet area with an underlayer of peat and a dominant community of sphagnum moss—but that does no justice to the wide variety of bog types, or the many ways they form. Some bogs came about when retreating glaciers left huge chunks of ice embedded in the soil; when the ice melted it formed a kettle-hole pond, over which, in the course of several thousand years, grew a floating layer of sphagnum, eventually thick enough to support shrubs and trees. Other bogs, known as raised peatlands, actually grow into vast domes, frequently with concentric series of ponds dotting their surfaces.

On younger kettle-hole bogs, the sphagnum mat often occupies only the outer rim of the old depression, with open water in the center. In such situations it is easy to observe the successive rings of plant communities, from the newest sphagnum to the encroaching forest, closing in like a drawstring bag on the shrinking pool. Bogs are almost always dominated by a mix of three conifers: black spruce, which is tolerant of the cold, acidic soil and is the most characteristic bog tree; tamarack, the only deciduous conifer in the Northeast; and balsam fir, which unlike the similar spruce bears its cones upright on its branches.

In places where the sphagnum mat covers a lens of water, visitors may suddenly find the ground beneath their feet giving way in a most alarming manner, like a giant waterbed sloshing and shimmying underfoot. In such "quaking bogs" even small trees may sway as you pass by—a decidedly spooky experience.

Because they are unique habitats, it should be no surprise that bogs hold a large number of plants and animals found nowhere else. Birders love to hunt through the black spruces for such bog specialities as olive-sided flycatchers, while amateur botanists revel in carnivorous plants like common pitcher-plant and round-leafed sundew, or orchids like the arresting beauty known as *Arethusa,* which blooms in midsummer.

The harsh conditions of the bog make life extremely difficult for plants. The acidic soil and water retard decomposition and result in a growing medium that is almost devoid of nutrients, while the high acidity actually retards the absorption of water by the plants; surrounded by huge amounts of liquid, many bog plants must fight a constant battle against dehydration—the reason many have rolled leaf edges and fuzzy coverings.

Because nutrients, particularly nitrogen, are in such short supply, a few famous bog-dwellers have taken to hunting. The pitcher-plant is especially easy to observe in northern bogs, with

Pitcher-plants, common in Northeast bogs, use their upright, water-collecting tubes to trap and digest insects.

Glistening droplets of sticky liquid coat the hairs of the sundew leaves, a trap for insects that blunder too close.

its green or bronze tubes, flared lips and well of water inside. Insects that slip into the reservoir are unable to climb out because of the lining of short, down-curved hairs; chemicals in the water reduce surface tension so the bugs sink and drown. They are eventually "digested" by the plant, which absorbs its nutrients through the reservoir wall.

The sundew has an even more elegant method of capturing insects. The tiny, paddle-shaped leaves that form a basal rosette are covered with dozens of small hairs, each tipped with a glob of sticky liquid. When a small insect touches against a hair it becomes mired, while its struggles cause the leaf to curl, bringing the other hairs into contact with the victim.

Not every plant in the bog is so blood-thirsty. One of the most striking in June is rhodora, a member of the rhododendron, or heath, family that bears lovely, pink-purple blossoms in great abundance, especially in the sunlit edge of the forest layer. Several other heaths are in evidence in the summer bog, among them leatherleaf, with a long raceme of white, bell-shaped flowers; Labrador tea, which bears clusters of gauzy white blossoms; and sheep laurel, a small, deep pink-flowered species known as lambkill because its foliage is poisonous to grazing animals.

The animal community in the bog is no less unusual, ranging

from the semi-aquatic water shrew, weighing less than 10 grams, to bull moose. For most naturalists, however, birds are the real attraction, since there are more than a dozen species of songbirds that nest primarily in and around bogs. Among them are the rusty blackbird, olive-sided flycatcher, palm warbler and black-backed woodpecker. The *see-weet see-weet* song of the Nashville warbler is one of the most typical sounds of the summer bog.

CAUTION: *Especially in some of the larger bogs mentioned here, it is easy to become confused and disoriented, losing your sense of direction. Make it a habit to always flag your entry point with a strip of surveyor's tape or a colorful handkerchief (removed, naturally, when you leave).*

Never explore a bog by yourself. There may be hidden pockets of water or peat slurry just under the fragile surface, and if you break through it's essential you have someone around to help pull you out.

HOTSPOTS

In Vermont's Northeast Kingdom, **Moose Bog** at the **Wenlock WMA** is an outstanding example of boreal peatland,

Stunted spruces, blooming Labrador tea and other wetlands plants form a dense mat over Moose Bog, in Vermont's Northeast Kingdom.

with pitcher-plants, sundew, blooming Labrador tea and rhodora, as well as spruce grouse, warblers and (as the name suggests) moose. From I-91 take Exit 28 (Route 5/105, Newport/Derby Center), following 105 East through Island Pond, a distance of about 21 miles. Eight miles beyond town 105 crosses a railroad line; go another 1.5 miles (past a sign for the wildlife management area) and turn right on an unmarked, gated dirt road. Park on the right .2 mile farther, walk about 100 yards down the road and enter the trail on your right.

The trail, actually an old woods road, skirts the northeast edge of the bog. Watch to your left; when you first catch sight of open water, look for one of several paths that lead to the open heath.

Just a few miles to the north are the much larger and wilder peatlands known as **Yellow Bogs,** reached after several miles of travel on dirt logging roads. Directions to Yellow Bogs can be found in Chapter 49, but use caution bushwhacking here, because it is empty, lonely country where it is easy to get lost. Have and use a good map and compass, flag your entry point well, and carry emergency food, water and rain clothes.

Maine is justly famous for its many bogs. In central Maine, **Caribou Bog** outside Orono stretches for miles along the eastern shore of Pushaw Lake, but the most accessible portion is known as **Orono Bog,** less than a mile from I-93. Get off at Exit 50 (Kelly Road/Orono); if coming from the south, turn left off the exit ramp and cross the interstate, while if coming from the north turn right off the ramp. Go .6 mile, turn left at the stop sign onto Stillwater Avenue and drive another .3 mile, parking in the dirt pull-off on the left. The tamarack, spruce and maple bog begins across the road to the northwest. There are no trails, so use an entry point marker.

Great Heath, north of Harrington in the Down East country, is Maine's largest raised bog, and is best explored by canoe, traveling up along the Pleasant River. To reach the put-in point, take Route 1 through Harrington and drive 2.4 miles north from the junction of 1 and 1A. Turn left at the yellow blinker light, drive 3 miles, go straight at the crossroads, then another 1.5 miles to the bridge. With a good map is is possible to navigate the maze of unmarked dirt roads that snake across the extensive blueberry barrens to the north and west of here and to put the canoe in for a downstream float, but be aware that during June the barrens are alive with millions of honeybees, and the fruit-growers who work the area frown on passersby.

The Maine Chapter of the Nature Conservancy has pre-served a number of the state's best bogs, and while some like Crystal Bog and Woodland Bog are closed to the public to prevent disturbance, others are open to visitors.

One of them is **Saco Heath Preserve** just north of the town of Saco in southern Maine. Known as a raised coalesced bog, it is one of the most southerly raised bogs in the United States and has the state's largest stand of threatened Atlantic white cedar. The preserve covers the eastern half of the heath, and the only access is across private property, for which advance permission is needed. If you are interested in visiting Saco Heath, contact the Maine chapter at the address listed in the Appendix for specific directions and more information.

The many bogs of the **Great Wass Island** archipelago south of Jonesport make it a wonderland for exploring naturalists; the Conservancy owns the southern two-thirds of 1,500-acre Great Wass Island, as well as owning or holding conservation easements on fifteen other surrounding islands. Peatlands here include shrub-slope heaths, raised heaths and a unique jack pine bog, the only one of its type known in the United States.

Great Wass Island is accessible by road from Beals Island; from Route 1 take Route 187 North to Jonesport, then follow the signs across the bridge to Beals Island. This is Great Wass Island Road, which becomes dirt on Great Wass itself, traversing private land before reaching a parking area at the Conservancy boundary. Nearby Mistake Island, across Mud Hole Channel to the east, can be reached by boat, and has a boardwalk to prevent damage to the shrub heath. For maps and more information on Nature Conservancy preserves in Maine, see the state chapter's excellent book *Maine Forever*.

In Acadia National Park, **Seawall Bog** (also known as the Big or Great Heath) has long been a popular attraction with naturalists, providing typical peatland plants and birds. The bog lies to the north of Route 102A, just south of the Seawall Campground.

Remnant bogs can be found much farther south of the peat belt in northern New England, however. They are common in the Adirondacks, but even more surprising are Emmons Bog Preserve in central New York, and Black Spruce Bog in northwestern Connecticut.

Emmons Bog, a Nature Conservancy property, is on a high ridge above the Susquehanna River, just south of Oneonta, and holds such typical bog species as pitcher-plant and sundew, rose pogonia orchids and leatherleaf, as well as songbirds like blackburnian and black-throated blue warblers. To get there, take I-88 to Exit 15 (Routes 23/28), turning onto Route 23E/28S. Go .2 mile and turn onto 28 South, drive another .7 mile, turn right and immediately left onto Southside Road. Drive 1.1 miles, make a right onto Swart Hollow Road and go 2.8 miles to White Hill Road, a left. Drive another 1.1 miles and pull off by the preserve sign on the left. The bog is visible in the bowl below the fields.

Black Spruce Bog, part of Connecticut's Mohawk State Forest, is a small wonderland of balsam fir, spruce, hemlock and highbush blueberries, threaded by a short boardwalk. From Route 63 west of Torrington take Route 4 West 2.9 miles to Allyn Road, a left that enters the state forest. Drive 1.7 miles and park by the maintenance sheds, being careful not to block access. The trailhead is across the road, and the bog is within an easy 5-minute walk.

34

Whale-Watching

More than 20 miles off the Maine coast, the sea had an oily smoothness beneath a slate sky, and gathering mist quickly sealed off the Mount Desert Rock lighthouse as we headed back toward land.

The day had been a long and fruitful one aboard the *Island Queen*, one of the many whale-watch vessels that cruise the Northeast coast each summer. We'd been escorted from the outer islands by harbor porpoises, sleek and black in the morning sun, then found minke (pronounced "minky") whales, the smallest of the baleen whales in the northern Atlantic. Later, as the day turned cloudy and foggy and the sea softened to dead calm, we'd cut our engines and drifted, hunting the great finback whales by the whooshing sound of their breath.

At last we'd gotten a close view; the ocean bulged and a finback split the water, flowing in a smooth arc along the surface, firing off an explosive blow that rose in a steamy white column in the air. Then the head sank again, replaced by the back and the small dorsal fin that knifed down as the whale disappeared once more.

Soon thereafter the boat had turned toward port, and the twenty-five or thirty whale-watchers aboard had settled down to nap or talk quietly on the long return trip. Only a few still watched the horizon fading behind the fog—and so were lucky enough to spot the distinctive, V-shaped blow of a right whale.

The news electrified everyone, for the northern right whale is one of the rarest marine mammals in the world, with a

North Atlantic population of perhaps only a few hundred individuals. For the next hour we drifted with silent engines as the 45-foot whale swam around and beneath the ship, at times sliding only a few feet beneath the keel, at others rolling on its back and waving a stubby flipper in the air. It was the kind of magical, once-in-a-lifetime encounter that makes whale-watching so exciting and rewarding.

The Northeast coast is one of the world's premiere whale-watching regions, with more than fifteen species of cetaceans (as whales, dolphins and porpoises are more properly known) and dozens of commercial boat operators willing to take visitors out for a closer look. The season (depending on the boat) may last from mid-May through October, but the peak is June, July and August.

While there is always a chance of sighting a rare species like a right whale, watchers more often see humpback, finback and minke whales. All three are, like the right, baleen whales—that is, instead of teeth they have plates of fibrous baleen hanging from the upper jaw, through which water is strained and food (mostly small fish and crustaceans) is filtered out.

Humpbacks are far and away the most popular species with whale-watchers, for they are big, curious and acrobatic; this is the species that lobtails its flukes high in the air, or breaches from the water like a missile only to fall back in an eruption of spray. Humpbacks range up to 60 feet in length, have a pointed, elongated head and long, curved flippers that give it its genus name *Megaptera,* or "big wing." The bumpy back peaks in a small dorsal fin, and the tail flukes are wide and scalloped along the trailing edge, with distinctive combinations of markings and scars that biologists use to distinguish individuals.

Like most of the whales along the Northeast coast, humpbacks are migratory; the western North Atlantic population breeds in the Atlantic off the Dominican Republic in late winter, then swims north in spring to the rich feeding grounds that stretch from Montauk to Greenland. Here humpbacks pursue small fish like capelin and sand launce that form dense schools.

Fishing techniques may be as simplistic as gulping, or involve cooperation with other whales, but doubtless the most spectacular method is bubble-ring feeding. Diving deep, the whale exhales while swimming in a circle below the school of fish, which are trapped and concentrated by the rising curtain of bubbles. The whale lunges straight up through the mass, breaching at the surface with thousands of gallons of water and fish cascading from its open mouth. It is one of the most awe-inspiring sights a naturalist can witness.

Next to the blue whale (almost never seen on New England or New York whale-watches), the finback is the largest animal in the world, with adults measuring as much as 70 feet long. This is a lean, streamlined animal with a narrow, lance-shaped head, proportionately small flippers and a tiny, curved dorsal fin; it is unusual in that its coloration is asymmetrical, with a light patch sweeping back from the right lip over the head. Finbacks are not as acrobatic as humpbacks, and most sightings involve the slow, majestic rise and dive of the breathing whale.

Similar in shape to the finback, but less than half its size, the minke whale is a common species, although it is not as obvious as the larger whales and is often overlooked. Other smaller cetaceans often seen on whale-watches include a number of the toothed whales, such as the very common harbor porpoise, about 5 feet long and blackish, and the beautiful white-sided and white-beaked dolphins.

HOTSPOTS

Because the best places for whale-watching may lie several hours offshore, it is best to sign up for one of the many commercial operations on the coast from Montauk Point to northern Maine. These are relatively inexpensive, and the captains know how to find whales. A list of whale-watch cruises, by state, can be found in the Appendix.

Be aware that not all whale-watches are created equal. Some may involve a 90 foot boat loaded with more than a hundred passengers and last only a couple of hours; others, like the **Maine Whalewatch,** which runs the *Island Queen* out of Northeast Harbor on Mount Desert Island, takes a limited number of people on all-day cruises that are as much research trips as recreational outings. Be sure to ask how long the trip lasts, the size and capacity of the boat, and whether or not restrooms and sheltered cabins are available.

Even in midsummer it is a good idea to bring plenty of warm clothing, since air temperatures on the open ocean can be 15 or 20 degrees colder than on land, along with the chill of an offshore breeze. In almost every case you'll need to supply your own food and drink, and of course don't forget film. Binoculars are always a good idea, not just for the whales but for the many species of pelagic seabirds that will also be found offshore.

NOTE: *If you're prone to seasickness (or if you don't know if you are), err on the side of caution by taking a motion sickness remedy; your doctor can recommend the best brand for you. Remember that to be effective, they must be taken before motion sickness sets in, usually before leaving land. Novices sometimes fast in the hopes of staving off sickness, but that may make it worse; try eating, but avoid dairy products or greasy foods. A light breakfast before leaving is always a good idea.*

If you do feel seasick, watch the horizon, sit away from diesel fumes from the engine, and try to concentrate on something else; the appearance of a whale is often enough to take your mind off your stomach and let the spell pass. If the sickness proceeds to its final, heave-over-the-side conclusion, take comfort from the fact that losing your lunch may actually make you feel better.

35

June Shorttakes

Moose-Watching

Although they look scruffy after the long winter, moose are easy to see in June, when they move into lake shallows and grassy roadsides to feed; later in the month the new calves will appear, too. The three best areas are the **upper Connecticut River** in northern New Hampshire, **Sandy Stream Pond** in Maine's **Baxter State Park,** and **Yellow Bogs** in Vermont. See Chapter 49 for directions and cautions.

Spruce Grouse

Although incredibly tame, the spruce grouse can be the very devil to find, a fact that has frustrated many birders trying to add this northern speciality to their lists.

This month, though, females with broods of chicks become a regular sight along roads and paths, where they feed on insects and take dust baths. Among the regional locations are Yellow Bogs (Chapter 49) and **Moose Bog** (Chapter 33) in Vermont, and in Maine the perimeter road through Baxter State Park (Chapter 49), **Quoddy Head State Park** (Chapter 45), and the Schoodic Summit path on the Schoodic unit of **Acadia National Park** (Chapter 40). Also in Maine, birders have long sought spruce grouse along two stretches of wooded coastal road—Route 191 between East Machias and Cutler, and Route 187 north of Jonesport.

See also:

Chapter 16, Nesting Bald Eagles. Chicks in the nest at **Moosehorn NWR**, Maine, will be near fledging this month, and should be actively exercising their wings.

Chapter 28, Nesting Peregrine Falcons. Chicks at regional eyries should fledge late this month, although the families usually stay close to the nest site until early autumn.

Chapter 37, Heronries. Nesting activity reaches a peak this month at regional heron colonies.

36

Breakout: Bringing Back the Puffin

Few birds have so much raw appeal as an Atlantic puffin. With its natty black-and-white plumage, portly banker's figure and outsized, multicolored bill of orange, blue and yellow, a puffin is almost cosmically cute.

Unfortunately, this seabird has become a rare sight on the Northeast coast. In presettlement days they were common as far south as Maine's Muscongus Bay, but uncontrolled hunting and egging during the nineteenth century, combined with the depredations of cats, dogs and rats, eliminated all the puffin colonies on Maine's islands. In recent years the largest outpost has been Machias Seal Island off Jonesport—an island that technically lies in Canadian waters.

Many people mourned the passing of Maine's puffins, but one man was moved to act. Stephen Kress, a National Audubon Society biologist, theorized that it should be possible to move young puffins from the large, healthy colonies in eastern Canada and repopulate the old breeding sites in Maine.

Kress launched "Project Puffin" in 1973, taking chicks from Great Island, Newfoundland, hand-raising them until fledging age, then releasing them on Eastern Egg Rock in Muscongus Bay. Over the next nine years, Kress' team transplanted more than 770 puffin chicks to Eastern Egg, not only bringing in the birds but constructing artificial nest burrows for them.

Success was not immediate, because of a peculiarity in the puffin's life cycle. Young puffins spend their first two or three years wandering at sea, and no one was certain that when the transplanted chicks reached maturity they would return to Eastern Egg Rock. To help lure them back to their adopted home, Kress made puffins decoys and bunched them on the rocky shore—a visual clue for the returnees.

The plan worked, and the maturing puffins began returning to the island in 1977. By 1981 a pair had nested on Eastern Egg, ending a century of exile. In recent years the colony has grown to several dozen breeding adults. What's more, similar Project Puffin introductions have brought the birds back to other Maine islands, particularly Seal Island south of Vinalhaven and nearby Mantinicus Rock, which with 150 puffins is the largest colony in Maine's waters.

The same biologists that have restored the puffins are also working to rebuild Maine's other flagging seabirds, notably common and arctic terns, which have suffered grievously as gull populations have exploded. By controlling gulls on several nesting islands, and using many of the same decoy techniques pioneered for the puffins, the biologists have achieved a remarkable rate of success; on Eastern Egg Rock, where arctic terns had disappeared in the 1930s, a mixed colony of nearly one thousand terns now nests.

The greatest public attention has been on the puffins, however. Puffins are social birds, nesting in tightly packed colonies where the adult males dig the burrows, which may be as much as 4 feet deep; naturalists who have watched the excavations report that the puffins use their huge bills to hack at the soil, which is kicked out with the webbed feet. The single chick spends about 40 days in the burrow, being fed as much as its weight in fish each day.

Then, without warning, the parents abandon the baby, which will fast for 6 or 7 days before hunger finally forces it from the security of the nest onto the open sea. If the chick survives its first days of freedom, when predators like great black-backed gulls are a constant menace, it will learn to fly and feed itself with no further assistance from an adult.

To protect the birds from disturbance, Maine's restored puffin colonies are closed to visitors, but naturalists can easily observe puffins by signing up for one of several puffin cruises now offered by commercial boat operators, some of whom share their proceeds with Project Puffin. A list of puffin cruises can be found in the Appendix, as well as the address for Project Puffin, which is supported solely by contributions.

JULY

July Observations

37

Heronries

It's hard to imagine a placid marsh at daybreak, the sun turning the mist orange, without your mind putting a great blue heron in the picture, silhouetted against the dawn. This long-legged, long-necked, long-billed bird is, for most people, the epitome of wetlands and soggy places.

Which is why so many people are surprised to learn that great blue herons nest high in trees, building flat platforms of sticks where they sit like gangly gargoyles. In fact, they usually nest in large colonies, filling the trees with dozens and even hundreds of nests.

In the southern portions of the region, great blues may be fixing up their nests by early April, while to the north they must wait several weeks for spring to catch up with them. Regardless, by midsummer the chicks are growing rapidly, demanding constant feedings, and the colony becomes a beehive of activity.

The first week of July is a good time to watch one of the big heronries (as such colonies are correctly known). Heron chicks' ravenous appetites press all the parents into hunting and feeding, and there is an endless procession of adults soaring in and out, legs trailing and necks tucked, flapping on wings that may stretch 6 feet.

The nest may be refurbished from the previous year or built anew, but the finished product is a large saucer, up to 3.5 feet across, made of thick sticks and lined with smaller twigs, and finally with a layer of green leaves. (Leaves are common in the nests of many large birds, including raptors, leading some biologists to suspect they are chosen for their insecticidal qualities.)

The eggs hatch after about 28 days of incubation, and the young grow rapidly on a diet of fish. Great blue heron clutches average three to five chicks, and unlike some closely related egrets, there is little vicious sibling rivalry. Biologists, intrigued at this dramatic difference between close relatives, once switched chicks from the nests of great blue herons and great egrets, which usually show a high degree of sibling rivalry. To their surprise, they found that the herons chicks moved to the egret nests became much more aggressive, while the egret chicks in the heron nests remained highly belligerent.

The reason may rest with food; both species feed their young fish, but egrets bring small fish that are easily monopolized by one aggressive chick, while herons tend to catch larger fish that are harder to hog. Placed in the grab-it-or-lose-it environment of an egret nest, a heron must fight or starve—while a egret moved to a heron nest retains its instinctive aggressiveness, cowing its foster siblings.

Even in the relative calm of a great blue heron nest, there is always some scuffling and pushing as the youngsters outgrow their small home. Through a spotting scope, an observer can see them standing up in the nest, exercising their wings as the time of fledging approaches. Young great blues have a certain charm, but they are far from classically cute; they are if anything even more gaunt-looking than their parents, with a crown of fluff that thins, as they mature, into something resembling a monk's tonsure. They are at once ridiculous and immensely appealing.

Great blue herons are by no means the only species of colonial wading birds nesting in the region, although they are the only one to be encountered regularly inland. Along the coast, colonies of wading birds may include great and snowy egrets, little blue herons, glossy ibises and black-crowned night-herons—the last a species that also nests inland at spots like the Niagara River and Lake Champlain.

Heronries are also quite unpredictable. While great blue heron colonies tend to be fairly stable, colonies of other species may grow, shrink, appear or disappear with no warning, or even any apparent reason. On Long Island numbers of cattle egrets have declined substantially in recent years—a surprise, since this alien species had been spreading across North America at an astonishing rate. Conservationists have also been worried by repeated oil

For all their attachment to water, great blue herons nest in tall trees, and watching their colonies can be a fascinating way to spend a summer day.

spills in New York harbor, whose tidal zone is the feeding grounds for many species of wading birds, and contamination of which may account for declines on nearby heronries.

HOTSPOTS

Because heron colonies are so sensitive to disturbance, the hotspots that follow are for those that can be viewed from a safe distance without disturbing the birds. Under no circumstances should you enter a heronry, since your presence may keep adults from feeding the young or cause them to leave the chicks exposed to hot sun and predators. Human disturbance may even cause complete abandonment. Obey any signs closing areas near the colony. Respect and circumspection are particularly needed at those island colonies that can be approached by boat. Stay well offshore and use binoculars—if the birds are reacting to your presence then you are too close.

Great blue herons are among the most common of the communally nesting wading birds, and there are a number of fine colonies in New York that can be watched without bothering the herons. At **Montezuma NWR,** at the north end of Cayuga Lake, a large heronry containing about 150 pairs can be seen across Tschache Pool from the observation tower. For directions to the refuge, see Chapter 19; to reach the tower from headquarters take the auto tour route, which ends here, or go west on Route 5/20 and then north on Route 89. The tower parking lot is just beyond the I-90 overpass.

Another colony of about 150 pairs of great blues can be found at **Iroquois NWR** in northwestern New York. See Chapter 19 for directions to the refuge, then follow Casey Road past headquarters for .9 mile, turning right onto Route 77. Drive 2.3 miles to the parking area on the right overlooking Cayuga Pool; the heronry is in the woods across the lake. Backtrack half a mile and watch on the left for the footpath leading between Cayuga and Mohawk pools, which will take you closer to the heronry.

Not far above the maelstrom of Niagara Falls, a colony of black-crowned night-herons nests on the **Dufferin Islands,** very easily seen from shore on the Canadian side of the Niagara River. For complete directions and parking hints, see Chapter 2; because July is high tourist season, a weekday visit is strongly encouraged.

Along New York's northern perimeter, the heronries on **Little Galloo Island** and neighboring islets in Lake Ontario west of Watertown have long been monitored by biologists, who in recent years have been concerned by growing numbers of double-crested cormorants, whose harsh guano kills the trees in which the herons nest. Little Galloo and **Calf Island,** west of Stony Point, and **Bass Island** and **Gull Island** in Henderson Bay, also support large colonies of gulls.

> CAUTION: *The islands are too far offshore for small cartop boats to reach safely, and weather conditions on the Great Lakes can change abruptly. The islands are privately owned and absolutely no landing is permitted. Observe from well offshore.*

Many of the same precautions apply to the remarkable bird colonies on **Four Brothers Island** in Lake Champlain, about 2 miles east of Willsboro Point. Here, birders can see large numbers of nesting black-crowned night-herons and egrets keeping company with ring-billed and herring gulls, as well as a colony of double-crested cormorants numbering hundreds of pairs, and still growing. Boat launches and rentals are most convenient from Willsboro Point, New York; from Route 22 at Willsboro take Farrell Road north to the village.

> NOTE: *Landing is absolutely prohibited on any of the four islands, and boaters should stay far enough away to avoid disturbing the birds.*

Last, small-boat owners or canoeists can—with discretion—visit the large great blue heronry at **Missiquoi NWR** in northern Vermont, where more than two hundred pairs nest in the flooded woodlands along the Missiquoi River delta, forming the largest colony in New England. To reach the refuge, take I-89 North from Burlington 32 miles to Exit 21 (Swanton), then follow Route 78 West 3 miles to the headquarters building. Another 2.2 miles west along Route 78 the road crosses Charcoal Creek, and there is a boat launch area on the right. Be sure you have a good refuge map, available at headquarters, before setting out.

38

Summer
Wildflowers

Spring is the season most closely associated with wildflowers, and for good reason; the open forest canopy of April and May allows many woodland species to bloom in bright sunlight that is later intercepted by the trees. But as summer takes hold of New England, naturalists can look forward to two unique wildflower spectacles—the bloom of the great rhododendron in New Hampshire, and the American lotus in Massachusetts.

The great rhododendron (also known as great laurel or rosebay rhododendron) is primarily a southern plant; the huge colonies in the southern Appalachians are justly famous. The species reaches its northern limit in New England, in a few places where the climate and growing conditions are more akin to the gentler south.

One such place is the rolling woodlands of southern New Hampshire, where a magnificent, 15-acre stand has been protected as Rhododendron State Park. The largest and healthiest of the nineteen known rhododendron colonies in central and northern New England, the stand was designated the state's only official botanical site in 1946.

Great rhododendron is an elegant shrub, growing here to near-tree size. The foot-long leaves are leathery and glossy green above, paler and buffier on their lightly furred undersides. The flowers, which appear in abundance in mid-July and linger for nearly a month, form large white clusters lightly tinged with pink, and stand out regally against the gloom of the forest.

The New Hampshire site is luxuriant; in many places along the main trail, vigorous rhododendron shoots arch out over the path, enclosing it like a tunnel. The soil here is damp and the air cool, even in midsummer, punctuated with the songs of ovenbirds foraging among the thick ground cover of bluebead lily and bunchberry—for the other wildflowers of the state park (best seen on the short Wildflower Trail) are more typical of cold, acidic north woods, species like goldthread, pyrola and dewdrop.

Approximately 40 miles to the southeast, in eastern Massachusetts, a summer flower spectacle of a very different nature is also taking place this month. On the wide impoundments of Great Meadows NWR, a tremendous bloom of the rare American lotus turns the lakes brilliant gold and green.

While *Nelumbo lutea* is fairly common in parts of the upper Midwest, it is a very local species in the East, and the Great Meadows colony is one of the largest and finest on the Atlantic Seaboard. The plant is easily recognized by its large, round leaves (up to 2 feet in diameter), which rise a foot or two above the surface of the water—unlike the floating leaves of the much more common fragrant water lily.

The flowers are the real eye-catcher, though. Starting in July and lasting through early autumn, the lotus raises a lemon-yellow bud, which opens in bright sunlight into a huge blossom of exquisite beauty, with pale petals framing a golden pistil.

The American lotus is a sun-worshipper; on blue-sky days the flowers open wide and flat, dancing gently in the breeze, but as soon as clouds begin to build the petals quickly close to protect the flower's precious pollen from sudden rainstorms. For this reason, try to time your visit for a sunny day, although the lotuses, covering many acres of the lakes, are impressive even when closed.

HOTSPOTS

To reach the rhododendron colony at **Rhododendron State Park** from the east, take Route 119 West to the town of Fitzwilliam, a perfect vision of the quintessential New England village. Just west of town turn right at the sign for the state park and go 2.1 miles to the parking area. The best stands will be found along the Rhododendron Loop Trail, an easy .6-mile hike.

Approaching from the west, take I-91 to Exit 1/Route 5 at Brattleboro, Vermont; follow Route 5N through Brattleboro, then pick up Route 119 East across the bridge in New Hampshire. Go

20.5 miles to Fitzwilliam Depot, drive another half-mile beyond town and turn left at the sign for the park, which is 2 miles farther.

The American lotus colony occupies much of the two large impoundments in the Concord unit of **Great Meadows NWR** in eastern Massachusetts, just north of the historic town of Concord. From the Boston area, take Route 2 West from I-95 approximately 5 miles, turning right (north) at the sign for Concord Center. Go 1.2 miles, bearing right at the yield sign onto Main Street, and turn left onto Route 62 East. Go another 1.5 miles and turn left onto Monsen Road, then left again .3 mile farther at the sign for the refuge. Park in the lot by the observation tower, and follow the Dike Trail separating the upper and lower pools of the impoundments. The lotuses are stunningly obvious, especially to the left in the upper pool.

An American lotus blossom closes before an oncoming storm at Great Meadows NWR, Massachusetts, where this uncommon species is unusually abundant.

39

Pelagic Seabird Trips

Far from land, on the open ocean where wind and surging waves are the only constants, lives a community of birds most people— even experienced naturalists—know little or nothing about.

Only briefly do these birds come to shore, lingering on land only long enough to rear their young before taking to the high seas again, roaming the Earth's oceans in journeys that are nothing short of epic. They are the pelagics—the petrels, jaegers, shearwaters and others most at home in a world of water.

Land-based observers never get to see pelagic seabirds except on rare occasions when storm winds blow them close to shore. Finding them entails a long trip by boat—but the rewards more than make up for the inconvenience.

Naturalists in the New England and New York who want to find pelagics are fortunate that whales are such a popular tourist attraction in the region, because many of the commercial whale-watch cruises also produce a good variety of seabirds. What's more, there are several ferry routes (most notably the famous *Bluenose* between Maine and Nova Scotia) that run through prime pelagic seabird areas.

The group of birds collectively known as pelagics are actually members of several diverse families, all of which have made the evolutionary compromises necessary for a life at sea. One of the biggest hurdles is drinking water; because ocean water is three times more saline than blood, a bird drinking seawater would have to excrete more water than it drank—a recipe for disaster.

Seabirds get around this problem with a unique set of salt glands resting above the eyes. Such glands are common in birds that eat a salty diet or drink salt water, but they are largest and most efficient in seabirds like storm-petrels and albatrosses. Within a couple of hours of ingestion, the salt is concentrated by the glands, which act as a sort of filter for the blood stream, and is ejected through the nostrils. A lot of energy is required to filter out the salt—but the alternative is obviously much worse.

In summer, more than two dozen species of pelagic seabirds may be encountered off the Northeast coast. Among the most common are the greater, Manx and sooty shearwaters, three acrobatic fliers with the long, thin wings characteristic of many pelagics. Greater and sooty shearwaters breed on remote islands in the South Atlantic, moving north in the boreal summer to feed off the Canadian and American coasts. Manx shearwaters, on the other hand, breed in the North Atlantic, including a handful on the North American side of the ocean.

The tiny storm-petrels, including Leach's and Wilson's, seem almost ludicrously delicate for a life at sea, dabbing at the surface like small, black swallows, yet they, too, undertake vast journeys. Wilson's storm-petrel is another Antarctic breeder that heads north in our spring, just as the weather is deteriorating in the austral ocean, while Leach's storm-petrels breed abundantly on islands off the Northeast coast, moving to and from their nest burrows under the cover of darkness.

Among the other pelagic species routinely sighted in the region are northern gannets, the huge, white boobies that plunge-dive spectacularly when feeding; red and red-necked phalaropes, small shorebirds that migrate and winter at sea, congregating off the Northeast coast by midsummer; common and arctic terns; parasitic, long-tailed and pomarine jaegers, predatory relatives of the gulls; great and south polar skuas, likewise large and piratical; and northern fulmars which, despite their gull-like appearance, are related to the shearwaters.

One of the attractions of pelagic seabird-watching, though, is the large measure of the unknown; so few people have seriously studied offshore birdlife, and for such a relatively short time, that much is still being discovered. Rare species like black-browed albatrosses and band-rumped and white-faced storm-petrels are occasionally seen in the region, and many experts predict that the growing popularity of pelagic trips will add even more species to the list of North Atlantic visitors.

HOTSPOTS

See the Appendix for a list of pelagic seabird cruises. Remember that most offshore trips for whales will also produce seabirds, but you will probably be on your own in wrestling with identification, whereas trips specifically for pelagics will probably have an experienced naturalist aboard.

It's also a good idea to check in regularly with coastal rare bird hotlines, on which specially scheduled pelagic trips are often advertised, and with local Audubon Society or bird club chapters (listed in the Appendix), which often charter boats for weekend cruises.

40

Exploring Tidal Pools

Knees grating against the abrasive layer of barnacle shells, I leaned down to the water and peered through my own reflection to the miniature world below. Bristling mats of Irish moss shone purple next to the deep blue of a mussel bed, each shellfish busily siphoning water through its intake valves. A green sea urchin moved with painful slowness across the rocky floor, while a small hermit crab lugged its empty periwinkle shell around on its back.

Where waves and shore meet in the thin zone not fully land or ocean, life faces difficult challenges. Exposed twice each day to frigid water and drying air, an animal or plant must be able to withstand the worst of both environments.

Tidal pools are refuges from these harsh conditions, where sea life is cupped in a natural aquarium during low water. Tidal pools may form anywhere, including on mud flats or sand beaches, but the best occur on the rocky coast of New England, where the ebbing tide exposes myriad nooks and crannies.

The intertidal zone—the area extending from the extreme low-water point to the top of the "splash zone" at high tide—is neatly divided into layers, as you can easily see when the tide is falling. Like the life zones on a mountainside, each intertidal layer has its dominant species of animals and plants.

In the splash zone, for example, blue-greens (often known as blue-green algae) are the most obvious organisms, forming a dark coating to the rocks; they are in turn grazed upon by millions of periwinkles, small snails that can survive for long periods out

Surf pounds the tidal zone in Acadia National Park, Maine, one of the most accessible locations for tide pool exploration in the Northeast.

of the water. Below them, at the uppermost reaches of the water, are bands of rock barnacles. Below, where the sea lingers a bit longer, are dense beds of blue mussels, which are not as tolerant of drying as the barnacles.

This central area of the intertidal zone is known as the midlittoral, and here many of the seaweeds grow in profusion. Knotted wrack and rockweed are among the most common, their brown fronds buoyed underwater by air bladders in their stems. Irish moss, with its short, palmate fronds, forms thick mats just below the rockweed zone—and all the species conceal an abundance of animal life, including pugnacious rock crabs. On most days dead low tide comes just to the edge of the kelp zone, with its leathery strands of edible kelp in ribbons as much as 10 feet long.

The animal life of the tidal pool is no less fascinating. There are sea stars, hunting for shellfish, which they pry open with their muscular arms and digest by inverting their stomachs into their prey's shell; their relatives the sea urchins, those hedgehogs of the ocean covered in bristling spines; and the bizarre sea cucumbers, which have the strangest defense of any tidal pool resident. When roughly handled, a sea cucumber responds by discharging its internal organs in a messy rush all over your hands—then patiently begins to regenerate a whole new set!

Bear in mind that high and low tide will be an hour later each day, and try to time your exploration for the new or full moon each month—these produce so-called spring tides, which rise higher and (more important) drop lower than at any other time during the month.

> CAUTION: *While the tidal zone is an exciting place to explore, you need to be aware of the hazards. Falls are the biggest danger, since wet, algae-slicked rocks are slippery as ice, and rockweed is especially treacherous to walk over. Move carefully and pick your way, and wear a pair of old work gloves and kneepads to prevent cuts from the sharp barnacle shells.*
>
> *Also be very aware of the changing water level, particularly if you are exploring along cliffs or in sea caves. The tide can come in with surprising speed, and it is easy to become cut off from dry land. All these precautions take on special significance if you choose to explore the tidal zone at night with*

*flashlights, when even more creatures will be visible.
It's a good idea to leave a lantern on shore to mark
your entry point.*

HOTSPOTS

There may be no better place for exploring the tidal zone
than **Acadia National Park** in Maine, where the sea has created
untold cracks and clefts in the pink granite of Mount Desert Island,
and the tide rises and falls as much as 10 feet with each change.

Virtually the entire island (as well as most of the **Schoodic
Peninsula** and **Isle au Haut** units) has rocky shoreline, but
especially productive areas are **Seawall** and the **Wonderland
Trail,** off Route 102A between Southwest Harbor and Bass
Harbor; the west shore of **Otter Cove** below Blackwoods Camp-
ground; and the shore from **Sand Beach to Otter Cliffs.**

At low tide it is possible to walk from the town of Bar
Harbor to **Bar Island,** the western half of which is part of the park,
and in the process enjoy a different sort of tide pool adventure.
Here the departing tide exposes a vast mud flat, pockmarked with
depressions in which shellfish, seaweeds and sometimes fish
become stranded. Wear old shoes and shorts, because this can be
muddy fun.

The Schoodic Peninsula unit of Acadia, just east across
Frenchman Bay from Mount Desert Island but almost 40 miles
away by car, is lightly visited in comparison to the main unit and
offers some wonderful tidal exploration, particularly on **Schoodic
Point** itself; be careful (as should always be the case) of powerful
waves, especially on days of strong east winds. From Ellsworth
take Route 1 North to Route 186 North at West Gouldsboro, turning
right toward Winter Harbor 7.3 miles away. The entrance to the
one-way park loop road is clearly marked; 5 miles into the loop
bear right at the fork marked for Schoodic Point.

Also part of the Schoodic Peninsula unit is **Little Moose
Island,** lying just off the southeast shore. At low tide the island can
be reached by foot and, like the flats at Bar Island, the muddy
expanse provides a rich hunting ground for intertidal creatures.

Along the central Maine coast the gentler shores of **Rachel
Carson Salt Pond Preserve,** a Nature Conservancy property,
provide a marvelous look at intertidal life and, for naturalists,
something of a shrine, for Carson did field work here that led to
her classic book *The Edge of the Sea.* Salt Pond itself, about a
quarter-acre in size, largely empties at low tide, allowing easy

exploration. From Damariscotta take Route 130 South to New Harbor, then go north on Route 32 about a mile; Salt Pond is on the right, although the preserve encompasses almost 70 acres of old farmland across the road.

Great Wass Island, another Conservancy preserve south of Jonesport, also offers tidal pools, especially at the south end of the island near Red Head; for directions, see Chapter 33.

The sandy beaches and tidal flats of southern New England and New York make for rather poor tide-pooling, but at Long Island's dramatic east end, **Montauk Point SP** has excellent pools full of shellfish, seaweeds and crabs. The best pools are to the northwest of False Cape; Montauk Point SP can be reached by taking Route 27 (Sunrise Highway/Montauk Highway) East from the Southern Parkway for 76 miles.

Stranded by the departing waves, a tide pool on Maine's Schoodic Peninsula holds a wealth of sea life for the exploring naturalist.

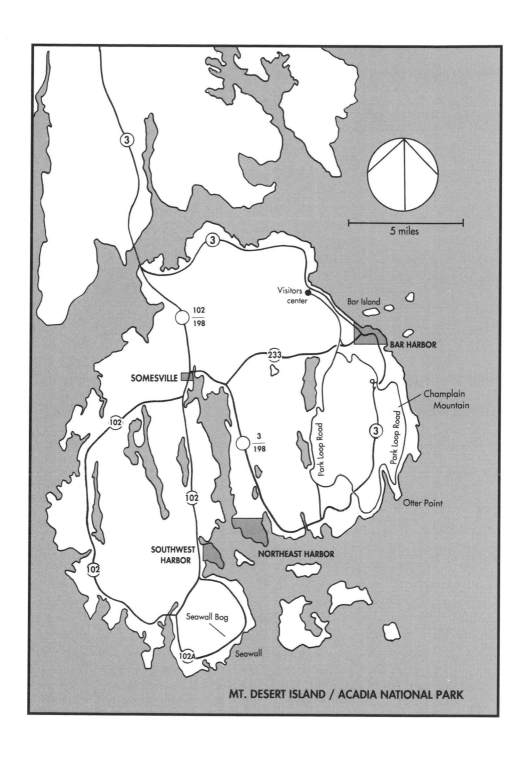

5 miles

Visitors
center

Bar Island

BAR HARBOR

$\frac{102}{198}$

233

Champlain
Mountain

SOMESVILLE

Park Loop Road

Park Loop Road

102

$\frac{3}{198}$

3

102

Otter Point

SOUTHWEST
HARBOR

NORTHEAST HARBOR

102

Seawall Bog

102A

Seawall

MT. DESERT ISLAND / ACADIA NATIONAL PARK

41

July Shorttakes

Bird Banding

Each week from mid-June through the end of August, the public can get a fascinating glimpse of biology in action by joining bird banders surveying local songbird populations at the **Wells Reserve** near Wells, Maine. Programs are usually held on Wednesday mornings; for information contact: Wells National Estuarine Research Reserve, RR2 Box 806, Wells, ME 04090.

Early Shorebirds

The "autumn" migration of shorebirds is already underway this month, and a good place to watch for it is **Rachel Carson NWR,** also near Wells, Maine; as many as nineteen species and thousands of individuals have been spotted on the refuge's mud flats and tidal river channels at low tide. For directions to the refuge, see Chapter 7. For more information on other late-summer shorebird sites, see Chapter 43.

Blueberry Picking

Although blueberries are more closely associated with Maine, with its huge commercial blueberry barrens, the luscious fruit grows in suitable habitat throughout the region. In Vermont, portions of the **Green Mountain NF** are managed for blueberry picking, burned off periodically to provide optimum growing conditions. One such place is the **Robert Frost Nature Trail** near

Ripton, but there are others, and the best locations vary from year to year. For current hotspots and directions, contact the Green Mountain NF at the telephone number listed in the Appendix.

See also:

Both nesting bald eagles at **Moosehorn NWR,** Maine (Chapter 16) and peregrine falcons in several locations (Chapter 28) will be active this month, with the young falcons already fledged and the eaglets about to leave the nest.

42

Breakout: Seeing the Forest for the Trees

It's normal to talk about "the woods" or the "the forest" as though it were a monolithic thing, but a naturalist quickly sees this for fallacy. This is no less true in New England and New York, where the woodlands are a patchwork of different forests, each with its own distinctive community of plants and animals. What is found where depends upon the mix of climate, topography, latitude, geology and a host of other factors, both obvious and subtle.

Ecologists once divided North America into broad "life zones," painted like swaths across the continent and shading from the subtropical to the arctic. But that left too much out of the equation; for example, the same ridge may have southerly species on the south slope, where the sun shines more warmly and the soil is drier, and northerly types on the shady, damp north slope.

Today, it's recognized that ecological communities are too diverse and dynamic to be so easily pigeonholed, and classifications now tend to be drawn along the lines of natural communities, usually named for the dominant trees. While many of these communities follow the broad patterns of the old life zones, there is more flexibility to the new method, which more fully reflects the remarkable mix of habitats that have evolved.

New York, bridging north and south, is a good example of the challenge specialists have in classifying "the woods." In the southeastern bootheel where the ridges of the Appalachians cross the state, oak forests more typical of central Pennsylvania dominate, while on Long Island, scrub oak and pitch pine—in part the remnants of a large oak/pine barrens ecosystem—hold sway. In the Appalachian Plateau region that covers most of the state's south and midsection, northern hardwoods, oaks and hemlocks comprise the primary forest mixture. The Adirondacks are more akin to southern Canada and northern New England, with forests of spruce, fir and hardwoods at the higher elevations, and aspen and birches in the foothills. The milder, wetter plains along the Great Lakes and St. Lawrence are largely forested in red maple, elms and other hardwoods, and in many other parts of the state, white pines take the fore.

Each forest type has its own distinctive blend of living things. Some species are found in many habitats; a good example is the great horned owl, one of the most adaptable of birds, and one that is capable of making a living in situations as varied as deep forest or suburban backyards. Others are much more specific in their habitat requirements—so much so that ecologists refer to them as indicator species.

Birders and amateur botanists both have a keen sense of forest types and the characteristic organisms they hold, since much of their hobbies rely on looking in the right place. To find a spruce grouse you must look in a boreal forest, that community made up

Bunchberry, a diminutive member of the dogwood family, is an indicator species of the boreal forest, growing best in the acidic shade of spruces.

of white and black spruce, balsam fir and such hardwoods as aspen and paper birch; likewise, a naturalist that hears the *quick-three-beers!* call of an olive-sided flycatcher can be relatively sure there's a bog hidden somewhere close by—for the flycatcher is one of the best indicator animals of the bog ecosystem.

But just as one uses several field marks to identify a bird, so should you look for a number of indicators before you decide what habitat you're in—particularly since nature is rarely clear-cut, and some species are found in several related communities.

The boreal conifer forest, for example, is indicated by the trees mentioned earlier, along with such characteristic wildflowers as clintonia (bluebead lily), bunchberry, starflower, Canada mayflower, and understory shrubs like striped (moose) maple. A boreal bog may have the same mix of spruce and fir trees, but the understory will be moisture-retentive shrubs like leatherleaf and Labrador tea, and an abundance of sphagnum moss studded with sundews and cottongrass.

The northern hardwood forest, one of the great woodland communities of the Northeast, is indicated by the presence of sugar maple, yellow birch and American beech, although they are usually joined by such cold-tolerant deciduous species as paper and gray birch, pin cherry and balsam poplar, as well as hemlock and white pine. On the ground you're likely to find painted trillium, wood sorrel and pink lady's-slipper—along with flowers like Canada mayflower that also grow in primarily coniferous woods. Among the indicator birds are solitary vireos, American redstarts and hermit thrushes, and while moose are dominant in boreal forests, white-tailed deer do better in northern hardwoods.

As you climb through the hardwood forest up a high mountain slope, you'll pass through noticeably distinct life zones, leaving the beeches down below, for instance, and seeing a great increase in the number of birches. Eventually the broadleafs give way to conifers, but not (in much of the region) the black and white spruces of the lowlands. These high-altitude trees are usually red spruce, a montane species found in the higher reaches of the Appalachians and in much of New England. Exceedingly tolerant of cold, they can live where few other trees can survive—another example of life's diversity and adaptability.

AUGUST

August Observations

43

Fall Shorebirds

Wild animals have their own sense of the season, and it is frequently at odds with human calendars. Few people, for instance, would consider August part of autumn, yet for millions of shorebirds, fleeing the increasing cold of the Arctic, the peak of the fall migration comes this month.

Shorebirds—the sandpipers, plovers and their relatives—have some of the longest, most arduous migrations of any of the birds. The Hudsonian godwits that gather this month on Monomoy Island south of Cape Cod, for example, commute twice each year from their breeding grounds on the shores of Hudson Bay to the estuaries of southern Argentina, covering much of the distance over the Atlantic. (Actually, the vast majority of the godwits never even alight in New England, instead flying out to sea off eastern Canada, and apparently not setting down until they pass the Orinoco River in South America.)

Semipalmated sandpipers likewise travel from the coastal plain of the Arctic Ocean to the northern coast of South America, while the tiny semipalmated plovers make a single, nonstop leap from New England to the Lesser Antilles each fall. Others do not fly as far, or in such a pell-mell rush. Dunlin may withdraw no farther than southern New England, and the purple sandpiper goes no farther than it has to to avoid coastal ice, staying throughout the winter as far north as Newfoundland.

For the most part, however, shorebirds seem to spend their lives in almost constant motion, settling down for only a few weeks in the Arctic to breed, taking advantage of the near-total daylight during the tundra summer, then lighting out again for the south; on the wintering grounds they have barely any more time to feed and rebuild their fat reserves before turning around to head north once more. Yet despite these exertions, shorebirds as a group are among the most long-lived of wild birds.

New England and New York are not as well-known for their shorebird concentrations as the Chesapeake Bay ecosystem to the south, but the naturalist who knows where to look can find some spectacular gatherings in August. Remember, though, that your actions can have a profound effect on the birds you've come to watch. Many of the shorebirds face an overwater trip of thousands of miles, and any disturbance burns energy and reduces their chances for survival. Watch from far enough away that your presence has no noticeable impact, and keep any pets in your car; even on a leash, a dog is much more disturbing to wild animals than a human.

HOTSPOTS

Without doubt, the vast **South Lubec Flats** in extreme eastern Maine are one of the region's premiere shorebird sites, providing a migratory refueling stop for thousands—sometimes tens of thousands—of sandpipers, plovers and other species. At

Low tide exposes the vast, fertile South Lubec Flats near Eastport, Maine, a mecca for southbound shorebirds in August.

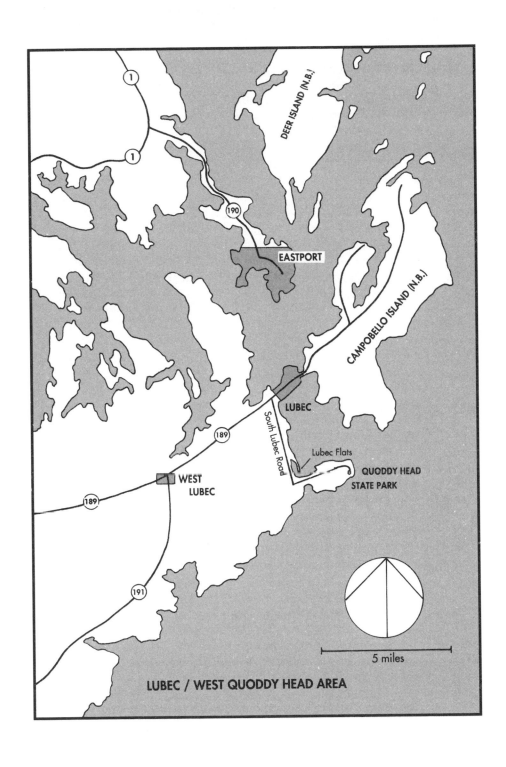

DEER ISLAND (N.B.)

①

①

⑲⓪

EASTPORT

CAMPOBELLO ISLAND (N.B.)

LUBEC

South Lubec Road

Lubec Flats

⑱⑨

WEST LUBEC

QUODDY HEAD STATE PARK

⑱⑨

⑲①

5 miles

LUBEC / WEST QUODDY HEAD AREA

low tide the waters recede into Lubec Channel, exposing an immense mud flat that can seem, at times, alive with shorebirds, gulls and an occasional bald eagle. Just across the channel from New Brunswick, this area is part of the Bay of Fundy ecosystem, now considered globally crucial for migrant shorebirds.

Although low tide is best for the birds, since it permits them to feed on marine invertebrates, a rising tide is better for visiting naturalists, since the fast-moving water reduces the space available to the birds, compressing the flocks into steadily denser concentrations until, at high tide, they are jammed together in solid ranks.

To reach the Flats, take Route 1 North to Route 189 East at Whiting. Go 10.3 miles to Lubec and turn right at the sign for Quoddy Head State Park. Another 1.8 miles along watch for Forest Service Products on the right; roughly 100 yards beyond it on the left, just past a house, is a dirt road leading out to the water and extending along the Flats for more than a mile. Do not block this road, which is used by local residents for clamming. Return to the macadam road and turn left, and in less than a mile the road swings east along the lower edge of the Flats.

Also in Maine, the **Scarboro River** marshes near Portland can be excellent, as can the tidal flats at **Wells** and **Biddeford Pool** to the south along the coast. For directions to Biddeford Pool and Scarboro River see Chapter 26, at Scarboro be sure to check Ferry Beach, on Ferry Road off Route 207 north of Prout's Neck. Directions for Wells are in Chapter 7.

Other shorebird hotspots in August include **Monomoy NWR** in Massachusetts, particularly North Island, just a short distance from the mainland; local charters are available, as well as regularly scheduled trips run by the Massachusetts Audubon Society and Cape Cod Museum of Natural History. See the Appendix for addresses, including the refuge headquarters, which can make recommendations on boat arrangements.

Shorebirds in large numbers and excellent variety can be found at Plum Island near Newburyport, Massachusetts, especially the area known as the salt pannes in **Parker River NWR,** and the beaches of **Plum Island State Reservation** at the extreme south end of Plum Island. For directions to Parker River NWR see Chapter 2; the salt pannes are less than a mile south of the entrance, while the Plum Island State Reservation lies at the far end of the access road, a distance of about 6 miles.

In the Concord area, the impoundments of **Great Meadows NWR** can be excellent for shorebirds, especially in a dry year or when the pools have been drawn down for management reasons. For directions, see Chapter 38.

In Rhode Island, **Charlestown Beach** and nearby **Quonochontaug** are locally famous for their fall shorebirding. Both are accessible from Route 1. To reach Charlestown Beach take Charlestown Beach Road south to the Charlestown Breachway Campground, park in the day use area and walk north to the mud flats. To reach Quonochontaug, return to Route 1 West, then take West Beach Road south. A dirt road beyond the public parking area hooks north along the channel; bird north along it toward the Bills Island flats. Low tide is best at Quonochontaug, and a rising tide is best at Charlestown.

Along the Connecticut coast, shorebirds often mass in sizable numbers at **Milford Point,** at the mouth of the Houstatonic River. From I-95 take Exit 35 to Route 1 South, go .2 mile and turn left at the light onto Lansdale Avenue. Drive another half-mile and bear right onto Milford Point Road, then follow it about 2 miles to the intersection with Seaview Avenue. Turn right toward the Milford Point Sanctuary and McKinney NWR. Low tide is best on the mud flats here, and a spotting scope is very helpful.

Inland, the shores of **Lake Champlain** in late summer can host good shorebird flocks from the first week of August on, provided the lake level drops a bit, as it often does. See Chapter 9 for general directions to the Vermont side near Addison and Button Bay; on the New York side, try the area near Westport Beach on North West Bay, just off Route 9N/22.

In central New York, **Sylvan Beach** on the east end of Lake Oneida provides some of the best shorebird-watching away from the coast, although sunbathers can be more plentiful than sandpipers on nice weekends. From I-90 at Canastota take Route 13 North 9 miles to the bridge across the Erie Canal. Park near the breakwater on the left and walk north along the beach.

Few locations attract as many birds within easy reach of as many people as **Jamaica Bay WR**, part of Gateway National Recreation Area in Queens. Shorebirds may be found anywhere near water in Jamaica Bay, including the heavily birded West Pond, but the most consistently productive area is East Pond, on the east side of Cross Bay Boulevard, especially if water levels are low. The greatest numbers of adult shorebirds pass through Jamaica Bay during the first week of August, while the peak of juveniles—and the greatest diversity of species—comes in the last week of August and the first week of September.

To get to Jamaica Bay, take I-495 (Long Island Expressway) to Woodhaven Boulevard and head south about 3.5 miles to Atlantic Avenue. Cross Atlantic onto Cross Bay Boulevard, which carries you out across Jamaica Bay. The refuge headquarters and parking is on the right.

44

Late Summer Wildflowers and Ferns

As summer moves to the indolent days of August, a sense of lethargy settles over the woodlands and fields of New England and New York; the katydids chirp lazily in the long twilight, and there's an almost palpable sense of richness on the land.

One of the best places to while away an August evening is an old meadow, where nature is slowly erasing the handiwork of man beneath a quilt of native grasses and wildflowers. Dominating the scene are goldenrods, whose pillars of yellow are emblematic of late summer, and wild bergamot, one of the loveliest flowers of this or any other season, with its graceful coronets of pale purple blossoms.

In the forests, on the other hand, summer is the season of the ferns, which thrive in the moist, shady environment that the canopy of trees provides. Stretching out on the ground in a woodland glade, surrounded by the high, heady smell of hay-scented ferns, is one of August's sweetest pleasures.

One site stands head and shoulders above the rest for late summer wildflowers and ferns—Bartholomew's Cobble, tucked away in the extreme southwestern corner of Massachusetts. Twin outcroppings of limestone (known as "cobbles" locally) makes the soil exceptionally rich, and the preserve's mix of woodland, forest and Houstatonic River edge make for a remarkable diversity of species.

In fact, more than seven hundred species of plants have been recorded on the 278 acres of Bartholomew's Cobble, including 450 species of wildflowers and 125 trees, shrubs and vines—an incredible total, especially considering how far north this site is. What's more, botanists have tallied fifty-three species of ferns and fern allies, making it probably the greatest natural community of its kind in the United States.

Among the ferns found at the Cobble are the purple-stemmed cliffbrake and walking fern, two rare, local species found only on dry limestone outcroppings, as well as more common species like maidenhair spleenwort, ostrich fern, bulbet fern, Goldie's fern and lady fern.

The importance of Bartholomew's Cobble has been recognized for years, and in 1948 it was purchased by the state's Trustees of Reservations, protecting it for future enjoyment and study. The Cobble is crisscrossed by a network of trails, none of them difficult and all liberally endowed with flowers and ferns. Harebells nod at the base of lime cliffs, while perennial phlox, pale jewelweed and New England asters grow at the edge of the trees. The meadows are especially striking, blanketed in goldenrod and wild bergamot, flickering with butterflies and ruby-throated hummingbirds. This is a place to spend at least a day in quiet exploration.

HOTSPOTS

To reach **Bartholomew's Cobble,** take Route 7 south from Great Barrington; 5 miles south of Sheffield, follow Route 7A, which splits to the right. Go .5 mile and turn right across the railroad tracks onto Rappano Road, drive another 1.6 miles, bear right and turn into the parking lot on the left. Signs for the Cobble usually mark each turn from Route 7A. Once at the site, first-time visitors should consider taking the Ledges Interpretive Trail, which focuses on the Cobble's plant life.

45

Whales from Land

As outlined in Chapter 34, whales are fairly common off the Northeast coast in summer—but to see them usually requires a long boat ride on a commercial whale-watch vessel.

But in late summer, at the uttermost end of Maine, it is possible to see whales feeding remarkably close to shore. Near the town of Lubec, jutting into Lubec Channel, is the bulbous peninsula known as West Quoddy Head. Finback, minke and northern right whales come near to shore here in late July and August, feeding on the rich assortment of marine life in the channel separating Quoddy Head from Campobello Island in New Brunswick. Whales also frequent the wider waters of the Bay of Fundy just to the northeast, and several nearby observation points in Canada are well worth a visit.

Unlike a whale-watch cruise, where there is usually a trained naturalist on hand to identify what's seen, here you will be on your own. A good identification guide will help you sort out the sometimes subtle differences in fin shape, blow pattern and skin coloration; one especially good book is *A Field Guide to the Whales, Porpoises and Seals of the Gulf of Maine and Eastern Canada* by Steven K. Katona, Valerie Rough and David T. Richardson.

The most common whales seen from shore are finbacks, minkes and right whales, along with smaller species like harbor porpoises. Finbacks are enormous—the second largest animals in the world, with a maximum size of 70 feet—but because they are rarely acrobatic, an observer only sees a small bit of the whale at any given time, usually the sleek back sliding up and arching down through the water. Minkes, the smallest of the region's baleen whales at 20–30 feet, are common but hard to spot because of their size and lack of a visible spout.

Right whales, the real attraction near Quoddy Head, are among the rarest marine mammals in the world; it is a true red-letter day when you spot the low, V-shaped blow of a right whale. The waters off Passamaquoddy Bay appear to be important to right whales both for feeding and mating, and females with calves are frequently sighted here.

HOTSPOTS

An excellent observation point on Grand Manan Channel is **Quoddy Head State Park,** where bluffs give a fine view of the waters to the east, and (on clear days) of Grand Manan Island 10 miles offshore. Another possibility is the **West Quoddy Biological Research Station** just outside the park, which has a small interpretive center open to the public, and good views of Lubec Channel; because of the proximity of the critically endangered right whales, the station has been researching their vocalizations.

To reach West Quoddy Head, take Route 1 North to Route 189 East at Whiting. Go 10.3 miles to Lubec and turn right at the sign for Quoddy Head State Park, bearing left 2.8 miles later. The biological research station is on the left a mile farther on, and the entrance to the park a mile beyond that.

Although just out of the New England and New York region, there are also good vantage points on the Canadian side of the border, and weekend visitors would do well to explore them. Cross from Lubec to Campobello Island, New Brunswick, and head north on Route 774 toward East Quoddy Head, the northern terminus of the island; the headland, which pokes out into the Bay of Fundy, is also good for seabirds and gulls.

You can also take a ferry from Blacks Harbour, New Brunswick, to **Grand Manan Island,** where the North and South Head cliffs can provide good overviews of whales feeding in the sea below. Although impractical for a whale-watch cruise, a tripod-mounted spotting scope is invaluable for shore-based observation.

46

Northern Blazing Star

When the glaciers melted back across New England, ushering in this most recent interlude of climatic warming, they left vast quantities of smashed rock, gravel and sand in their wake. Along parts of the Maine coast, sand deposits may be 60 or more feet thick, underlying unique natural communities known as sand plains grasslands.

One of the most unusual is found in extreme southern Maine, just a few miles from the ocean. Known as the Kennebunk Plains, it holds a number of rare plants and animal species, many at the edge of their range. But the show stealer on the Plains is the northern blazing star, which turns hundreds of acres into a sea of purple each August.

The blazing stars of the genus *Liatris* are a diverse group of prairie plants, all sharing upright flower stalks bearing clusters of pink-purple flowers. There are dozens of species, including the dense blazing star *(Liatris spicata),* which has long been popular with wildflower gardeners.

While dense blazing star is found across a wide swath of the eastern and northcentral states, northern blazing star *(L. borealis),* is restricted to New England and New York and south through Pennsylvania and New Jersey. Its distribution is spotty, since it prefers dry, open woodlands and clearings. Obviously conditions on the Kennebunk Plains suit it perfectly, however, for this is believed to be the largest colony of the species anywhere, and the only place in Maine where it grows.

Instead of the tall, tightly packed spike of flowers characteristic of other blazing stars, the northern blazing star has fewer, larger flower heads attached to the central spike by short stalks. This makes the individual plant less spectacular than other, related species, but the tremendous aggregation at the Kennebunk Plains more than makes up for any individual failings.

The bloom is nothing less than astounding, since blazing star is one of the dominant plant species across the more than 1,500 acres of sand plain. This is all the more remarkable when one considers the abuse these plains have taken; for years this area was a commercial blueberry barrens, and was sprayed in the 1980s with the herbicide Velpar, which decimated many of the native plants. Fortunately blazing star is resistant to Velpar, and since the area was protected by the state and the Maine chapter of the Nature Conservancy several years ago, the wild plants have staged an encouraging comeback.

HOTSPOTS

The **Kennebunk Plains** lie just a few miles from I-95, one of Maine's busiest arteries. From Exit 3 (Kennebunk) turn left after the toll booth onto Route 35 South, go .2 mile and turn right, then follow signs for Route 99. Turn onto Route 99 West, drive 1.8 miles and you'll enter the plains, a dramatic expanse of grassland studded with purple blazing star. Route 99 cuts through the plains for a little more than a mile; you can turn left onto McGuire Road, a partially hidden dirt track that doubles back through the area. To return to Route 99 continue on McGuire to Wakefield Road, turn left and go .6 mile.

Because the Kennebunk Plains are home to Maine's largest nesting population of grasshopper sparrows, one of the state's most threatened birds, stay on the sand roads and do not bring pets into the area, even on a leash. Although August is after the peak breeding season, a few late pairs may still be nesting—and with a bird as rare as the grasshopper sparrow, every nest is precious.

47

August Shorttakes

Tree Swallow Hordes

Each August huge flocks of tree swallows gather on the marshes of the Hudson River in southern New York, particularly at evening when clouds of them swirl in to roost. One of the best places to see this spectacle (as well as to learn about the unique tidal estuarine environment here, beneath the looming Palisades) is **Constitution Island Marsh Sanctuary,** an Audubon Society property. From I-84 take Exit 11 to Route 9D South, then go 10 miles to the town of Cold Spring; alternately, from the Taconic Parkway take Route 301 West 9 miles into town, then turn left onto 9D South. Just south of town turn right onto Indian Brook Road and drive half a mile to the parking area; the road sloping down to the right leads to the visitors' center and boardwalk trail through the tidal marsh.

Tree swallows are also often found in massive flocks on **Plum Island** and **Monomoy NWR,** both in Massachusetts, and **Braddock Bay State Park** in New York. For directions to Plum Island see Chapter 2; access to Monomoy is by boat, and visitors should talk to refuge staff before trying to charter one. See the Appendix for the address and phone number. Directions to Braddock Bay can be found in Chapter 13.

Loosestrife

In August it's hard to miss the great splashes of purple across the landscape, especially in southern New York and parts of southern New England. Casual passersby are apt to smile admiringly at the almost solid stands of flower spikes that fill marshes and damp meadows, but naturalists are more likely to grind their teeth in frustration—for as spectacular and beautiful as purple loosestrife may be, it is a noxious invader.

A European species, loosestrife thrives in wet or moist environments, quickly spreading in dense, choking mats that force less competitive native species right out of the picture. Even worse, loosestrife has little food or cover value for wildlife, so an infested wetland becomes much less productive once the loosestrife takes over. Nor is it easy to remove, once established; even the tiniest bit of rootstock will regenerate, so it must be laboriously hand-dug, then burned. Ironically, it is freely sold in many garden shops, and is often transplanted to new areas by unsuspecting gardeners. Fortunately, entomologists have isolated an insect pest that feeds on loosestrife, offering the possibility at last of control.

Red-Necked Phalaropes

Through the 1970s and early 1980s, an astonishing natural spectacle occurred each year in late July and August on the chilly waters of **Passamaquoddy Bay** between Maine and New Brunswick—the gathering of up to 2 million red-necked phalaropes, a delicate shorebird that winters at sea.

For reasons that remain a mystery, however, the phalaropes began to decline in the mid-1980s, dropping to eight thousand in 1986 and disappearing altogether by 1990; surveys of plankton, on which the birds feed, suggest that it, too, suffered a serious decline, perhaps forcing the phalaropes away. Likewise affected were Bonaparte's gulls, which once flocked by the tens of thousands in this area in August. This might be part of a natural cycle, and birders hope that one day the vast flocks will again return to the Passamaquoddy. For this reason, visitors to the area to look for whales (Chapter 45) may want to watch for phalaropes offshore as well.

See also:

Chapter 52, Autumn Landbird Migration. Heavy flights of migrant warblers, particularly adult warblers, which leave the breeding grounds several weeks before the immatures, occur this month.

Chapters 50, 56 and 61, Fall Hawk Flights. The earliest movements of bald eagles, ospreys, kestrels and broad-winged hawks start in late August, generally after passage of strong cold fronts.

Chapter 39, Pelagic Seabird Trips. Late summer is one of the best times to sign up for a pelagic seabird trip or schedule a ferry crossing on the *Bluenose* with large numbers of shearwaters, petrels and other oceanic migrants moving through offshore waters.

48

Breakout: Endangered Places

Ever since environmental protection became a major concern in the 1960s, some of the most controversial and expensive actions have revolved around endangered species. The list of organisms qualifying for government protection and recovery programs is hundreds of species long and getting bigger by the year—and the price tag for saving them is growing exponentially as well.

But conservationists are increasingly convinced that such a piecemeal approach isn't the answer. They point out that many threatened plants and animals come from habitats that are themselves under siege, like wetlands. Save the habitat and you save the species—and often for far less money and time. Instead of waiting until an organism is so far gone that it requires the conservation equivalent of intensive care, many now argue it is better to take a preventive approach, by identifying habitats in trouble and working to save them.

The Kennebunk Plains, which flame into glory this month with the bloom of the northern blazing star, are just one example of a unique ecosystem that is being crowded out of existence. Sand plains grasslands like those at Kennebunk, which occur where retreating glaciers left thick deposits of sand and gravel, could once be found in many areas along the Northeast coast. But unfortunately for the many plants and animals that depend upon them, the sand plains are coveted by people, too, who look at the flat, well-drained, coastal sites and see building lots.

The blazing star may be the best-known inhabitant of the Kennebunk Plains, but there are dozens of other grassland species of plants and animals that are protected there—species that have lost out to development on other sand plains. Botanists are especially interested in toothed white-topped aster, found at only one other site in Maine, and upright bindweed, a small, white member of the morning glory family. Unlike the abundant alien species, field bindweed, upright bindweed is a beleaguered native; on the Kennebunk Plains it took a terrible beating from herbicides used when the area was a commercial blueberry barren, and it wasn't even seen here until 1988.

Nor are plants the only benefactors when the sand plains are preserved. The Kennebunk tract holds Maine's only colony of state-endangered black racers, and one of New England's largest concentrations of nesting grasshopper sparrows. Another eighty-six species of birds nest in the grasslands and surrounding pitch pine/scrub oak woodland—itself a threatened habitat across much of the coastal Northeastern United States.

To the south, on Long Island, a similar story has been taking place, with formerly expansive habitats now greatly reduced in size, placing in jeopardy a number of unique plants and animals.

Here the focus is on the Long Island Pine Barrens, actually a mix of several distinct natural communities, including what was once the largest prairie east of the Appalachians. The prairie, known as the Hempstead Plains, and 60,000 acres of pitch pine/oak barrens known as the Oak Brush Plains, once covered much of central Long Island, but their proximity to New York City and the ease with which this flat, fairly open ground could be developed all but sealed its fate. Fortunately, nearly 1,000 acres of the oak brush have been preserved near the site of the old Edgewood state hospital, providing a home for such characteristic barrens species as birdsfoot violets and the buck moth, an unusual autumn-flying insect listed as a species of special concern in New York.

Protection has come too late for some creatures, however. The Long Island barrens were once home to the heath hen, the eastern race of the greater prairie chicken, as were coastal scrub oak plains and inland blueberry barrens from Massachusetts south. By the 1840s the heath hen was eliminated virtually everywhere but Martha's Vineyard, due to heavy shooting, fire and (it seems likely) disease. The subspecies became extinct in 1932, when the last Martha's Vineyard male disappeared.

By targeting threatened habitats, environmentalists are hoping to avoid repeating the heath hen's story with other plants and animals. In addition to state and federal efforts, private organizations—most notably the Nature Conservancy and its local chapters—place a priority on acquiring unusual or rare habitats, thereby extending protection to the many species found within them.

The Nature Conservancy was instrumental in preserving part of the Kennebunk Plains, and has been active in saving such disparate places as Bergen Swamp in western New York, home to small white lady's-slippers and massasauga rattlesnakes, and Clinton Prairie Bluff on the Nashua River in eastern Massachusetts, where a number of state- and globally endangered plants are found. The Conservancy usually works with governmental agencies, often transferring ownership of the land, and responsibility for its protection, to the state once the purchase is complete.

SEPTEMBER

September Observations

49

Moose

If northern New England has a symbol, it is the moose—and an unmistakable symbol it is, with those long, gangly legs, drooping Roman nose and (on the bulls) the impressive rack of palmate antlers.

Moose are visible throughout much of the year; early summer, in fact, is the best time for seeing cows and their new calves. But autumn may be the best season of all for moose-watchers, when the bulls are coming into the rut, or mating season, and both sexes are looking their fittest and best, glossy and fat for winter.

Moose were once found as far south as the Adirondacks and perhaps even northwestern Pennsylvania, but during the eighteenth and nineteenth centuries the twin onslaughts of logging and unrestricted shooting took their toll, and the species faded into Canada and northern Maine. The worst damage may not have been inflicted by bullets, but by a much more insidious threat, the brainworm. This parasite commonly infects white-tailed deer, which seem unaffected by it, but in moose it causes behavioral changes and death. When the North Woods were clear-cut of their spruce, the second-growth hardwood forests that replaced them made a fine home for deer, which in turn established brainworm and decimated the local moose population.

Over time, however, the forests of northern New England have matured, and as deer herds have declined the number of moose have rebounded strongly. Moose have been moving back into many areas from which they have been absent a century or more, providing unexcelled opportunities for observant naturalists.

Today, good numbers of moose can be found in Maine (the traditional core of the species' Northeast range) as well as northern New Hampshire and Vermont. During the late 1980s moose reappeared as well in the Adirondacks, although the total population is perhaps no more than twenty-five.

There is no mistaking a moose for anything else. This is the largest deer in the world, exceeded only by the great, extinct Irish elk of the last ice age. Bulls stand as much as 7 feet at the shoulder and weigh 1,200 to 1,400 pounds; the antlers of a mature male may be 4 or 5 feet across. The nose is long and flabby, and beneath the chin hangs a "bell" of hair, like a beard.

Beginning early this month, bulls begin to clean the velvety skin covering from their antlers as preparation for the rut, which lasts in some areas until late November. This is a period of high activity for moose, particularly the bulls, which are much more visible now than during the rest of the year as they seek out females. Should two dominant bulls meet, they may engage in ritualized combat—an epic clash of lowered heads and locked antlers. For all the violence, however, the battles rarely result in injury or death to the combatants.

CAUTION: *Moose may look a trifle silly, but they are potentially dangerous animals, especially*

A young moose forages along the shores of Sandy Stream Pond, one of the best places in Baxter State Park, Maine, to see this giant deer.

*during the rut, when bulls can become highly ag-
gressive toward intruders. An enraged moose is
deadly serious business, since it is bigger, stronger
and faster on foot or in the water than any human.*

*Most important, observe moose from a safe
distance, whether on foot or in a car (angry bulls
have been known to attack automobiles). If the
moose is showing any signs of disturbance—rolling
its eyes, vocalizing, thrashing its head against
brush—back off immediately. If you surprise a moose
and are charged, try to climb the nearest tree. Do not
imitate a moose's calls, and be aware that a cow
moose may be just as aggressive as a bull if she feels
her calf is threatened.*

HOTSPOTS

Moose can be found almost anywhere in interior Maine, and
across much of New Hampshire and Vermont, but for all their bulk
these massive animals can be amazingly shy. Still, there are several
places where moose are both common and easily observed.

Baxter State Park in central Maine has long been the best
moose-watching spot in the region, with a large population that,
protected from hunting, is quite unafraid.

There are two entrances to the park—the Togue Pond
gatehouse in the south, 16 miles from Millinocket, and the
Matagamon gatehouse in the north, accessible from Patten 24
miles away. Connecting them is a 50-mile dirt perimeter road with
several side branches to campgrounds, and a network of nearly
175 miles of foot trails reaching into the interior of the park.

The surest bet for moose is **Sandy Stream Pond,** near the
Roaring Brook Campground in the south of the park. This fairly
shallow, muddy-bottomed lake is rich in aquatic plants, and it is
not unusual for visitors to see four or five moose wading and
feeding in its waters, or wandering in the spruce woods surrounding it. And unlike those in most other areas, the Sandy Stream Pond
moose are usually active even in midday. From the Togue Pond
gatehouse turn right at the first fork and drive 8 miles to the Roaring
Brook camp and park, then follow the South Turner Mountain
Trail, which passes Sandy Stream Pond; this is an easy, fairly level
hike that takes only about 15 minutes. Take your time and watch
the woods—there may be moose anywhere, although the scenic
overlooks along the pond are always good possibilities.

Moose are liable to show up anywhere in the park, and their tracks are common along almost every mile of the perimeter road, but several other sites consistently produce good numbers in autumn, including **McCarty Fields,** the **Grand Matagamon Lake** deadwater, **Nesowadnehunk Field** and **Nesowadnehunk**

The bulk of Mt. Katahdin rises above a small pond in Baxter State Park, which has one of the highest moose populations in Maine.

Lake and the open fields at **Trout Brook Farm.** Hikers can reach some exceptionally good moose habitat by taking trails to **Dwelly Pond** along the McCarty Mountain fire road, and **Russell Pond,** the latter 7 miles from the closest trailhead.

Although better in summer than fall, a trio of lakes in the extreme southwest of Baxter can also can be good for moose in September: **Daicey Pond** at the Daicey Campground, and **Tracy and Elbow ponds** on Katahdin Stream; a trail leads past the last two on its way from Katahdin Stream Campground to Daicey Pond Campground, and a nature trail circles Daicey Pond.

Just outside the Matagamon entrance are **Sawtelle Deadwater** and **Scraggly Lake,** both known locally for the numbers of moose they attract; from the Matagamon gatehouse drive east on Grand Lake Road, turning north on Huber Road about a mile before crossing the Seboeis River. There is a boat launch and camping sites at the southeast end of Scraggly Lake, a Maine Public Reserve tract.

In northern New Hampshire, the **upper Connecticut River** from First Connecticut Lake to the Quebec border is famous for its evening moose show, although the numbers drop off somewhat in autumn compared to early summer, when visitors may see a dozen or more while cruising this empty stretch of Route 3. Most of the moose are cows and calves spotted while feeding brazenly along the shoulders of the road, but if you drive slowly and peer carefully into the forests—especially into small clearings in the spruce woods—you'll be rewarded with moose that the others miss, including some of the larger, shier bulls. From Pittsburg drive north on Route 3 to the entrance of George D. Roberts Park (Connecticut Lakes State Forest); from here to the Canadian border, a distance of about 12 miles, is prime moose habitat. Explore on foot the boggy area around **Moose Falls Flowage,** on the left just past the Deer Mountain Campground.

Moose are also common in much of Vermont's Northeast Kingdom, especially the huge peatlands known as **Yellow Bogs,** near the town of Island Pond. A network of private logging roads, which can be used by the public, permit access to this sprawling tangle of second-growth hardwoods, dense spruce forest and bogs.

CAUTION: *Before heading into the Yellow Bogs area, be aware of several potential problems. These are working timber company routes; the log-ging trucks act like they own the road because they do. There is little room for a truck to squeeze by, and little time to get out of the way, given the speed many are driven. Be exceedingly careful going around turns, keep your speed very low, and at the first hint of an approaching truck get as far to the right side as you possibly can. Never stop your car in the middle of the road and leave it, even for a few moments, since you are endangering others by doing so.*

While most of the road is in fairly good repair, several stretches are rutted badly enough to make passage difficult for a low-slung family sedan, especially if it's heavily loaded. And make sure you have sufficient gas for the trip.

This is also very easy country in which to get lost, on the road and off. Logging operations may open new roads, creating intersections not covered below, while foot travel can be confusing in the thick, fairly flat bogs. Have a good, detailed map (such as a USGS topographical quad or a DeLorme atlas), and for hiking flag your entry points and route, and carry and use a good compass. It would also be prudent to carry extra water, food and rain gear, in case you become "misplaced" for the night.

The 16-mile route that follows skirts the outer edge of Yellow Bogs through prime moose habitat, although the bogs themselves are rarely in sight. From I-91 take Route 105 East to Island Pond. Stay on 105 several miles past town, noting the local airport; go another 4.2 miles beyond it and, just before a railroad crossing, turn onto the dirt road on the left. Although unmarked, this is Lewis Pond Road. Drive 5.2 miles and bear right at the fork, then drive straight another 2.1 miles; there are numerous small side roads splitting off in this area, but use common sense and follow the main track.

Cross a small bridge and turn right at the T-intersection, then go 2.6 miles to another T-intersection with a power line corridor. Turn right, using caution for the next several miles, since this stretch is heavily pitted with ditches and deep holes. Follow this road for 4.2 miles until it bears right away from the utility lines, then turn left .4 mile later onto Black Branch Road. This leads within 2 miles back to Route 105.

A nearby area that can also be good for moose is Moose Bog in **Wenlock WMA;** see Chapter 33 for directions to it and several other moose hotspots.

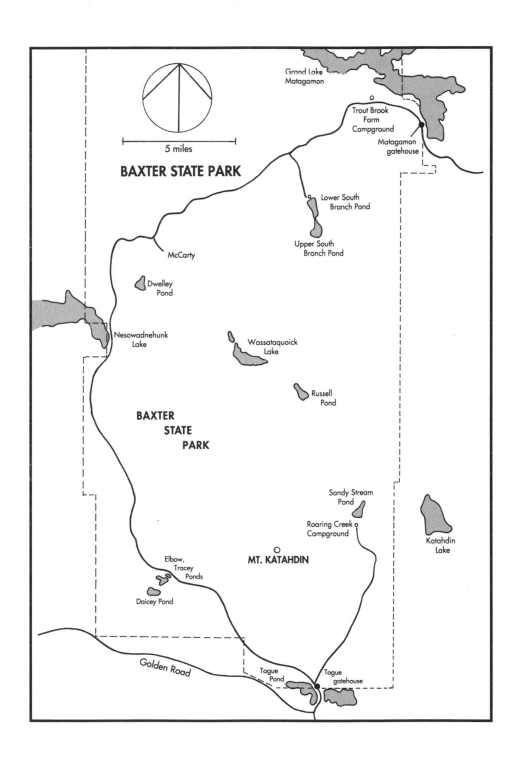

50

Fall Hawk Flights—Part 1

Each autumn they come, like far-flung tributaries joining to form a river—broad-winged hawks from the woodlands of New England, goshawks from the spruce woods of Quebec, peregrine falcons from Labrador, even rare golden eagles from the far Ungava Peninsula.

The autumn migration of hawks is one of the Northeast's finest wildlife spectacles, stretching from the earliest days of September until November's bitterly cold end. Each month the character of the flight changes, as some species peak and others fade; for this reason, it will be dealt with as well in Chapters 56 and 61.

And because, unlike the spring flight, the fall hawk migration touches almost every part of the region, the hotspots are likewise divided among chapter entries for the three months. This chapter details inland hotspots in New England; Chapter 56 covers the best places along the coast; and Chapter 61 focuses on ridge overlooks in interior New York.

The autumn flight actually starts in mid-August, when the first ospreys, bald eagles and kestrels begin to drift south. Of these earliest migrants, the eagles may be the most intriguing, because band recoveries suggest that the bald eagles that migrate through the region in early autumn breed in Florida and wander as far north as Canada after the conclusion of their nesting season in May. Strangely, not all the Florida birds go north, and there does not appear to be a correlation with age or sex. The northern bald

Ospreys are among the vanguard of the autumn hawk migration, with the peak of their movement coming this month along the coast.

eagles that actually nest in the Northeast do not usually begin to migrate until late October or November.

As dramatic as eagles may be, the star of the September hawk flight is the broad-winged hawk, a small, rather chunky bird that belongs to the group known as buteos, or soaring hawks. A hardwood forest species found over most of eastern Canada and the United States, the broadwing is among the most migratory of hawks, traveling as far as Peru each winter. It is also remarkably social, a trait found in no other eastern hawk. When a naturalist in the Northeast spots hundreds of hawks swirling around inside a rising thermal—a congregation known as a kettle—there's no doubt that they are broadwings.

Singly, broad-winged hawks can be somewhat harder to identify. Adults seen in good light will have horizontal chestnut barring across the undersides, and a tail striped with wide black-and-white bands. Immatures look much like other young buteos, with a tail finely barred in brown and with brown streaking on the belly. Experienced hawk-watchers look at the shape of the bird (often all you can see in silhouette anyway), noting the broadwing's wide wings that taper neatly to a point, and the flat trailing edge when the bird sets its wings to glide to the next thermal.

The broadwing migration gets under way in earnest in the first week of September, and builds very quickly to its climax. The passage of a low pressure system through eastern Canada and northern New England usually sets off the heaviest flights, prodding the hawks south and providing good winds. Broadwings seem less tied to strong winds than other hawks, however, and will sometimes move on days with little breeze at all.

A heavy broadwing flight is a sight unmatched in the region, with thousands—sometimes tens of thousands—of hawks passing by in a single day, boiling up in huge kettles, then streaming out in level ranks. Unfortunately, although the timing of the broadwing migration is predictable (the peak usually comes in Massachusetts around September 10, for instance), the exact flight path year to year is anyone's guess. While all the inland count sites usually record good numbers of broadwings each autumn, only one or two spots usually have a "Big Day" with more than ten thousand hawks—and it's almost never the same spot each year. Some seasons, the big plug of broadwings misses the manned sites completely, leaving the expectant crowds wondering where they went.

Hoping for a Big Day adds spice to fall hawk-watching, but even if you never catch the heaviest flights, the spectacle is always gripping. There is something about seeing a hawk maneuver against the clouds that is endlessly fascinating, and always uplifting.

HOTSPOTS

The hotspots in this chapter cover inland hawk-watches in New England; for coastal locations throughout the region, see Chapter 56, and for inland sites in New York see Chapter 61.

In Connecticut's southwestern panhandle near Greenwich, the **Quaker Ridge** hawk-watch at the Audubon Nature Center produced an astonishing 30,535 broadwings on September 14, 1986, a fall record never surpassed among any of the eastern hawk-watches. While there's no guarantee you'll see anywhere near that many hawks (broadwing flights are notoriously fickle), Quaker Ridge is a good choice for a visit during September. To get there, take the Merritt Parkway to Exit 28 (Round Hill Road). Take Round Hill north for 1.4 miles, then turn left on John Street for 1.5 miles. Watch for the entrance to the Audubon Center on the right by the corner with Riversville Road.

Some of the best hawk-watching in New England takes place in central Massachusetts—at **Mt. Tom** between Holyoke and

Northampton, and **Wachusett Mountain** north of Worcester. Both are easily accessible.

Mt. Tom rises more than 1,200 feet above the Connecticut River valley, commanding a north-south ridge system that provides a pathway for migrating hawks. From I-91 take Exit 17A, turning left at the first light onto Routes 5/202 North, then left again at the next light onto Route 141 West. Drive 2.4 miles to the entrance to Mt. Tom State Reservation on the right; the turn is hidden, but comes immediately after a large "Entering Easthampton" sign.

Follow the entrance road 2.2 miles to park headquarters, then bear right 1.4 miles to Goat Peak parking lot. From here a short, rocky trail leads uphill to the right to Goat Peak Tower, the site of the hawk-watch.

Birders can drive right to the top of Wachusett Mountain, another state reservation about 15 miles northwest of Worcester. Approaching from the south take I-190 to Route 140 North 13 miles; from the north, take Route 2 to 140 South and go 2.2 miles. From either direction, turn off 140 at the sign for the Wachusett Mountain Ski Area and drive another 2.2 miles (past the ski area) to the entrance to the reservation. Follow signs for the summit. Hawk flights here can be exceptionally good, especially during the broadwing migration in early September.

While Vermont, New Hampshire and Maine lack the heavy autumn flights that characterize the southern half of the region, there are a number of locations that nonetheless can offer exciting hawk watching.

One of the oldest manned lookouts is **Mt. Agamenticus,** about 10 miles north of Kittery, Maine, a popular hawk-watch with local birders; seasonal counts have exceeded ten thousand hawks here in recent years. To reach the mountaintop, take Route 1 North from York about 5 miles to Cape Neddick, turning left onto Mountain Road. Go another 3 miles to Agamenticus Village, continuing west on Mt. Agamenticus Road 1.4 miles to the access road up the mountain, a right.

In New Hampshire, **Pack Monadnock Mountain,** a 2,300-foot hill about 10 miles north of the Massachusetts line near Peterborough, is used as a hawk lookout in autumn. From Peterborough, take Route 101 East 3.7 miles to the entrance of Miller State Park, a left; the scenic access road leads to the summit of South Pack, the best hawk-watching spot.

In Vermont **Mount Philo,** south of Burlington and overlooking Lake Champlain, is one of the best choices for fall hawk-watching, with annual counts commonly around eight hundred. From Burlington take Route 7 South through Charlotte, a distance of 10 miles, then continue about another 3 miles south on Route 7 to a left turn for **Mount Philo SP.** The toll road to the summit is open to car travel through the middle of the fall, and by foot after that.

Even though ornithologists have known about the fall hawk migration through New England for more than two centuries, much remains to be learned—and there are undoubtedly many good lookouts still unknown. This is especially true in New Hampshire and Vermont, where each year birders find one or two new locations that hold promise. Prospecting for unknown hawk-watches can be exciting, a worthwhile contribution to our knowledge of birds—and you just might strike the motherlode in the process.

51

Fall Foliage Routes—Part 1

Autumn in the Northeast is so famous it is almost a cliché, but the sight of sugar maples burning across a mountain's flanks in fabulous oranges, or a stand of red maples standing crimson against golden tamaracks, is guaranteed to move even the most jaded.

Because the region encompasses such a huge land area— almost 450 miles from north to south, with lowland river valleys and mountains rising to more than 6,000 feet—it's no surprise that the leaves change at different times in different places. In the highest hardwood stands of the Adirondacks and Presidential Range, the leaves will be nearing their peak in mid-September, while on Long Island (admittedly not famous for its foliage) the trees won't turn until almost a month and a half later.

The region's premiere foliage tree is the sugar maple, one of the dominant members of the northern hardwood forest community that covers much of the land. Sugar maple is valuable from almost every human standpoint, providing an extremely high-quality lumber, backyard shade, famous maple syrup—and, in autumn, a natural spectacle beyond compare.

Not every maple in the Northeast woods is a sugar maple, however; there are five other native maples, all with generally the same lobed leaves arranged opposite each other on the twig. Sugar maple leaves generally have five lobes, with moderately deep sinuses (as the indentations between the lobes are called). The bark is dark, with vertical grooves, and the shape of the tree—

especially one that has been growing for decades in a front yard, or along an old stone wall—has a distinctive symmetry, with low-hanging branches and a fine, round crown. An old sugar maple at any time of the year is nobility given form.

The red-orange of sugar maples is autumn's theme in the Northeast, but there are infinite variations, thanks to the many other hardwoods (and one remarkable conifer) that change color with the season. In wet lowlands, red maple (also known as swamp maple) lives up to its colorful name by turning brilliant scarlet—the more acidic the soil, the redder the foliage. On exposed ridgetops, American mountain ash likewise turns red, although the most eye-catching part of the shrub are the clusters of bright orange berries, enjoyed by waxwings and other fruit-eating birds.

Yellows are common, especially in the forest understory, where striped maple and witch hazel take on a delicate, translucent shade of the color. Big-toothed aspens have a more golden tone, accentuated by the constant flickering of their leaves in even the slightest breeze, while the birches, especially paper birch, bears an intense yellow that covers large areas of the high slopes.

Some of the season's most subtle color doesn't even come from a hardwood. The tamarack, or American larch, is the only conifer in the Northeast to lose its leaves in winter, and before the needles drop they turn a subdued gold, brightening the bogs and moist woods where this odd softwood grows most commonly.

Timing is crucial to seeing the best of the fall display, but predicting when the peak will come is an art, not a science. Generally speaking, by the middle of the month there is a smattering of orange sugar maples on the mountaintops, with lots of red maples in swamps and along rivers already turning. The peak in color, however, comes to Vermont's Northeast Kingdom by mid-to-late September, and to the Adirondacks, the northern Green Mountains and northern New Hampshire the last week of September or the first week of October. Remember that temperature, altitude and even how wet or dry the preceding months have been can effect the timing of the foliage. If you're traveling any distance to see the display, it's usually best to call one of the fall foliage hotlines, listed in the Appendix, provided by the various state tourism offices.

HOTSPOTS

Although the directions that follow (here and in Chapter 58) are for routes that cover lots of gorgeous terrain, they can also attract lots of like-minded tourists, especially the last week of the month when color in these areas is at a peak.

The easiest way to avoid the crowds is to get out of your car and walk. Autumn is a marvelous time to hike, with a nip in the air and the bugs a memory; most of the best foliage regions also have unparalleled networks of trails—far too many to list here. You won't cover as much ground as you would in a vehicle, but you'll have a chance to see the details that you miss behind the wheel, and you'll be spared the numbing sight of bumper-to-bumper traffic on a crowded weekend. If you plan on doing any climbing, however, be sure to read the high-altitude cautions on page xx.

For hiking in the Adirondacks, there are no better guides than the 11-volume *Discover the Adirondacks* series, published by Backcountry Publications of Woodstock, Vermont. Each book covers a different region, and each contains hike descriptions, maps and background information.

Other excellent resources for the region are *Guide Book of the Long Trail* (Vermont) and *The Hiker's Guide to Vermont,* both published by the Green Mountain Club and Northlight Studio Press. Also helpful are the *Fifty Hikes* series by Backcountry Publications, including guides to Vermont, New Hampshire, central New York and Maine.

If you do decide to enjoy the show from the road, try to schedule your trip for the middle of the week, when the crowds are smallest. Even then, it's a good idea to have lodging reservations.

One of the best areas for late-September foliage is New York's **Adirondacks,** the largest wilderness area in the East and one of the most ruggedly beautiful regions anywhere. For a two- or three-day loop (allowing plenty of time for side trips, short hikes and maybe a woodland picnic), leave I-90 (New York Thruway) at Amsterdam and head north on Route 30 to Long Lake, a distance of 108 miles. This section takes you along Great Scanandaga and Indian lakes, and beneath peaks like Snowy, Little Moose and Hamilton mountains, all more than 3,000 feet high.

At Long Lake turn east on Route 28N toward Newcomb for 19 miles (stopping along the way at the **Newcomb Adirondack Park Visitor Center,** which has a nice trail system), then take the left turn for Tahawus; go about 1.5 miles and bear right on Boreas Road toward Blue Ridge and North Hudson, another 19 miles through lovely, empty forest.

Ignore the interstate and head north on Route 9 for 10 miles, picking up Route 73 to Keene, a distance of 13 miles. Two miles beyond town turn right onto Route 9N and drive to Keeseville 28 miles away, getting onto I-87 South for 4 miles to Exit 33. Get off and follow Route 22 (eventually 22/9N) south. This road winds its way for 51 miles through woodlands and farms on the edge of the Champlain Valley to the village of Ticonderoga; from here, take Route 9N South along Lake George for another 39 miles, ending the trip at I-87 at the town of Lake George.

New Hampshire's foliage may be a little too famous for its own good, especially if you've sat through near-gridlock in some of the small White Mountain towns. You can get away from the crunch, however, by traveling into the northern panhandle of the state, where the foliage turns earlier than in the better-known Presidential Range. Particularly attractive is Route 145 from Colebrook to Pittsburg, a drive of 19 miles, then Route 3 from Pittsburg to the Canadian border, another 26 miles along the upper Connecticut River.

Also try exploring the network of small roads south of Colebrook, under the shadows of the northern peaks like Blue Mountain and Muise Mountain. If you're traveling on a weekday when traffic isn't heavy, from Colebrook swing east on Route 26 the 22 miles to Errol, passing through the scenic Dixville Notch area.

The color in Vermont's **Northeast Kingdom** also hits a peak in the last week of September—and this is the state's emptiest and least-visited quarter, even during the big tourist season. Much of the forest here is boreal conifer, but the patches of sugar and red maple, birch and aspen set off by spruces (and mixed with golden tamarack) have a special beauty of their own. **Mt. Pisgah** and the **Willoughby Cliffs,** overlooking spectacular Lake Willoughby and the Vermont countryside rolling north to Canada, is a great place to stretch your legs and enjoy the foliage. From I-91 take Route 16 to Route 5A South, then go 5.6 miles south to the trailhead. The route is nearly 7 miles long and, in places, quite steep, ending with a walk back north along the lake to the starting point.

If exploring the Northeast Kingdom by car, continue south on Route 5A through the Willoughby valley, joining Route 5 for about 7 miles, then turning north on Route 114 for 39 miles, through Island Pond to Norton at the Quebec border; this stretch passes through what ecologists call the "spruce-moose" ecosystem, so watch for the huge deer along with areas of fall color, and see also Chapter 49, which suggests moose-watching hotspots in the Island Pond area. At Norton, Route 114 veers east for 13.9 miles to Canaan, passing Great Averill Pond. At Canaan turn south on

Route 102, which follows the scenic upper Connecticut River for almost 50 miles to the juncture with Route 2 West; follow Route 2 a final 30 miles to St. Johnsbury, where you return to I-91.

Farther south in Vermont, fall color comes earliest to the high deciduous forests of the Green Mountains, just below the alpine spruce zone. One of the nicest hikes is the climb up **Camel's Hump,** described in detail in Chapter 31. Vermont, in fact, is one of the best states in New England for hiking, especially in **Green Mountain NF;** detailed trail guides and maps for the various ranger districts are available by writing to the national forest headquarters at the address listed in the Appendix.

52

Autumn Landbird Migration

No one knows how many hundreds of millions of songbirds pass each autumn through New England and New York—flocks that dance across the face of the full moon in an instant or drop call notes out of the night sky like loose change, waves of warblers and vireos flickering through the trees at dawn in a symphony of movement.

At no other time of the year are their numbers as high. Bolstered by the just-finished breeding season, the passerines turn south from their nesting grounds and begin what for many, like the blackpoll warblers, is an epic journey. Blackpolls travel from New England to South America in an eighty-six-hour, nonstop, over-water flight. It has been pointed out that this is the equivalent of a human running nonstop 4-minute miles for 3.5 days, but even that does not convey the enormity of the feat.

The migration takes the shape of a broad, thick front spreading down across the region, but along the way the birds are forced by circumstance—by strong winds, or by bodies of water, or the shape of the land—into narrow flight paths, or tiny island refuges. These places are known to naturalists as migrant traps, and in September they can make for some exciting bird-watching.

This is also birding at its most challenging. The majority of the birds are immatures (in part because the adult warblers usually migrate earlier, in August), and the immatures of many species bear only a drab resemblance to their colorful parents. Too, the adults of some species, like chestnut-sided and bay-breasted warblers, molt into less garish fall plumage that can fool a novice, as do some other nonwarblers like scarlet tanagers.

But if you're familiar with the spring adults, you shouldn't have too much trouble with fall immatures. Rather than looking for specific field marks, take in the bird's general shape, behavior and pattern—there's often enough of a resemblance between parent and offspring to narrow the identification quickly. Even though an immature Cape May warbler lacks the breeding male's orange-and-yellow face, it shares his slightly down-curved bill, slim build and general streakiness.

No one ever said being a naturalist was supposed to be easy—just fun. If you're a beginner and you find yourself overwhelmed by the difficulties of sorting out fall warblers, remember that there is no shame in letting a bird go by without a name. Sit back and enjoy the show for what it is: a remarkable chance to see the dynamics of nature in action.

The fall migration, sadly, isn't quite what it used to be. Both observations by birders, and more scientifically accurate assessments by biologists, point to a drastic decline in the numbers of many songbirds in the past several decades, particularly those that winter in the Neotropics, like many thrushes and warblers. Some of the information has come from the annual North American Breeding Bird Survey, in which more than two thousand sites across the continent are surveyed each summer; the survey shows clearly that most tropical migrants are decreasing, while those that are year-round residents, or which do not leave North America in winter, are largely stable or increasing in number.

Even more telling, scientists have compared weather radar images from the 1960s through the 1980s. These pictures show the massive flocks of songbirds that pass over the Gulf of Mexico twice a year—flocks that have decreased by an astounding 50 percent in twenty years.

Much of the blame no doubt rests with the devastation of the tropical forests from southern Mexico through South America; most migrants have very specific habitat requirements on the wintering grounds, requirements that often fly in the face of what we expect. In New England during the summer, for instance, an eastern kingbird lives in open country feeding on insects, but while migrating to its wintering grounds in South America, it depends on fruit for most of its diet.

Nor does tropical deforestation deserve all the blame for the decline of songbirds. Here in North America, fragmentation of the once-vast forests into smaller and smaller pieces exposes deep-woods nesters like many warblers to predation by crows, blue jays and raccoons, and to nest parasitism by brown-headed cowbirds.

Fortunately, conservation groups and wildlife agencies have awakened to the urgency of the situation, and a number of far-reaching programs incorporating education, research and habitat protection have been started. With luck—and a lot of work—naturalists will always be able to look forward to the great flood of songbirds that washes through the region twice each year.

HOTSPOTS

In fall as in spring, Maine's **Monhegan Island** is well-known as a magnet to songbirds, including such regularly spotted rarities as clay-colored sparrows. And as an added bonus in autumn, the ferry ride can produce good pelagic birding, with shearwaters and storm-petrels a likelihood. See Chapter 25 for details and cautions about birding on Monhegan; the best time is the first two weeks of the month, when the warbler flight is at its heaviest. Also worth checking in autumn, and accessible by car, is **Bailey Island** on the Maine coast south of Brunswick; directions can also be found in Chapter 25. Finally in Maine, check **Fletcher Neck** near **Biddeford Pool.** General directions to Biddeford are in Chapter 26; **Maine Audubon's East Point Sanctuary** at the far end of the neck is the best bet.

Birders in Massachusetts have been combing the woods of **Marblehead Neck Wildlife Sanctuary,** east of Salem, for years, and they are rarely disappointed during the autumn songbird flight. Strong northwest winds are a coastal landbirder's ally, since they force the migrants to the shore, and sometimes result in amazing concentrations of birds at places like Marblehead Neck, where the land pokes out into the ocean. The list of travelers that use this small sanctuary is impressive, including such nominally "southern" species as hooded and yellow-throated warblers, and uncommon northern migrants like Philadelphia vireos. For directions, see Chapter 25.

Cape Cod can be considered a giant migrant trap, intercepting birds trying to cross the Gulf of Maine and needing a place to rest, as well as collecting those forced east by inland winds. One of the best locales for songbirds is the **Chatham area,** which forms the easterly elbow of Cape Cod. There is no one place to recommend here, unless it is Morris Island near the headquarters for Monomoy NWR. The best way to bird Chatham is to spend a few quiet dawns walking along wooded roads—most of the land is private, and residents do not look kindly to even the gentle intrusion of birders.

One of the finest landbird traps in New England is Block Island, about 10 miles off the coast of Rhode Island. Access is by ferry (although some lines shut down after early September). Be sure to have lodging reservations before you arrive. The best birding is often at the island's northern end, especially in and around **Block Island NWR,** a 46-acre tract near Sandy Point that adjoins locally owned conservation land. To reach the refuge, take Corn Neck Road to its end, then follow the path along the edge of Cow Cove and Sachem Pond toward North Lighthouse. The last two weeks of September and the first of October are traditionally considered the best for a Block Island visit.

Along the Connecticut coast, **Lighthouse Point Park** is perhaps better known for its fall hawk migration, but landbirds pass through this New Haven city park in excellent numbers too, including a tropical kingbird in 1990 that represented the state's first-ever record of a species that rarely strays north of Mexico. To reach the park from northbound I-95, take Exit 50 and go straight .4 mile to the second light, then turn right on Townsend Avenue. Go 1.8 miles, then right onto Lighthouse Road; the park is .6 mile ahead. From southbound I-95 take Exit 51, go .9 mile on Frontage Road and turn left on Townsend to Lighthouse.

Inland, Lake Champlain acts as a barrier and a guide for migrants, which sometimes pile up on south-pointing peninsulas like **Kill Kare SP,** near St. Albans in northwestern Vermont. From St. Albans take Route 36 North for 3.9 miles, turning left onto Hathaway Point Road; the park is another 3 miles south.

On the New York Lake Ontario shoreline, the **Sandy Pond** area can be a first-rate migrant trap on days with strong northwest winds, especially on the southern sand spit bracketing North Pond. From I-81 at exit 37, go west on Route 15 (Lake Road) about 6.5 miles to the village of Sandy Pond. Park at the boat launch and walk north along the wooded peninsula.

On Long Island, a relatively short stretch of trees and bushes near the **Short Beach Coast Guard Station,** at the west end of Jones Beach, is known for phenomenal songbirding in September, especially one or two days after passage of a cold front. Warblers, vireos, flycatchers, cuckoos and other Neotropical migrants mass in the vegetation on their way south, with eager

naturalists waiting to watch them. Take the Meadowbrook Parkway South to Jones Beach SP, bearing right on the island to the
Coast Guard station.

Also worth a visit in autumn are the many urban parks and
cemeteries in the region, which, as in spring, act as havens for
migrating birds. A list of suggestions can be found in Chapter 25.

53

September
Shorttakes

Endangered Terns

One of the largest concentrations of endangered roseate terns in the United States can bc found roosting each evening this month on **Monomoy NWR,** Massachusetts, along with even greater numbers of common terns and other species; some years the total of roseates exceeds seven thousand. For information about visiting Monomoy Island, see Chapter 7.

See also:

Chapter 43, Fall Shorebirds: September is a prime month for shorebird migration along the coast, with large numbers at several spots, including **South Lubec Flats**, Maine, **Monomoy NWR**, Massachusetts, and a number of sites along the south shore of Long Island, New York. See Chapters 26 and 43 for more details and suggestions.

Chapter 55, Great Lakes Salmon Runs: The autumn spawning run of coho and chinook salmon on several Great Lakes tributaries begins in earnest this month. See Chapters 15 and 55 for a detailed discussion and hotspots.

54

Breakout:
Animal Navigation

As dusk thickens along the coast of Maine, a stirring grows in the treetops. Flocks of songbirds that have been resting or feeding all day begin to take to the air, disappearing into the night sky, their path aimed to the south. Some will stay over land; others will launch themselves to sea, not touching ground again until they reach Venezuela sixty or eighty hours later.

Offshore, humpback whales are traveling south, too, from the summer feeding grounds off Mount Desert Rock and the Stellwagen Bank, heading for the waters near the Dominican Republic; with them are right whales returning to their traditional cold-weather haunts off the Carolinas, Georgia, Florida and Bermuda.

By day, monarch butterflies traveling to the Mexican highlands join broad-winged hawks bound for Peru, and Canada geese moving from James Bay to the Chesapeake. At night, hoary, silver-haired and red bats flee from the northern forests to the warmer climate of the Southeast, tracing their own ghostly migratory routes through the sky.

But how do they know where they're going? Animal navigation is one of the abiding puzzles of natural history—and what we've learned in recent years only makes it seem all the more remarkable.

Science has learned the most about bird navigation, in part because birds are easiest to study. Much of the navigation research has been done with pigeons, those master travelers, although wild birds are perhaps even more skilled. Band recoveries show that songbirds may return not only to their precise nesting site year after year, but also to exactly the same wintering territory.

It now appears that birds use a variety of clues to find their way from one place to another. Actually, the task has two parts—the bird must know where it is (orientation) and also where it is going (navigation). For short-distance travel, such as hunting in the area around the nest, birds appear to rely on local landmarks; likewise, larger features like mountain ranges and coastlines act as guides for migrants.

Landmarks are certainly important, but not exclusively so. Flying above heavy fog, birds can orient themselves with the sun, easily compensating for its steady march across the sky. At night, when many shorebirds and songbirds migrate, they simply switch to the stars, something that's been proven in planetarium experiments with captive songbirds. In spring, caged indigo buntings clearly orient themselves with the North Star, following it around the planetarium, even when the illuminated star map is reversed so Polaris is in the south. Not that the buntings are using only the North Star as their guide—experiments have shown that they can navigate by any of the constellations within a wide circle of it.

Some of the most intriguing research into bird navigation has dealt with birds' use of the Earth's magnetic field. Some birds, at least, are sensitive to extremely weak magnetic fields, making it possible for them to navigate not only over long distances, but also on short-range hops, perhaps using magnetic anomalies like iron deposits. But again, how can they sense magnetism? For some species at least, it may be because they literally have rocks in their head—magnetite, to be specific, a magnetically sensitive form of iron oxide. Deposits have been found in in the heads of homing pigeons and bobolinks, among others. More startling yet, some biologists now argue that birds may actually see the Earth's magnetic field.

Still other birds, again including pigeons as well as petrels, appear to use smells for some navigation. A Leach's storm-petrel, nesting in a burrow on an island off the Northeast coast, can find its nest in pitch blackness by its unique smell—but not if the bird's nostrils are plugged.

The list of navigational clues goes on. Birds seem to be able to hear extremely low-frequency sound of the sort generated by wind and ocean waves, and which can carry for hundreds, even thousands of miles. They may use subtle changes in barometric pressure, wind direction and even ultraviolet light to tell them where they are and where they're going.

None of this answers the question of how a three-month-old warbler knows that there is a safe, warm place thousands of miles away where it can pass the winter. Scientists argue that the bird "knows" nothing of the sort—it has a genetically encoded urge to fly in a certain direction at a certain time of the year, an urge most likely triggered by bursts of hormones themselves brought on by the changing length of the day. But even broken down to mere facets of biology, the results are no less wondrous. For creatures as mighty as the great whales and as delicate as dragonflies, the earth is an open book and an open road.

OCTOBER

October Observations

55

Great Lakes Salmon Runs

Successfully transplanting the magnificent salmon of the Pacific coast to the East was a dream long before it was a reality. As early as the 1870s, fishermen stocked chinook salmon in the Great Lakes, but early efforts sputtered, and it wasn't until the 1970s that fisheries biologists established large populations in lakes Erie and Ontario.

Today, salmon are one of the main attractions for anglers in the Great Lakes, as well as dozens of tributary rivers and streams in New York. Although not native to the region, the salmon provide quite a spectacle each autumn when they make their upriver spawning runs.

There are two species of Pacific salmon in the October rivers—the chinook, at more than 40 pounds the biggest (western sea-run chinooks sometimes exceed 100 pounds), and the smaller coho, which averages around 10 or 15 pounds. The two species look very similar, with their streamlined bodies and leaden color that deepens with maroon during the spawning run; in the hand, a chinook's gums are black at the toothline, while a coho's are white. For the casual observer it's enough to know that the very biggest specimens will be the chinooks.

The salmon spend most of their lives in deep water, feeding on alewives, a small herring that provides the forage base for larger predator fish. In late summer the adult salmon begin to move inshore, eventually congregating at the mouths of the spawning streams by September; at this time of year, the fishing boats are trolling just offshore, arrays of rods hooked to sophisticated "downriggers" that take the lures down to the salmons' level.

The first upriver movement starts around mid-September and peaks in October. The numbers are impressive; at the Salmon River Fish Hatchery in Altmar, about eleven thousand chinooks and five thousand cohos make it past the batteries of fishermen to reach the headwaters and spawn.

In the wild the salmon find a clean, graveled stretch of stream bottom where the female uses her tail to dig a redd, or nest, depositing the eggs which are immediately fertilized by an attendant male. While some of New York's salmon do spawn naturally, few of the eggs survive, and the fishery is almost completely dependent upon hatchery-reared fingerlings, raised from eggs collected from the adults. Whether they spawn naturally or with human assistance, the adults invariably die a short time later, their purpose fulfilled.

Salmon and salmon fishing are important to the economy of a number of Great Lakes towns—Pulaski, on the Salmon River, throws an annual Salmon Festival each September, and hordes of fishermen pump millions into local coffers. At the peak of the salmon run, hotel accommodations can be scarce, so be sure to call ahead for reservations, even during the week.

A word about snagging: When salmon were first established in New York, the state decided to permit fishermen to snag the fish in rivers using heavy rods and large, weighted treble hooks, on the theory that spawning salmon (which do not feed) couldn't easily be caught otherwise. In the years since then, however, fishermen have demonstrated that the salmon can be taken on a variety of sport tackle, including fly rods and spinning gear—and the controversy over snagging, which is viewed by many anglers as a perversion of the sport, has grown heated. Fortunately, New York has severely restricted snagging to a few small stretches of river, and intends to phase it out completely in the near future.

HOTSPOTS

As with spring steelhead, the best place to see the fall salmon run is on the aptly named **Salmon River** in New York, a tributary of Lake Ontario about 40 miles north of Syracuse. The river attracts thousands of fishermen each fall, but for non-anglers the prime viewing location is the state's **Salmon River Fish Hatchery** at Altmar, where the great fish end their spawning run by ascending Beaverdam Brook to the long fish ladder and finally into the hatchery holding ponds. Here it is possible to see chinooks of up to 30 pounds, as well as a lesser number of cohos, stacked thickly in the quieter pools of the fish ladder, resting after their exhausting swim from the lake.

Directions to the hatchery can be found in Chapter 15. The visitors' center is open every day from 9 A.M. to 4 P.M., and the fish ladder area is open from dawn to dusk. When hatchery employees are at work visitors can see the spawning process, which involves gently "stripping" the eggs and milt from the adult salmon; the fertilized eggs hatch during the winter, and in spring the finger-lings, about 3 inches long, are stocked in the river to begin a new cycle.

A surprising number of salmon, steelhead and brown trout get past the water gate at the hatchery and continue up Beaverdam Brook a short distance to a dam, where visitors can see them in a more natural (and less crowded) setting. Walk past the hatchery on the road about 100 yards, then follow the path to the right, which leads to the dam.

With a fisherman's map of the river (available at most sporting goods stores), you can easily find the following over-looks, which provide good views of the salmon. **Clark Falls,** near the Schoetler paper plant, is good during mornings and evenings, when salmon are trying to jump the low falls; because of posted property, access is along the river from the west. Other good locations are the cliffs above the **Black Hole** in Pulaski, the **Route 2A Hole** and the **Smoke House Hole** downstream from Altmar.

> *CAUTION: The Salmon River's level fluctu-ates dramatically with releases of water from an upstream hydroelectric dam. If you are walking along the river, be sure to read the warning posters, and if the water starts to rise, move back to higher ground.*

Other New York rivers with chinook and coho salmon runs include **Cattaraugus Creek** near Silver Creek, **Eighteenmile Creek** near Hamburg, **Canadaway Creek** near Dunkirk and **Chautauqua Creek** near Westfield, all on Lake Erie. On the Lake Ontario shore, runs occur in the **Oswego and Genesee rivers**, **Black River** near Watertown, **North and South Sandy creeks** just to the south, **Oak Orchard Creek** north of Albion, and

Eighteenmile Creek north of Lockport. On these streams, however, seeing the salmon themselves will take a great deal of luck; watch from bridges if the water is fairly clear, and be sure to wear polarized sunglasses to cut the surface glare.

56

Fall Hawk Flights—Part 2

In New England and New York, October arrives with a crash, as the riot of foliage and crisp days bring droves of tourists north. But the same presaging of winter also drives many residents south this month—raptors fleeing the oncoming cold, migrating along the interior ridges and coast.

September's hawk flight is dominated by broad-winged hawks, traveling in huge flocks. By the opening days of October, however, the broadwings are a memory, and the focus shifts to accipiters and falcons, which race down the mountaintops and dunes in general solitude; in fact, two sharp-shinned hawks flying together are more apt to be dogfighting than flapping companionably.

Accipiters are almost supernaturally agile forest hawks, adept at threading their way through dense thickets at high speeds as they chase fleeing birds. The most common, the sharp-shinned hawk, is about the size of a blue jay, while the somewhat rarer Cooper's hawk is roughly as big as a pigeon—although (as in most raptors) the females of each species are noticeably larger than the males.

With fairly rounded wings and long tails, accipiters have excellent maneuverability and quick bursts of speed. They also have a distinctive flight pattern, a series of quick wingbeats and a shallow glide, which experienced hawk-watchers use to identify them at long distances. Separating sharpshins and Cooper's from each other, however, can be tough, because the two hawks have virtually identical plumage—brown above with vertical streaking underneath in immatures, and blue-gray above and horizontal rusty barring below on adults.

Relative size helps, especially if a sharpie and a Cooper's are flying together, but size is less useful on lone birds. Expert hawk-watchers look for the somewhat slower wingbeat, proportionately longer wings and tail and more rounded tail tip of the Cooper's, and the heavily marked underparts of the young sharpshin compared to the fairly light breast of an immature Cooper's. After you've watched enough accipiters, you'll know almost by feel what a distant hawk will be.

Sharp-shinned hawks dominate early October both in the mountains and along the coast, but coastal locations have a lock on October's other big raptor attraction—falcons. Ranging from the diminutive American kestrel to the rare and powerful peregrine falcon, these swift birds trace the outline of the shore on their migration south, thrilling naturalists at such beach lookouts as Lighthouse Point Park in Connecticut and Jones Beach State Park on Long Island.

Falcons are built for speed, their every line and angle molded by evolution to slip freely through the wind. The kestrel, by far the most common North American falcon, is lightly structured, with delicately tapered wings and a buoyant flight; because of its size, it preys on small mammals, sparrows and large insects. Only slightly larger but much more robust is the merlin, a bird of the boreal forest that is simply dazzling in the air, blasting low across the backdunes in pursuit of songbirds. The peregrine is bigger still, the size of a crow, and perhaps the fastest creature on Earth, a master of the scorching dive, capable of speeds in excess of 175 mph. It is no wonder that, for many hawk-watchers, the peregrine alone makes October worthwhile.

And as if accipiters and falcons aren't enough, October offers up a smorgasbord of raptors for the watching naturalist; of the three-month fall hawk migration, this period has the greatest variety. Early in the month, the leftovers of the broadwing flight are still passing through, along with fair numbers of bald eagles and ospreys. Toward the end of the month, red-tailed hawks, goshawks and golden eagles appear with increasing regularity, especially on the interior ridges. It is enough to make any birder long for October twelve months of the year.

Accipiters like this Cooper's hawk take center stage during October's hawk flights, especially at coastal hawkwatches like Lighthouse Point Park in Connecticut.

HOTSPOTS

The hotspots that follow are a few of the best coastal locations throughout the region—sites that offer some of the best hawk-watching in October. But they are not the only options this month. For suggestions for interior New England, see Chapter 50; for inland New York, Chapter 61.

Lighthouse Point Park in New Haven, Connecticut, is one of the best hawk lookouts in the region, averaging an impressive seventeen thousand raptors a year, with totals some years running much higher (more than twenty-seven thousand birds in 1990, for instance). Although some broadwings pass through here, Lighthouse Point is busiest during the last week of September and first two weeks of October, when large numbers of accipiters and falcons (primarily kestrels and merlins, but with tantalizing numbers of peregrines) come through.

As an added bonus, this is an excellent location for songbirds in September and early October, and some of the agile bird-eating hawks, like merlins and sharpshins, are often hunting the park in early morning. For directions, see Chapter 52; the hawk-watch is next to the parking lot at the park's east side.

In Massachusetts, falcons and accipiters travel along the beaches and barrier islands on their way south, sometimes in impressive numbers. **Plum Island/Parker River NWR,** east of Newburyport, is a good spot to intercept the flight; see Chapter 2 for directions. There is no formal hawk-watch here, although many observers prefer the region near and south of Hellcat Swamp. Simply find a raised vantage point and watch for passing hawks.

Napatree Point, in Rhode Island's western "toe," has a growing reputation among New England's hawk-watchers during the accipiter season. From Route 1 at Westerly, Rhode Island, take Route 1A south to Avondale, then follow Watch Hill Road 2.2 miles to the town of Watch Hill, parking near the harbor. The best hawk-watching is west of here, near the neck of the peninsula.

The Bronx may seem a most unlikely place for a hawk-watch of any sort—much less a fabulously productive one like **Pelham Bay Park,** where in 1990 more than twenty-two thousand hawks were counted, 15,459 of them on a single September day. Unlike most of the region's coastal hawk-watches, Pelham Bay is at its best in mid-September during the broadwing flight, when winds are out of the northwest with a scattering of clouds.

Pelham Bay Park is also one of the best places in North America to see migrating ospreys, ranking only behind Lighthouse

Point and Cape May, New Jersey, in total counts. It is, however, by far the best place to watch ospreys make their stunning, feet-first hunting dives—during one two-week period, more than 220 such attacks were witnessed. The peak period for the osprey migration is also mid-September.

To reach the park, take I-95 to Exit 9, getting onto the Hutchinson River Parkway and driving north across the river to the Pelham Bay Park exit, the next interchange. Go straight through the traffic circle into the park, following signs for Orchard Beach parking.

A long-established hawk-watch can also be found along the south shore of Long Island, on **Fire Island.** Northerly winds are the best here, and flights of kestrels and merlins can be heavy, with seasonal totals for all species running around five thousand birds. To get to Fire Island, take the Robert Moses State Parkway to the Moses Causeway, following signs for Fire Island. Once over Captree Island and Fire Island Inlet, turn west on the island to Democrat Point, which overlooks the inlet. Hawk-watching can also be good 14 miles to the west, near Short Beach close to Parking Lot 2 of Jones Beach State Park. See Chapter 52 for directions.

57

A Potpourri of Migrant Birds

Autumn is one of the most exciting times of the year for a naturalist, in large part because of the mass movements of migrating birds. The fall hawk flights are covered elsewhere, but this chapter will detail some of the more unusual land-, water- and shorebird concentrations that can be found this month.

HOTSPOTS

It's odd to list an inland lookout for coastal species, but **Derby Hill Bird Observatory** along Lake Ontario in New York, is the most reliable inland site in North America for jaegers, normally only seen well offshore on pelagic boat trips. The best conditions are during a northwesterly gale, when the gull-like seabirds can be spotted flying out over the lake, so plan on miserable weather and dress accordingly. The payoff can be spectacular—in early October 1979, more than two hundred jaegers, most of them parasitics, were seen.

In less drastic weather, Derby Hill is a prime waterfowl corridor in October, and here again it produces a surprise, with significant flights of scoters and brant, birds normally associated with the ocean coast. Their migration peaks from mid-October through November. Heavy flights of gulls are also passing Derby Hill this month, including some of the rarer "white-winged" species so eagerly sought by birders. For directions to Derby Hill, see Chapter 13.

Throughout autumn, the impoundments and marshes of **Dead Creek WMA** in western Vermont are a magnet for waterbirds

October is a prime month for waterfowl concentrations, including large numbers of ducks (canvasbacks among them) on Lake Champlain and nearby Dead Creek WMA in Vermont.

of all sorts. The Champlain Valley, in which Dead Creek sits, is a major migratory route for snow geese heading south, and starting in the middle of October large flocks of these dazzling white birds can be found here, along with a variety of other waterfowl, lingering great blue herons and the first wintering red-tailed and rough-legged hawks. The numbers can be amazing, with as many as fifteen thousand snows at a time.

Nearby **Lake Champlain** is also very good at this time of year for migrant waterfowl, and visitors can expect to see large flocks of diving ducks. For directions to Dead Creek and a number of nearby Lake Champlain points, see Chapter 1.

On Long Island, birders have long known that the vegetation around the **Short Beach Coast Guard Station** at the west end of Jones Beach is a terrific trap for migrant landbirds. After the September warblers waves are history, attentive naturalists find large numbers of migrating sparrows here, including, on an almost annual basis, such rarities as lark and clay-colored sparrows. For directions, see Chapter 52.

Combine a visit to the Coast Guard station with a stop at **Zach's Bay** to the east, which attracts many of the same species.

From mid-October to the end of November, the Zach's Beach area also holds good numbers of shorebirds—largely dunlins and black-bellied plovers, but also including such enticing species as marbled and Hudsonian godwits and lesser golden-plover. To reach Zach's Bay, drive east from the Meadowbrook State Parkway entrance to parking lot 5; the bay is just to the east.

58

Fall Foliage Routes—Part 2

It started as a hint of red on the highest hills, then grew to an orange blanket in the peaks of the Adirondacks and the Green and White mountains as September came to a close. But now, as October billows in on cobalt-blue skies and chill northwest winds, the autumn color is unleashed from the highlands, washing across the Northeast in a fiery rush of changing leaves.

And with the rush of color comes a rush of tourists, the "leaf-peepers" that choke the weekend roads of Vermont and New Hampshire, western Massachusetts and upstate New York. The first week of October on one of the more popular main roads, you're likely to spend most of your time watching the bumper in front of you than the mountains.

But New England and New York are a big region, and because of the abundance of sugar maples, there is good fall color almost everywhere. The hotspots that follow are especially scenic, but use them as starting points only. Get a good map or a DeLorme atlas and strike off on your own, picking small back roads off the beaten track. You will leave most of the crowd behind, and have the special thrill of discovery when you round a bend and find a magnificent vista spread out before you like a glorious surprise.

Another, even better option is to abandon your car entirely and head out on foot. You'll still see the sweeping views, but without the madding crowds. More important, you'll enjoy the small tableaus the season sets, which the car-bound miss: a single, blood-red maple leaf on a bed of moss, or the burnished copper of dying ferns against a screen of tamarack. For suggestions on hiking guides (and areas), see Chapter 51.

Timing is always the trickiest part of seeing the best fall color, and while the timetable that follows is generally accurate, each season is a little different; an especially cool autumn may bring the color on more quickly, for instance, as will a summer drought, which can cause the trees to shut down for the winter several weeks earlier than usual. A large body of water will hold heat and warm the surrounding land, also delaying the change compared to other areas in the same general area.

As a general rule, look for the peak foliage the first week of October in the Allegheny Highlands of southwestern New York, at altitudes from 2,000 to 3,500 feet in the White Mountains of New Hampshire, and across most of the higher elevations in the Green Mountains in Vermont. October's first two weeks bring the best show in the Catskills, while across central New York and in elevations below 2,000 feet in Vermont and New Hampshire, the ideal time is usually the second and third weeks of the month. The last two weeks of October are usually the best in the Hudson Valley. It's always a good idea to check with the local foliage hotline (listed in the Appendix) before making your visit.

> CAUTION: *This is one time of the year that you shouldn't travel without lodging reservations, especially in the White and Green mountains. Motels and bed-and-breakfasts fill up quickly, so try to make your plans as far in advance as possible.*

HOTSPOTS

In Vermont, Route 100 runs north to south down the spine of the Green Mountains, providing unparalleled views—and a good jump-off point for side road explorations into the **Green Mountain NF,** which lies generally to the west of the road. Starting at Wilmington and heading north to Troy, in the shadow of the Cold Hollow Mountains, the road runs for nearly 190 miles through deep forests, picturesque farms and small towns.

Other good fall drives in Vermont include **Route 2** across the northern half of Vermont early in the month, and later in October, **Route 4** from Rutland east to White River Junction on the New Hampshire border, and **Route 9** across the southern edge of the state from Brattleboro to Bennington.

The **Lake Umbagog** region in northeast New Hampshire is also good for early October color. Starting at the town of Errol you can travel north on Route 16 into the Rangeley Lake area of Maine, or around the southern end of Umbagog on Route 26. South on Route 16 from Errol is the scenic Androscoggin River valley.

In New Hampshire's White Mountain NF, the **Kancamagus Highway,** which runs for 37 miles between Lincoln and Conway, can be astonishingly beautiful in autumn—and astonishingly crowded, particularly on weekends. Still, the scenes of dramatic mountains, especially around 2,890-foot Kancamagus Pass, make the jostling crowds worthwhile. Top off a low gas tank before entering, however, because there are no services on the highway.

In New York, early October brings subtle colors to the farmlands and woodlots of the **St. Lawrence River Valley,** between Cape Vincent and Ogdensburg; follow routes 12E, 12 and 37 along the river, with views of the Thousand Islands region. Mid-October can be spectacular along Route 97, which follows the **upper Delaware River** past the dramatic overlook known as Hawk's Nest; the colors here are most intense in mid-October, with the splashy red and orange of maples and the dark counterpoint of white pines and hemlocks.

In the **Catskills** the peak color often comes the first week of October. Two drives along branches of the Delaware can be exceptionally attractive, especially if the oaks are having a good color year. On the main branch of the river, follow Route 10 from Deposit east to Delhi, along the Cannonsville Reservoir; farther south on the east branch of the river, take Route 30 from Route 17 north along the Pepacton Reservoir to Route 28, which then loops east through the heart of the Catskills.

The glory of the Green Mountains in autumn often overshadows their neighbors to the south, Massachusetts' **Berkshire Hills**, but there's plenty of color in this patchwork of mountains and farms. For a weekend drive, start in Northampton, along the heavily industrialized Connecticut River valley. Head west on Route 9 toward Pittsfield, a 41-mile drive that leads through increasingly mountainous and scenic terrain.

Just before Pittsfield, at the village of Coltsville, turn north on Route 8 along the Hoosic River for 19 miles to North Adams, then turn east on historic Route 2. This road traces the old path known as the Mohawk Trail, dating from a 1663 war between the Mohawk and Pocumtuck Indians; today it passes through **Savoy Mountain** and **Mohawk Trail** state forests on its 35-mile way to Greenfield.

59

October Shorttakes

Rutting Whitetails

Each autumn, hundreds of white-tailed deer can be seen early in the morning and just before dark in the vicinity of **Rachel Carson NWR,** near Wells, Maine. At this time of year the deer are at their physical peak, the bucks well into the mating season, or rut, and sporting swollen necks and fine racks. For general directions to Rachel Carson NWR, see Chapter 7; deer-watching is especially good in the area of Laudholm Farm, part of the Wells Reserve. From Wells drive north on Route 1 for 1.5 miles and turn right at the second blinker light onto Laudhold Farm Road, then left at the fork.

See also:

Chapter 62, Snow Geese. Snow geese numbers grow quickly at **Dead Creek WMA** in Vermont this month, peaking near the end of October or early November. Some years as many as fifteen thousand pass through on their way down the Champlain Valley.

Chapter 63, Pelagic Birds From Shore. The gannet migration along the coast is also building in late October, and northeasterly storms may bring incredible concentrations of these and other pelagic birds to shore at places like **Point Judith**, Rhode Island, toward the end of the month.

Chapter 52, Autumn Landbird Migration. Early October can be prime time for migrant songbirds; **Block Island**, for instance, is often at its best the first week of the month following a frontal passage.

60

Breakout:
Fall Foliage Mysteries

It may seem magical, but the annual change from subtle green to brilliant color that makes the northern forests famous is rooted in chemistry, not alchemy.

A leaf, at its simplest, is a food factory; here the tree combines water and carbon dioxide, using sunlight to provide the needed energy. The results are sugar compounds—and the chemical that makes this photosynthesis possible is chlorophyll, which gives green plants their characteristic coloration.

Throughout spring and summer, deciduous trees process vast quantities of water and carbon dioxide, building their sugar reserves and (not incidentally) producing a great deal of oxygen in the bargain. But as autumn approaches the tree must shift strategies. In the northern winter, with the ground frozen, liquid water becomes almost impossible to obtain; in addition, the low humidity of winter would quickly dry out the leaves—and the trees.

So to protect itself from lethal desiccation, the tree must shed its leaves for the winter (conifers avoid this because their leaves have been reduced to thin needles heavily coated in protective, waxy layers).

As the temperature begins to drop in early autumn, the tree essentially shuts off the tap. Much of the chlorophyll is withdrawn into the twig, and the rest begins to break down chemically. Cells at the juncture between the twig and the leaf stem cut off the flow of sap, and the joint weakens.

With the chlorophyll greatly reduced, other pigments that it masked in the leaf all summer become evident. These are many of the browns and yellows that show up in autumn foliage, colors that were simply hidden through the growing season. But the most spectacular colors, such as the deep red-orange of a sugar maple glowing in the sun, are the result of chemical changes in the sugars trapped in the now-isolated leaves.

In fact, the intensity of the final color will be determined to a large degree by the amount of sugar in the leaf—and here weather again becomes vitally important. A good growing season encourages sugar production, but even more important is a succession of mild days and cool, but not freezing nights in early fall (Jack Frost and below-freezing temperatures are actually the enemies of a good foliage display). Mild days prod the leaf into making sugar, while cool nights retard its withdrawal into the stem. The sugar, trapped in the leaf, is converted to a pigment called anthocyanin, the source of the red color; once it in turn breaks down, it may produce bronzes, purples and other subtle threads in the autumnal tapestry.

If science knows the fundamental chemical reactions that produce fall color, it cannot yet make any but the most general predictions about how a particular autumn will turn out. A hot, dry summer puts the trees under a lot of stress, forcing many to shut down for the year earlier than usual and greatly reducing sugar production; in such years a poor display can be expected. Likewise, a coolish, well-watered summer may enhance leaf sugar levels, although too much water can be as bad as too little. Some years the trees confound all prognostications and light up the hills, despite the worst of conditions. Perhaps, after all, there's still a little magic involved.

NOVEMBER

November Observations

61

Fall Hawk Flights—Part 3

This month marks the conclusion of the autumn hawk migration, but (in the minds of many naturalists, at least), the best is saved for last—for November is the month of the great raptors of the north.

These are birds like red-tailed and rough-legged hawks that need winter's cold breath to get them moving south, and they fly, for the most part, along the interior ridges, shunning the coast. And with them comes the finest of November's birds, soaring on 7-foot wings, the rare eastern golden eagle.

Hawk-watching in November is not for the faint-hearted; when an icy gale is raging, raking the mountains with 30 mph gusts and windchills that may dip toward zero, it take perseverance to stick out the day. But the rewards are in keeping with the sacrifice—the sight of redtails streaming down the ridge, wings half-tucked in the blast, riding the chaotic winds as easily as a quiet summer's day. Or a goshawk spooking through a snow squall like a boreal ghost, or a rough-legged hawk, black as soot and fresh from the Arctic.

As the autumn migration runs its course from September through the closing days in November, the number of birds passing each week steadily declines. Don't expect the staggering counts of broadwing season when, on an exceptional day, ten thousand or more hawks may pass a count site. Depending on the location, a good day in November may be a few hundred birds, perhaps a thousand—but instead of straining to see specks wheeling in the stratosphere, as is often the case with broadwings, November's migrants tend to hug the ridges, affording marvelous views.

Red-tailed hawks make up the bulk of the late fall migration. Big, solid birds, redtails are ubiquitous across most of North America, where they breed in woodlands but hunt most often in open or brushy terrain—a perfect description of much of the Northeast. These are buteos, well suited for soaring with their wide wings and tails, but in migration they most often ride the deflection currents produced when strong winds strike the sides of the ridges and billow upward. The redtail flight begins in late October, when most of the individuals moving are immatures; the adults, identified by their brick-orange tails, tend to wait a week or two more, peaking in early November. Stragglers may continue well into December, however.

The golden eagles that pass through the region are among the most enigmatic of birds, and the rarest of eastern raptors. Even their historical breeding range is subject to dispute; golden eagles were once thought to have nested as far south as Tennessee, but a careful review of old accounts has led biologists Walter Spofford and David Lee to reject any claims of golden eagles nesting south of the Adirondacks, where five or six pairs nested until the 1970s. The species disappeared as a resident from New Hampshire nearly a century earlier, with the last apparently a pair that raised two chicks on White Horse Ledge near Conway in 1876. In recent years, only northern Maine has had breeding golden eagles—just one or two pairs in locations kept carefully secret by ornithologists.

The eastern golden eagle is a bird apart from its more common and widespread western counterpart. Although an eastern and western bird are physically almost identical, they are worlds apart ecologically. While the western eagle is a bird of open spaces and arid lands, feeding most heavily on small mammals, the eastern golden is tied to wetlands, nesting on cliff faces in the forest and hunting bogs and marshes for a diet heavily dependent on birds; among the prey species recovered at eastern eyries were bitterns, great blue herons, cormorants and mergansers.

It seems likely that we know less about eastern golden eagles than virtually any other raptor in North America, largely because of their scarcity. In all, there are fewer than fifteen breeding records for the Northeast in the twentieth century, far too few to account for the number of goldens seen each fall during migration.

Most of the migrants, it seems, come from Canada, where a small, isolated population survives among the stunted boreal forests and tundra of northern Quebec and Labrador, and the mountains of southern Quebec and the Gaspé Peninsula. Each fall some of them (or all, since it is not known if the Canadian birds are primarily residents or migratory) head south into the United States, following the interior ridges for hundreds of miles. Judging from a fairly scanty selection of band recoveries, it appears the adults tend to winter inland along waterways, while immatures most often fetch up along the coast from Massachusetts south.

A golden eagle is a majestic bird, with wings that may stretch more than 7 feet across. First-year immatures are chocolate colored, with a great deal of white at the base of their black-tipped tails; as they age, the white disappears. Unlike western golden eagles, eastern immatures frequently lack any white on the undersides of their wings, a field mark unfortunately often stressed in guides. All ages have the distinctive, brassy cast to the feathers of the crown, nape and shoulder—the reason a golden eagle almost glimmers in the late-day sun.

Nor are goldens the only eagles that November may serve up. Northern bald eagles from Canada and New England wait until winter is breathing down their necks before they head south, although many tough out the season in the region (see Chapter 67). A day with an eagle, bald or golden, is a red-letter occasion, and makes the freezing winds more tolerable.

HOTSPOTS

The best locations for November hawk-watching are the inland ridges of the Appalachians and southern New England; generally speaking, the coastal locations that were so productive during the peak of the accipiter and falcon flight in October fade from importance as the focus shifts to mountain migrants like redtails. In addition to the following sites, check Chapter 50 for interior New England suggestions.

In inland New York, most of the fall hawk-watches are concentrated in the state's bootheel, where the Appalachians cut across the Hudson and north along the Massachusetts and Vermont borders.

Perched above the Hudson River is **Hook Mountain,** a fine overlook reached after a fairly strenuous hike from the road, with usual fall totals of around fifteen thousand hawks to make it worthwhile. From the New York Thruway on the west side of the

Hudson take Route 9W North 2 miles, parking at the base of the hill and watching for a blazed trail on the right, which leads to the lookout.

To the northwest of Hook Mountain is **Mt. Peter**, near the village of Greenwood Lake. From I-87 take Route 17 north or south to 17A North; follow this 7.5 miles to Greenwood Lake, then go another 2.1 miles on 17A North. Watch for the Appalachian Trail crossing and pull off in the defunct restaurant parking area on the right immediately after it (a new establishment is planned for the site). The hawk-watch is on the ridge less than 100 yards beyond the lot. Flight totals are lower here than along the Hudson, running between six thousand and nine thousand hawks a year.

Also in southern New York is the **Port Jervis** scenic overlook on I-84 just east of the Delaware Water Gap, between exits 1 and 2. The best views are from the parking area for the northbound lanes, so coming from the east drive on to Exit 1, turn around and backtrack about 1.5 miles to the overlook. This site is usually manned only during late October and early November, but has been good for redtails.

To the north, the **Petersburg Pass Scenic Area**, on the crest of the Taconics between New York and Massachusetts, offers hawk-watching in a spectacular setting, although the annual count here is not as high as at some other lookouts. From the Albany area take Route 2 East to the village of Petersburg and drive another 5.6 miles to the pass; park in the lot at the right. From the east take I-90 (Massachusetts Turnpike) to Route 20/7 North, then Route 2 West for 4.2 miles to the scenic area parking lot. There are good views both from the old ski building foundation south of the lot, and from a clearing on the hill to the north.

Central New York has few regularly manned hawk-watches, even though this area would seem a logical path for southbound hawks. Observations at **Franklin Mountain**, south of Oneonta, bear this out; one-day counts for red-tailed hawks have exceeded 1,200 birds, and golden eagle totals are nothing short of astounding—123 were counted in 1992, tying an eastern continental record, with daily counts as high as 19. Best of all, goldens at Franklin Mountain often pass exceptionally low and close.

To reach the Franklin Mountain hawk-watch, take I-88 to Exit 15 (Routes 23/28), turning onto Route 23E/28S. Go .2 mile and turn onto 28 South, drive another .7 mile, turn right and immediately left onto Southside Road. Drive 1.1 miles, make a right onto Swart Hollow Road and climb the hill for 1.6 miles to Grange Hall

Road, a sharp right. Go .3 mile and pull off onto a small road on the left below an old barn; this is the Delaware-Ostego Audubon Society Sanctuary. Follow the broad path left of the barn and up the hill. The hawk-watch is not at the top, but at a flat area about halfway up.

Not as productive as Franklin Mountain (and no longer regularly manned) is the **Oneida Hill** hawk-watch, about 15 miles south of Rome, New York; it is a broad, low hill overlooking the Oneida Lake valley. From I-90 take Route 365 West toward Oneida, turning left in the village of Oneida Castle onto Route 5 East. Go .8 mile and turn right onto Hamilton Avenue and drive 4.3 miles to a sharp left bend where Sullivan and Eaton roads join. Turn onto Eaton and go 2.4 miles to the intersection with Hatalla Road; go straight on Hatalla, which eventually makes a 90-degree bend to the left. Drive another .7 mile and pull over opposite the hulk of the local landfill, and watch the sky to the north.

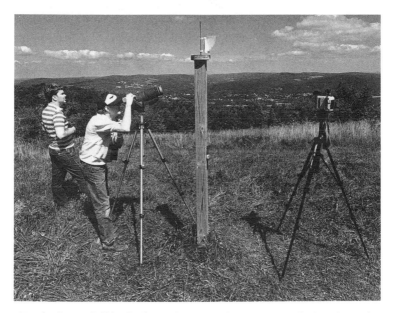

Perched on a hill high above the Susquehanna River, the hawkwatch at Franklin Mountain in central New York is the best place in the Northeast to see golden eagles in autumn.

62

Snow Geese

A flock of snow geese, seen against an autumn sky, does not appear to fly so much as ripple through the air, the flickering of the white bodies and black wingtips producing a surrealistic effect that is intensified by the birds' shrill, barking call, a sound that permeates the air wherever the flocks are found.

Each autumn, most of eastern North America's population of snow geese—the larger race known as the greater snow goose—leaves its breeding grounds on the frigid islands and Greenland coast ringing Baffin Bay and heads south, arrowing for the St. Lawrence Valley, then following the long Mahican Channel down the valleys of Lake Champlain and the Hudson to the Atlantic coast, to spend the winter from New Jersey to the Outer Banks.

Along the way the geese rest, sometimes in concentrations of twenty thousand or more. This storm of geese with the storms of winter on its heels provides unmatched opportunities for anyone who loves a natural spectacle.

The Champlain Valley is perhaps the best place to view this grand passage, for the waters of the lake and its nearby marshes provide safety, while the farms of the surrounding lowlands provide food in the form of waste grains and grazing.

Snow geese are all but unmistakable—the only wild, white goose found commonly in the East. Necks stretched in flight, adults are almost 2.5 feet long, bright white with black primary feathers on the wings; up close, look for the pink bill with its distinctive black "grin patch," and pinkish legs. Seen at near range, many snow geese also have rusty staining around the head, the result of a summer spent feeding in iron-rich tundra ponds.

The young snows are decidedly dingier than their parents, with gray legs and bills but black wingtips; seen alone, one can easily be dismissed as an odd domestic goose. Snow goose family units appear to last through migration, at the least, for two or three immatures are often seen in the company of one or two adults.

Snow geese are among the earliest of migrant waterfowl in the spring, returning to their Arctic breeding grounds well before the snow has melted. They tend to choose somewhat protected nest sites, places where the tundra terrain shields them from the worst of the wind; perhaps because such places are few and far between, snow geese are colonial nesters, jamming together by the tens of thousands, although protection from predators is another powerful incentive for colonialism.

Snow geese mate, if not for life, at least for the long haul, and as soon as they are back on the breeding grounds the established pairs reclaim their old nest sites. Younger birds mating for the first time must make do with less attractive positions near the edge of the colony, where the risk of chick and egg predation from arctic foxes, gulls and jaegers is much higher (snow geese may minimize this threat by nesting close to snowy owls, which aggressively defend the area against other predators).

The entire colony—indeed, the entire species—takes a gamble each spring with the fickle Arctic weather. If the spring is late or unseasonably cold and wet, nesting success will be poor, and it is not unusual for the breeding season to be a complete loss. Add to that the stress that nesting places on the adults, for the females fast during the twenty-three-day incubation period, and the gander stays close by the entire time defending the eggs.

Within hours of hatching, the family abandons the nest and heads for open water, where it is safer from land predators like foxes, but still vulnerable to aerial attack from jaegers, falcons, owls and hawks. Only when the chicks begin to approach adult size does the danger lessen, and within 6 weeks of hatching they have taken to the air, ready for the trip south.

Despite the many dangers and difficulties snow geese face each year, the eastern population has been growing at a remarkable rate, with recent estimates as high as 2.4 million. While this is wonderful for the birds and those who enjoy watching them, it has posed some serious problems, especially on the coastal refuges to the south where they winter in large numbers. Snow geese are "grubbers," not merely nipping off the tips of plants when grazing but pulling up the whole thing, roots and all. In tidal areas like the New Jersey and Delaware coasts, enormous (and increasing) flocks of snow geese, restricted by development to relatively small stretches of shoreline, have had a devastating effect on cordgrass, the foundation plant of the tidal marsh. Large areas have been grazed to the bare mud, destroying habitat for many other organisms.

Naturalists scanning a big flock of snow geese may occasionally see dark-bodied birds in the sea of white, geese with blue-gray torsos and necks, pale gray wings and white heads. These are the so-called "blue geese," once considered a separate species but now classified as a color phase of the lesser snow goose, which migrates most often through the Midwest and West. There is a dark phase of the greater snow goose, too, but for some reason it is rare, while the lesser blue phase is common and apparently becoming more so.

Experienced birders also carefully sift through snow goose flocks for white geese with the same general shape, but which are noticeably smaller. These are Ross' geese, a rare western species that sometimes shows up in the East. Ross' geese have the same white and black pattern as an adult snow, but are only about 23 inches long (compared to the snow's average of 28), with a smaller bill and no grin patch, and a proportionally shorter neck. Now that naturalists know to watch for Ross' geese, a few are spotted in the region almost every fall.

HOTSPOTS

With the bulk of the snow goose flight channeling down the Champlain Valley, it is no surprise that the two best places in the region to see the flocks are in Vermont—**Missiquoi NWR** at the lake's north end and **Dead Creek WMA** near Chimney Point.

The migration of snow geese through western New England is a prolonged affair, starting in mid-October and running through the third week of November. The number of geese funneling through the region is nothing short of remarkable; by one estimate, the figure is up to twenty thousand geese per week for five weeks.

Dead Creek is perhaps the easiest and most productive area to search, since it has good access and plenty of open farmland where the geese can be easily spotted. For directions to Dead Creek, see Chapter 1; pay particular attention to the areas of the lake south of Route 17, and roads like Nortontown Road that

Most of the greater snow geese in North America funnel down the Champlain Valley each fall from Canada, providing an amazing spectacle at places along their route like Dead Creek WMA in Vermont.

branch west from Route 22A below Addison. Missiquoi also attracts huge numbers of snow geese, but most of the access is by boat or foot; general directions can be found in Chapter 37.

During migration, snow geese may turn up anywhere along Lake Champlain; watch for large patches of white in the distance when driving through farmland near the lake. Other areas in Vermont worth checking for snow geese are the waters of **Shelburne Bay** south of Burlington, and **Grand Isle** and **Isle La Motte** in the northern lake; for the last two, follow Route 2 West to Grand Isle, exploring back roads on the island, then continuing on Route 2 to Route 129 to Isle La Motte.

On the New York side of the lake, snow geese and other waterfowl are especially abundant in the protected waters of **Whallon Bay,** between Westport and Essex. Take I-87 to Exit 31, then follow Route 9N South for 5 miles to Route 22 North at Westport. Just beyond town, turn right onto Shore Road and go 7 miles, then turn right onto Albee Road, which hugs the bay to Split Rock Point.

And although the numbers are much lower than in the Champlain Valley, snow geese are also found at **Jamaica Bay WR,** which sits between Brooklyn and Queens. At the peak in mid-November, up to one thousand snows may be seen here; check Chapter 43 for directions.

63

Pelagic Birds from Shore

Pelagic birding, while fascinating, is admittedly not everyone's cup of tea; the very idea of spending hours on a freezing, wildly pitching boat can be enough to deter even the most enthusiastic naturalist. Fortunately, this month there is a way to see many of the same birds without ever leaving land. In fact, you may even see a whale or two while you're at it.

Late autumn is the peak of the migration season for many species of seabirds. They are an odd mix of north and south— gannets, jaegers, kittiwakes and alcids that nest in the Arctic and Canadian Maritimes, great skuas that nest in Iceland and Europe, along with a few lingering shearwaters, petrels and south polar skuas that breed in the South Atlantic and are returning for the start of the austral summer.

This migration streams south well offshore of the Northeast coast, out of the sight and knowledge of most humans. But much as weather and geography conspire to form notable concentrations of migrant landbirds, so too do these forces sometimes bring the seabird flight within range of shore-based observers.

The best places to watch the parade—Race Point on Cape Cod, Point Judith in Rhode Island, or Montauk Point in New York—stick far out into the sea, close to the flight lanes. Add to this a strong northeast wind of the sort that boils up in many autumn gales, and you have the chance to witness a sight that is usually reserved for the open ocean.

Gannets and jaegers are the real attractions in the autumn pelagic migration. Gannets are magnificent seabirds, pure white except for black wingtips that stretch 6 feet apart, and a faint yellow tinge on the face. They are powerful fliers, and still more powerful divers, hurtling violently into the sea from a height of 50 or more feet, folding back their wings at the last moment so they become javelins. The plunge takes the gannets deep into the water, below the range of lighter fish-eating birds like terns, where they can prey on fish like sand launce.

In summer, the gannets gather in huge colonies on sea cliffs like those of Bonaventure Island on the Gaspé Peninsula, but they spend the winter at sea, ranging from southern New England to the Gulf of Mexico. During the migration the numbers of gannets that pass south off the region's coast is remarkable, and when a nor'easter is blowing, a lucky observer may see thousands close to shore. Even without bad weather, gannets offshore can often be spotted through strong binoculars or a spotting scope, wheeling and diving in the sun.

Jaegers are less common along the coast, although during strong northeast storms they, too, can pile up near land in great numbers. Members of the same family as gulls and terns, jaegers— the name is from the German word for "hunter"—are bold predators and thieves, feeding in summer on lemmings, voles and small birds on their Arctic breeding grounds, and in winter on fish, often taken by piracy from other seabirds.

Identifying jaegers can be exceptionally confusing, since the two most commonly seen species, the parasitic and pomarine, both have similar light and dark phases, and immature plumages that greatly resemble each other. For all but the most experienced birder, the best course is to log the bird as "jaeger spp." and let it go at that.

HOTSPOTS

Although you may see gannets even under clear skies, to stand the best chance of seeing migrant pelagics, try to catch the worst weather—a strong northeast gale, which will force the birds toward land. Generally speaking, mornings are more productive than afternoons. Be aware, however, that the shore—especially rocky bluffs like Halibut Point—can be dangerous places during violent storms; stay well back from the reach of even the highest waves, and avoid dropoffs made slick by sheets of rain. At the very least, you'll need to dress for the weather, with quality rain gear (pants and hat as well as a coat) and layers of insulation beneath.

A fierce wind lashes Halibut Point on Massachusetts' Cape Ann, a hotspot late each autumn for pelagic birds, which are blown to shore by northeast gales.

The great scythe of land known as **Cape Ann,** Massachusetts, curves well out into the ocean, giving the shore-bound watcher a way to get close to the migration path. **Halibut Point** and **Andrews Point** are traditionally the best locations; see Chapter 9 for directions. Just to the north, **Parker River NWR** and **Plum Island**, although not a peninsula, can also have good gannet-watching on strong east or northeast winds; directions are in Chapter 2.

Three sites on Cape Cod are normally excellent for pelagics. At the northern tip of the cape, **Race Point** is one of the region's outstanding pelagic hotspots during strong northeast winds, which blow many of the seabirds into Cape Cod Bay; those same winds may drive the birds close to **Sandy Neck Beach** on the inner arm, near Barnstable. Once the storm passes and the winds shift to northwest, the birds are blown back toward land again, this time appearing in good numbers at **First Encounter Beach,** on the bay side near Eastham.

To get to Sandy Neck Beach, take Route 6 onto the cape, turning immediately onto Route 6A; follow this to Sandy Neck Road, a left, which leads to the beach parking lot, the best observation point. To get to First Encounter Beach, take Route 6 onto the cape; go about 34 miles to Samoset Road and turn left, driving another 2 miles to the beach. For Race Point, take Route

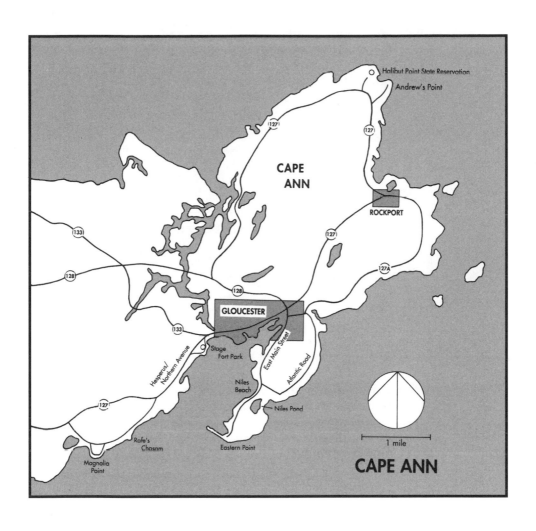

Halibut Point State Reservation
Andrew's Point

127

127

CAPE
ANN

127

ROCKPORT

127

127A

133

128

128

GLOUCESTER

133

Hesperus/ Northern Avenue

Stage
Fort Park

East Main Street

Atlantic Road

Niles
Beach

127

Niles Pond

Rafe's
Chasam

Eastern Point

Magnolia
Point

1 mile

CAPE ANN

6 all the way to the northern tip of the cape to Provincetown, another 23 miles past Samoset Road, turning right at the light onto Race Point Road, which leads to the beach parking lot.

In Rhode Island, **Point Judith** is as popular with birders as it is with surfers, who wear heavy wetsuits against the chill of autumn water when the wind churns up the waves. Sticking out between Rhode Island Sound and Block Island Sound, Point Judith is an excellent vantage point for pelagics passing by on easterly winds. To get there, take Route 1 to Wakefield, then follow signs for Point Judith onto Route 108 South for 5.8 miles. Pass the entrance on the right for Point Judith SP and go another .2 mile to the old restaurant, the best overlook to the east.

Also in Rhode Island, **Napatree Point** near Watch Hill can be good for gannets and other seabirds during November. See Chapter 56 for directions.

Montauk Point, at the east end of Long Island, provides exciting seabird watching opportunities each autumn, especially during storms, when the number of gannets can be spectacular; this site also can produce jaegers, and in late November and early December a heavy migration of scoters can be seen from shore. For directions to Montauk, see Chapter 40.

It would hardly seem worthwhile to look for pelagic birds hundreds of miles from the ocean, yet at two inland locations seabirds show up with enough regularity each autumn to make a visit—during the right conditions—worth considering.

Derby Hill Bird Observatory, on the shore of Lake Ontario in New York, is the most reliable inland site in North America for pomarine and parasitic jaegers, those gull-like predators of the Arctic that are most often seen at sea during the winter. Some, at least, do pass down the Great Lakes, and can be seen from the bluffs at Derby Hill from late September and October (the usual peak) through mid-November, generally during strong northwest gales. Dress for the weather, and be very careful near the edge of the bluff. Directions to Derby Hill can be found in Chapter 13.

Naturalists have also discovered that **Lake Champlain** also hosts pelagics during the same September-November period, with the list in recent years including parasitic and pomarine jaegers, gannets, Leach's storm-petrels, black-legged kittiwakes and Sabine's gulls, the last a species that normally winters at sea in the Southern Hemisphere. The incidence of sightings is much less frequent here than at Derby Hill, but it certainly pays to keep an eye open for anything unusual when visiting the lake.

64

Owling

Dusk comes on a chill November night, and the woods speak with the voice of an owl. It may be the whooping barks of a barred owl in a maple and hemlock forest, the scratchy whistles of a tiny saw-whet owl in a spruce stand, the stuttering whinny of a screech-owl in a farm woodlot or the ringing bass hoots of a great horned owl almost anywhere there are trees.

People have always been fascinated by owls—by their unsettlingly human faces, by their strange calls and nocturnal lifestyle. Although many species are quite common, they are rarely seen, one reason why the pastime known as owling is growing in popularity.

Owling depends on an owl's tendency to respond to (and investigate) imitations of its call. Most owlers use tape recordings, but anyone who can whistle or hoot can probably mimic an owl well enough to call one in by voice alone. There is a real thrill in carrying on a conversation with a wild bird.

There are seven species of owls that breed in part or all of New England and New York (leaving out migrants like snowy and boreal owls). Some, like the barn owl and long-eared owl, do not respond to call imitations, but fortunately for naturalists, the most common species—great horned, barred, screech- and saw-whet owls—do.

What species you'll find depends on location and habitat. Screech-owls, for instance, aren't found north of southern Maine, but in the rest of the region they are abundant in deciduous forests, including parks and wooded neighborhoods. Saw-whets, on the other hand, are wedded to conifers, preferring to stick to stands of spruce, hemlock or pine (they may also be found in mixed hardwood-conifer forests, especially near bogs).

Each species has a distinctive call—many of which sound nothing like the common perception of an owl hoot. The great horned owl, found in almost every corner of the region, has the most typically owlish call, a series of five to seven booming hoots: *Who-who-who, whooo-whooo.* Pairs (which mate for the long-term) will often call in tandem, even out of the breeding season, with the larger female having a paradoxically higher-pitched voice.

Few suburbanites realize the tremulous, descending whistle they hear in their backyard trees is an owl. The eastern screech-owl is very much at home around humans, snatching moths and katydids from around streetlights, even nesting in large birdboxes put up for their use. The screech-owl has two calls, the whinny and a long, monotone "throb" whistle. Either one can be easily imitated by a reasonably accomplished whistler.

Barred owls have perhaps the most otherwordly call of the regional species, a whooping phrase usually rendered *Who-cooks-for-you, who-cooks-for-you-aaaallll,* ending in something like a drawl. The barred owl's repertoire is infinitely varied, however, including an assortment of spooky barks, yips and yodels. On a dark night in a strange place, this does *not* sound like an owl.

Last, the saw-whet owl is the smallest and tamest of New England and New York's resident species, a little fluffball barely 8 inches long, with a round head, large yellow eyes and no ear tufts. It is rarely seen, since it perches in dense conifers, but its call—a series of flat, metallic whistles—carries for quite some distance. The bird's name comes from a fancied resemblance of the call to the sound of someone filing a saw—an analogy that means little to modern birders, most of whom have never whetted anything.

Finding a place to go owling is usually not hard, since almost any wooded habitat will have at least one species, and frequently several. There are no hotspots listed for this chapter, however, in part because owls are commonly distributed across the region rather than concentrated in a few spots, but largely because listing hotspots would place undue pressure on the owls found there—and as noted below, too much owling can be harmful to the birds.

Great horned owls, with their distinctively deep hoots, are easy to hear and easy to call on late-autumn nights.

There are a number of excellent recordings of bird calls on the market, from which you can tape owl calls for your own use. They include *A Field Guide to Bird Songs (Eastern and Central North America)*, which complements the *Peterson Field Guide to the Birds,* and *National Geographic Society's Guide to Bird Sounds,* likewise a companion to the society's field guide.

Studies have shown that the later at night it is, the better the owls respond—after midnight is good, and the final two or three hours before daybreak may be best of all. If possible choose a moonlit night so you can watch for the owl flying in, but the wind is more important; calm nights are far more productive, and a windy night will probably be a waste of time.

Try cruising a circuit of lonely back roads, stopping periodically to play the tape. Start with the calls of the smaller species first, because the larger birds like great horned and barred owls eat their smaller cousins, and the sound of their hoots may frighten a screech-owl or saw-whet into silence. (By the same token, don't be surprised if a big owl glides silently into your position when its hears what it thinks is supper calling.)

Play the call through several repetitions, then switch off the tape and listen. If you get a response, play just one or two calls at a time, allowing the owl a chance to approach you. Stay quiet and as motionless as possible, watching against the sky for the flying bird. Great horned owls tend to be skittish, but the smaller species may allow you to shine a flashlight on them briefly before they fly off.

NOTE: *There has been growing concern among naturalists over the potentially harmful effects of taped calls on owls, particularly the very real disruption it can cause during the courtship and breeding season and at any time when the same owls are harassed night after night by humans.*

Because many species of owls, particularly great horneds, begin to court as early as January, owling should be a strictly autumn and early winter activity, and has to be undertaken with a great deal of care and circumspection. In particular, avoid owling in places that you know attract many owl-watchers. Because great horned and screech-owls are fairly common, it should be relatively easy to locate them in areas unfrequented by other naturalists.

Always play taped calls at normal volume; an unnaturally loud call booming from a tape player may convince the owl that its territory has been invaded by the great-granddaddy of all owls, and that the best thing to do is leave. Remember, owls have exceptional hearing, so it's not necessary to crank up the volume.

Most of all, bear in mind that the owl isn't a sideshow, but a living creature whose life is being disrupted, however briefly, by your presence. While it sits and responds to your tape, it is not hunting or feeding or watching for predators—any of the things an owl usually does with its time. Stop calling after a few minutes, and allow the owl to get back to its life. This is especially true with smaller species like screech and saw-whet owls, which may be placed in jeopardy by excessive calling that can attract the dangerous attention of one of the larger owls.

65

November
Shorttakes

Thousands of Brant

In mid-November each year, huge flocks of brant, along with lesser numbers of snow geese and a fine mix of other waterfowl, descend on **Jamaica Bay WR** in New York; this is, in fact, one of the best places for brant north of the mid-Atlantic coast. For directions to Jamaica Bay, see Chapter 43.

66

Breakout: Vagabonds of the Sea

The migration of seabirds off the Northeast coast each autumn is part of a global shift that mixes bird populations from half the world—species constantly fleeing cold and darkness, and sometimes covering tens of thousands of miles in the process.

Consider the Wilson's storm-petrel, a delicate creature smaller than a martin. It breeds on the subantarctic islands of the south Atlantic and along the verge of the Antarctic mainland itself, where it numbers in the hundreds of millions and may be the most abundant wild bird in the world.

It arrives on its breeding grounds in December, just as spring is returning to the southern polar zone; as soon as the snow melts it locates a deep crevice or burrow and lays its eggs, which may fail to hatch because of late storms. By April the young storm-petrels have fledged, and as the weather begins to sour with the onset of the austral winter, the birds head north, crossing the Equator to arrive off the Northeast coast by early summer.

Storm-petrels spend the northern summer feeding—skipping and pattering along the waves with outstretched legs and high-held wings, a characteristic posture that led the oldtime sailors to dub them "Little Peters" for their apparent ability to walk on water. By autumn they have again begun the southward journey, returning to the breeding colonies after a round-trip of nearly 10,000 miles.

Nor are Wilson's storm-petrels the only transhemispheric migrants plying the sea winds in autumn. Leach's storm-petrels, which nest along the New England and Canadian coasts, are in their turn heading south to the waters off Brazil and the Gulf of Guinea, and sooty shearwaters and greater shearwaters are returning to their breeding grounds on islands scattered from the southern tip of South America far out into the south Atlantic.

No one is sure why these seabirds travel such incredible distances. Typically, migration is a result of poor food resources— a case of the grass being greener somewhere else. Some authorities suspect the long-distance migrations are an artifact of an earlier age, or may simply be an outgrowth of the normal, nomadic foraging techniques of most seabirds. Instead of hunting in a random pattern, the birds follow a genetically determined course that takes them farther than almost any other group of vertebrates.

Part of the reason they can travel so far is that seabirds have mastered the winds in a way unmatched by most other birds. Watch a shearwater skimming the waves on those long, thin wings, and you'll see an impressive demonstration of a flight strategy known as dynamic soaring.

The shearwater stays fairly low, near the waves, rising and falling as it flies, but almost never flapping its wings. The bird is taking advantage of the near-constant wind on the open sea, and the fact that interference from the waves slows the wind velocity the closer to the surface of the water the bird flies. Dropping down with the faster-moving upper air at its back, the shearwater accelerates, then bottoms out in the slower moving air near the water and relies on momentum to carry it up again. Rising, it banks into the breeze, catches the wind under its wings, and regains altitude. Thus, the bird is able to move effortlessly at right angles to the wind in a process that can be repeated endlessly.

Pelagic seabirds gather in such numbers off the Northeast coast because of the region's fecund waters, which abound with food. The smallest pelagics, the storm-petrels, feed on floating zooplankton plucked from the surface, while shearwaters, with their long, thin bills, are designed to capture fish at or just under the surface. Arctic terns, another pelagic migrant, plunge a few feet down to catch fish, while gannets powerdive from great heights, smashing deep underwater to attack schools.

There's still quite a bit unknown about the lives of pelagic birds while at sea; it isn't even clear exactly what species are found off North America's coasts. The occasional sightings of yellow-nosed and black-browed albatrosses may be the result of true vagrants, or a normal migration by some populations. Because it is difficult and expensive to travel out to the migration lanes, only a relative handful of experienced naturalists have done so, and for only a relatively short time.

As a consequence, almost every year brings a few electrifying sightings of birds that, according to conventional knowledge, have absolutely no business being where they are. It may well be, however, that the birds know their business better than we do.

DECEMBER

December Observations

67

Wintering Bald Eagles

Bald eagles never fail to attract attention. They are so big, so beautiful and so symbolic that seeing one makes any day special.

Fortunately, finding a bald eagle is easier in New England and New York than in many other parts of the country. Naturalists can see them in migration, even (at a few places) on their nests. But the best time to observe large numbers of bald eagles is the dead of winter.

Although eagles eat carrion, birds and smaller mammals, they are predominantly fish-eaters, and need open water in order to hunt. As winter grips the region that becomes an increasingly difficult need to fill, and many bald eagles migrate south, out of the area.

But for a large and growing segment of the Northeast's eagle population, the migration is relatively short; eagles move from their nesting territories to places where nature or man keep the waters open and food available. Here they are joined by bald eagles from farther away, migrating from northern Ontario, Quebec and the Maritime provinces.

Some of the largest concentrations of winter eagles are in southeast New York, along the upper Delaware River and the extensive system of nearby reservoirs. As many as 175 eagles pass the season here, and lucky naturalists can see the great birds gathered in trees like white-headed ornaments, or rowing up and down the river valley on their huge, chocolate-colored wings.

The eagles begin to arrive on the wintering grounds in November (most of the bald eagles that migrate through the region in early fall are southern birds, returning to their nesting sites in Florida after a summer spent wandering north). Research by endangered species biologists in New York has shown that the eagles tend to return to the same area winter after winter, displaying the same fidelity they show toward their breeding territories.

They stay through the winter, finally departing in March. So for almost five months, naturalists can enjoy a wonderful show— not just along the Delaware, but also in the St. Lawrence Valley of New York, parts of Connecticut and Massachusetts, even northern Maine. The criteria is open water, either churned free of ice by reservoir spillways, heated by power generation to just above freezing, or subject to tidal action.

It's also a good idea to check immature eagles closely. An adult bald eagle is unmistakable, but immature balds closely resemble golden eagles, a species that is occasionally seen at the wintering sites (Quabbin Reservoir in Massachusetts, for instance, has been attracting one or two goldens each winter for years). The trademark white head and tail take a juvenile bald eagle four or five years to acquire; instead, look for the relatively massive head and beak of a young bald, compared to the more buteolike features of a golden. Immature bald eagles frequently have white splotching on the belly and back, and large areas of white in the "wingpit," compared to the all-brown body of a golden. The white on a golden eagle's wings, if present, is confined to the base of the primary feathers. Both species can have white tails with black terminal bands.

NOTE: *Winter is a hard time for any animal, including eagles, and unnecessary disturbance should be strictly avoided, especially in areas where eagles may be perched near roads. Remember that most wild animals do not feel as threatened by people in vehicles as on foot, so stay in your car if the eagle is less than a couple hundred yards away.*

HOTSPOTS

The best eagle-watching in the Northeast can be found among the rivers and dams of southeastern New York, in the drainage of the **upper Delaware River**. Up to 175 eagles winter in this area, where the sight of the birds combines with the scenic mountains to produce a wonderful winter spectacle.

There is plenty of ground to cover here, and a birder can spend a weekend exploring back roads that thread their way among the hills and skirt the rivers and reservoirs. A good starting place, however, is the **Cannonsville Reservoir** and nearby stretches of the Delaware's west branch, about 25 miles east of Binghamton; this area is popular with both eagles and eagle enthusiasts. Take Route 17 to the town of Deposit, then go north about 2 miles on Route 8/10/48. Follow Route 10 North for 1.2 miles to a parking area just below the dam breast; this is a good place to watch for eagles, although the entire area from here back to Deposit is excellent, as the eagles hunt for alewives or harass ducks. Then continue north on Route 10 to Walton, a 24-mile trip that hugs the edge of the giant dam, then follows the bed of the river.

There are many areas along the road to pull off and scan, but the road can be narrow; be sure you are parked completely off the road. The eagles may be anywhere, perched or in flight—be sure to scan any suspicious lump in distant trees, but don't be surprised if you glance up and see one of the huge birds right overhead.

The main branch of the Delaware itself, from **Hale Eddy south to Port Jervis,** is also very productive for eagles, especially the 25 miles of river from **Minisink Ford to Port Jervis.** This stretch is paralleled by Route 97, a beautiful drive but a busy road, so choose your pull-offs with care. It is not unusual to see two dozen or more eagles in this area.

Just north of here is the **Mongaup River,** which has been described as some of the best winter eagle habitat in the United States—so good, in fact, that the state of New York recently purchased more than 13,000 acres in the area specifically to safeguard wintering eagles.

Three reservoirs—**Rio, Mongaup Falls** and **Swinging Bridge**—are strung out on the river from the Delaware north to Route 17B between Smallwood and Monticello. A DeLorme New York atlas will help sort out the maze of small roads in this area, but generally speaking, head north from Route 97 at Pond Eddy on Route 41 to Glen Spey, then drive along Route 42 for about 3.5 miles to Route 43 toward Forestburg; this road crosses the upper end of Mongaup Falls Reservoir. On the east side of Mongaup Falls at Fowlerville, you can head north to Swinging Bridge on Old Plank/Section B Road, or south along Rio Reservoir on Old Plank/Section A Road. Swinging Bridge is especially popular with local eagle-watchers because the state often attracts the big birds with bait for banding operations.

Other reservoirs in the area worth checking for eagles include **Pepacton** in Delaware County and **Rondout** on the Sullivan/Ulster county border. Both are very accessible for car viewing, although eagle numbers and locations vary with ice conditions.

Also in New York, lesser numbers of eagles winter along the state's portion of **St. Lawrence River,** the **lower Hudson River** near Peekskill, and **Great Sacandaga Lake** west of Glens Falls. Visitors who find themselves passing through these areas should keep a careful watch for eagles, although big concentrations are unlikely.

In Connecticut, eagle-watching has become a popular pastime on **Shepaug Dam** near Southbury, where a joint project between Northeast Utilities and the state chapter of the Nature Conservancy provides a chance to observe the birds from a blind. The hut is open three days a week from late December through the end of March, and reservations are required. For more information, contact the Connecticut chapter of the Nature Conservancy at the number listed in the Appendix. The eagles gather at the hydroelectric dam because the power generation keeps part of the Houstatonic River free of ice, and while the numbers fluctuate, as many as twenty-eight have been seen. The **lower Connecticut River** from Haddam to the ocean is also prime eagle wintering habitat.

Quabbin Reservoir in central Massachusetts has long been a mecca for those who want to see eagles, including rare but regular golden eagles. Quabbin has been the focus of an eagle-hacking project, so it is no surprise that the birds also winter on the giant lake, joined by migrants from farther north. To reach Quabbin take I-90 to Springfield, then take Route 21 North 11 miles to Route 202 North. Just past Belchertown take Route 9 East 2.3 miles to the Windsor Dam entrance to the park; check at the visitors' center for recent eagle sightings. The Enfield Lookout, about halfway around the park loop road, is normally the best place in Quabbin Park to spot eagles.

Bald eagles also show up regularly in winter along the **Merrimack River** between Newburyport Harbor and Haverhill, and on the Connecticut River from Springfield south to the Connecticut line.

In Maine, bald eagles regularly winter south of Bath, Maine, on the Nature Conservancy's **Bald Head Preserve,** where open water and high, pine-topped cliffs offer food and security for the birds. The conservancy prefers that visitors watch from the road to avoid disturbing the eagles; from Bath take Route 127 South to the bridge between Arrowsic and Georgetown islands and look to the south for eagles hunting over the marsh.

Also in Maine, the area around **Eastport**, at the state's easternmost point, may draw more than twenty-five bald eagles in winter, part of a large wintering concentration in scenic Cobscook Bay. There are many side roads and ocean vistas to explore, and a USGS topographical map or DeLorme atlas will help immensely.

68

Tracking

For much of the year, a naturalist needs a sharp eye to see the signs of an animal's passage—the scuffed leaves on the forest floor where a deer ran, scattered droppings, the nipped twigs where a hare fed. But when winter comes and the snow falls, the outdoor world becomes a clean page, recording in precise detail the dramas enacted on its surface.

At its most basic, tracking is simply finding and identifying tracks. This in itself can be a challenge, especially if you are a beginner trying to discriminate between the similar tracks of gray and red foxes, for example. But the track itself is only the beginning—a skilled tracker is a sleuth, reading not only the print in the snow but its context with the surroundings, the other tracks in the trail, his or her knowledge of the animal's habits, even the nearby trails of other species. Taken together, an experienced naturalist can guess a great deal about what the animal was doing, even what it was thinking, all from the tracks.

Actually, old-timers spoke most often about reading "sign," the catchall phrase for not just tracks, but any physical indication of a creature's passing, including droppings, feeding remains, beds, dens, scratchings and the like. Learning to see them is only the first step (and not always easy, since some of the most revealing signs are also the most subtle). Next comes a sense of imagination, putting yourself in the animal's place to figure out why it was doing what it was doing.

Following an animal trail through the snowy woods, puzzling out its motives and movements, is a natural detective story.

Little things mean a lot when you're trying to unravel an animal's trail. Does the fox trail show a long line of evenly spaced tracks arrowing through the woods for hundreds of yards? Could be the fox was heading back to a safe haven before daylight. Or does the trail go in fits and starts, long loping strides shortening to tentative steps, eventually marred by drag marks from the tail and the sweep of fur? Most likely the fox was stalking something, sinking low to the ground as it moved more and more slowly. Look ahead for the marks of a sudden rush—and the tracks of a grouse, perhaps, budding in an aspen blowdown, unaware of danger creeping closer.

The best tracking snow is soft and wet, not too fluffy and not too deep (otherwise you get a collapsed hole with no detail). If you have a choice, wait a night or two after the snowfall before heading for the woods, to give the creatures time to move around. By carefully examining the track, you should be able to tell if it was made recently or is a day or two old, with blurred edges or a drift of blowing snow inside the print.

Should you lose the trail on open ground or crusted snow, mark the last track with a hat and circle, in the hope of striking the trail once more. Here, too, intelligent guesses about the animal's habits and intentions pay off. And remember, a good tracker never steps on the trail being followed—you may need to backtrack to reexamine a section.

Novice trackers would do well to read two excellent books on the subject: Olaus J. Murie's classic A *Field Guide to Animal Tracks,* part of the Peterson field guide series from Houghton Mifflin, and *Tracking and the Art of Seeing* by Paul Rezendes. Both books cover the spectrum of sign, from tracks to scat to dens.

HOTSPOTS

The beauty of tracking is that a naturalist can find a challenge in even the most mundane surroundings; figuring out the amblings of a raccoon in a suburban park, or even a tunneling shrew in the backyard, can be as fascinating as tracking a bobcat in the mountains.

Still, there is a thrill in covering new ground, or tracking animals you rarely see. The national wildlife refuges listed elsewhere in this book are terrific starting points, and many have particular attractions. The huge impoundments, streams and marshes of **Montezuma** and **Iroquois NWRs** in New York, though frozen most of the winter, still attract foxes, raccoons and mink, and the runs, latrines and feeding stations of muskrats can be found near open water. For directions to Montezuma and Iroquois, see Chapter 19.

Wetlands and upland mammals are also common at **Great Meadows NWR** in eastern Massachusetts, both at the Concord and Sudbury units; directions can be found in Chapter 38. At **Moosehorn NWR** in Down East Maine, a tracking snow may reveal the signs of snowshoe hares, porcupines, mink and otters (although, ironically, few moose). See Chapter 22 for directions.

For a real wilderness tracking adventure, consider **Baxter State Park** in northcentral Maine. Moose are more common here than virtually anywhere else in New England, and the variety of other mammals—deer, otter, coyote, red fox, fisher, pine marten, bobcat, lynx, porcupine and snowshoe hare among them—makes this an exciting place to visit. It is also remote and challenging in winter, requiring cold-weather experience and the proper equipment. See Chapter 49 for general directions to Baxter; for information on winter visits, including regulations (which differ from many state parks) and cabin or bunkhouse reservations, write to the Baxter State Park administration office at the address in the Appendix.

69

The Raptors
of Winter

Far from being a slow season, winter is an exciting time for the naturalist—in part because this is one of the best times of the year for observing a variety of birds of prey, including hawks, owls and shrikes. To find them, simply look for open land that mimics the Arctic tundra from which many of them come.

The bread-and-butter hawks of winter are two buteos, the familiar red-tailed hawk and the Arctic rough-legged hawk. Both are largish birds, the redtail the more solidly built of the two. Perched at a distance, a redtail may be mistaken for a snowy owl or a pale gyrfalcon, since the white chest and undersides fairly glow in the sun; through binoculars or a scope, you should see a speckled belly band and the brown upperparts. Adults have tails that are brick-orange above but pale pink below, while immatures' tails are brown with fine barring.

Roughlegs come in several color variants, from light-phase birds with creamy chests, thick black belly bands and a black-tipped tail, to coal-black dark-phase roughlegs, against whose ebony plumage the bright yellow cere (the flesh around the beak) and feet stand out. Light birds usually have dark "wrist" markings, which redtails lack, and any roughleg will soar with a more pronounced and angular dihedral than a redtail.

Both redtails and roughlegs are open-country hunters, both feed primarily on mammals, and both would, at first glance, seem to be in competition with each other. But nature abhors direct competition between species as much as it abhors a vacuum, and so the hawks come at the problem of food from slightly different angles. Where the redtail is a generalist, adept at taking food as small as mice or as large as muskrats, along with birds like gulls or ducks that may be sick or slow, the roughleg is a mouse specialist. Its feet are roughly half the size of a redtail's, even though it has about the same body size—dainty little feet, feathered to the toes, that are perfect for snatching voles, shrews and mice. Roughlegs seem to take the more exposed hunting perches, and sit nearer the top of a tree; they also hover on flapping wings, something the redtail almost never does. A large hawk frantically hover-flapping in the distance is almost certainly a roughleg.

The winter fields and marshes are shared with several other raptors. In many areas kestrels, the delicate little falcons, linger through the winter, hunting mice from roadside utility wires. Northern harriers (once known as marsh hawks) likewise hunt mice and small birds with a characteristic approach, zig-zagging low across the fields, then pivoting suddenly and dropping when their eyes or sensitive ears detect prey. Harriers, with their oddly pronounced facial disks, resemble owls in some ways—and often as they retire for the evening, short-eared owls, their nocturnal analogs, take over.

The most sought-after of the winter hawks is the gyrfalcon, the largest and most powerful falcon in the world, and an Arctic hunter that only rarely strays south to the region; the discovery of one makes the rare-bird hotlines sizzle. Gyrs come in three basic color phases: almost pure white, pale gray and sooty brown-black. In New England and New York, gray gyrfalcons are the most frequently seen, although white and dark birds sometimes appear as well.

Gyrfalcons are capricious and liable to show up anywhere, but they are most often seen along the coast, or in the Champlain Valley. Immatures in particular can be exceptionally trusting, a trait of many northern species, perching on telephone poles or rooftops in shoreside communities.

Perhaps the oddest of the winter hunters isn't a hawk at all. It is a songbird—but one with decidedly predatory manners.

Northern shrikes look superficially like mockingbirds, with the same gray body and white flash-marks on the wings. But up close the similarities fade; a shrike is heavily built, with a chunky head, black mask and a strong, hook-tipped beak. Unlike virtually any other songbird, shrikes make their living hunting vertebrates, particularly mice and small birds, along with large insects in summer.

Because they lack the specialized feet and talons of a hawk or owl, shrikes rely on their heavy bills to do the killing, stunning their prey with strong blows, although northern shrikes may grab flying birds in their feet and force them to the ground for a coup de grace. Once the prey is dead, the shrike will usually impale it on a thorn or broken twig, or jam it in the tight fork of a branch, thus holding it more firmly than it could do with its feet while it eats. Or the prey may be left where it hangs as a sort of open-air cache, to be returned for hours, days or weeks later. Shrikes have been shown to have remarkable memories, with one loggerhead shrike (a related southern species) coming back for a frog it had stashed eight months previous. Unfortunately, there was nothing left but a mummy.

Northern shrikes breed in a thin band across the Arctic and, like many irruptive species, come south only when their winter prey base, small rodents, suffers a cyclic crash. Watch for shrikes perched on utility lines or high in trees, showing a distinctive tail-pumping movement similar to a kestrel's. Immatures, which are browner and more heavily barred on the breast than adults, are most common south of Canada.

HOTSPOTS

Wintering hawks, particularly roughlegs, may appear wherever there is open country and an abundance of food. Regular concentrations, however, can be found at a number of coastal and inland sites.

One of the best areas in New England and New York for winter raptors, as well as snowy owls and northern shrikes, is the **Champlain Valley** of Vermont and New York. This is wide, flat terrain of open fields crisscrossed by fencerows, brushlines and small woodlots—perfect for rough-legged hawks, which sometimes gather here in remarkable numbers. Particularly productive is **Dead Creek WMA** near Addison, Vermont, and the surrounding countryside, while on the narrower New York side of the lake, the area around **Willsboro** has long been known as a hotspot for winter hawks. See Chapter 1 for directions to both regions.

At the northern end of Lake Champlain, **Grand Isle** and **North Hero** island can be good for wintering raptors. From Winooski, Vermont, take I-89 North to Exit 17 (Lake Champlain Islands/Milton), then follow Route 2 West 7 miles to Grand Isle. From here, follow Route 2 as it winds north to North Hero and back to the mainland at Route 78, a distance of 24 miles. Be sure to check side roads along the way. At the juncture with 78, you can turn east on 78 back to I-89, or continue west on 2 to I-87 in New York.

Also good in winter is New York's **Finger Lakes region,** particularly the farmland between lakes Cayuga and Seneca. Here, too, on the uplands between the lakes, hawks find the wide horizons they like—and visiting naturalists find a gridlike network of small roads that makes it easy to wander without getting lost. For starters, try the area around the villages of Ovid and Lodi, reached from Ithaca by taking Route 96 North 26 miles to Ovid, then Route 96A/414 South for 5 miles to Lodi; from here work your way south and east back toward Route 96 on the network of squared-off country roads (a topographical map or DeLorme atlas will help). In addition to hawks, this area can be good for snowy owls during one of that unpredictable species' flight years, and for short-eared owls toward dusk.

Along the coast, good places to find roughlegs and other winter raptors include **Salisbury Beach** (Chapter 3) and **Plum Island** (Chapter 2) in northern Massachusetts, the latter including **Parker River NWR** and **Plum Island SR**.

Short though it may be, the coast of Rhode Island is another good area to explore, particularly **Sachuest Point NWR** (Chapter 10) east of Newport, and the region from Galilee east to Charlestown near **Trustom Pond NWR.** From Route 1 North take the Matunuck Beach Road exit (this exit can be reached only from 1 North; those going south will have to make a U-turn and come back to the exit). Go 1.7 miles to check the beach area, then backtrack .3 mile and turn left onto Card's Pond Road, drive 1.2 miles to a T-intersection and turn right onto Moonstone Beach Road.

Drive half a mile and turn left onto Matunuck Schoolhouse Road, then go .6 mile to Trustom Pond NWR, where there are several trails ranging over much of the refuge's 640 acres and two observation towers overlooking the Trustom Pond, the only coastal pond in the state to escape development. Leaving the refuge, turn left on Matunuck Schoolhouse Road and drive for several miles to Narrow Lane, a right, which returns you to Route 1.

Long Island's tidal marshes and dunes draw harriers, roughlegs and other midwinter raptors; see the list of suggestions in Chapter 1 for snowy owls, which use many of the same areas.

70

Christmas Bird Counts

In December 1900, Massachusetts ornithologist Frank M. Chapman—digusted by the tradition of a Christmas Day hunt in which anything was fair game, and the biggest bag won—started a quiet protest. Instead of going hunting, he would spend the day counting all the birds he could. Chapman enlisted others in about two dozen locations scattered across New England and elsewhere to do the same—and so the Christmas Bird Count (CBC) was born.

In the near-century since then, under the direction of the National Audubon Society, Chapman's idea has grown beyond anything he could have imagined. During the 1991–92 holiday season, there were 1,646 counts, including thirty-seven in the tropics and ten on far-flung Pacific islands, in which more than forty-three thousand people counted birds of 628 species. In New England alone, CBCs produced more than 1.8 million individual birds.

Each year, National Audubon's research journal *American Birds* publishes a compendium of all the counts, a volume that takes on the dimensions of a telephone directory. The counts are a snapshot of winter birdlife from around the continent and beyond, a valuable resource for scientists and a source of endless enjoyment for participants.

In New England and New York, the 1991–92 counts ranged from a high of 135 species on the Brooklyn, New York CBC (including such rarities as a Pacific loon, western kingbird and yellow-breasted chat), to the count in aptly named Misery Township, Maine, which recorded just twenty-seven hardy species including gray jays, boreal chickadees and a bald eagle.

In all, there are 145 counts in New England and New York, with new areas being added almost every year, making it one of the most thoroughly covered regions in North America. New York, with sixty-six, has the most, and (not surprisingly) tiny Rhode Island has the fewest, three. Generally speaking, CBCs are most often found near large population centers or traditional birding hotspots, but many others are scattered across the map, wherever a few people decide to take some time over the holiday season to head outdoors.

Each CBC covers a circle 15 miles wide. Sometime during the last two weeks of December and the first week of January, almost always on a weekend, teams of birders fan out across the count circle for a twenty-four-hour period and tally not just species but individual birds. Some years the counts run as high as 190 million birds for the North American counts alone.

All of the counting is done by volunteers, either in the field or watching home feeding stations. The work often begins hours before dawn, with counters armed with tape recorders listening for owls. Come daybreak, the volunteers are usually assigned a small, manageable chunk of the count circle that will be their responsibility for the day. Parties may strike out on snowshoes or skis if the snow is deep, and some imaginative CBCers have even hitched rides with Coast Guard patrols to count wintering seabirds.

The count ends with the traditional compilation dinner, a chance to add up the totals and share the triumphs and disappointments of the day. There is usually excitement (and at times, stunned disbelief) over unexpected rarities, and frustration over missing birds that normally show up every year. The total, however, is just a benchmark for the day, and not its reason; the important thing is the comradeship and fun, the chance to hone birding skills and take part in a little friendly competition.

HOTSPOTS

There are few count leaders who wouldn't be delighted to have new, enthusiastic help on their CBC. First, check the state-by-state listing of counts in the Appendix to see which is closest to you, or contact the local birding club or nature center for the name of the count compiler. Or you can write to the Christmas Bird Count editor, *American Birds,* National Audubon Society, 700 Broadway, New York, NY 10003, and ask for a list of counts and compilers in your state. If there are no CBCs in your area (and if you enjoy organizing), ask National Audubon for help in starting one.

There is a participation fee (five dollars at this writing) to cover the cost of printing the annual CBC issue. Be prepared for an entire day outdoors, regardless of weather, since CBCers never let minor inconveniences like snowstorms or sub-zero cold stop them. Be honest about your birding abilities—beginners are often teamed with experienced counters, which is a good way to learn. And if you aren't up to fighting the elements but live within the count circle, consider signing up as a feeder watcher, which allows you to take part from indoors.

There are nearly 150 Christmas Bird Counts conducted each year in the Northeast, in which participants tally not just species, but individuals like this flock of Canada geese.

71

December
Shorttakes

Diving Ducks

From December through January, large rafts of diving ducks can be found sheltering in quiet coves and bays of **Cayuga Lake** north of Ithaca, New York; species include redheads, scaup and ring-necked ducks. See Chapter 9 for details and directions. This month can be good for waterfowl at a number of locations, depending on ice conditions; see Chapters 9 and 62 for suggestions.

See also:

Chapter 1, Snowy Owls. By early December, snowy owls may be appearing at traditionally productive sites like the Champlain Valley, although the number of owls varies greatly from year to year.

Chapter 2, Rare and Unusual Gulls. December is usually the peak for enormous flocks of Bonaparte's gulls at the mouth of the Niagara River.

Chapter 3, Red-throated Loons. Common and red-throated loons can be found this month, sometimes in very large numbers, at many wintering areas.

Chapter 63, Pelagic Birds From Shore. Watching migrant and wintering pelagic birds from shore continues to be productive this month, especially on strong east or northeast winds.

72

Breakout:
Winter in the Mountains

Winter is merciless in the mountains of the Northeast. It comes early, settling into the highest peaks by late October and spreading a veil of white farther down the slopes with each passing day.

By December the beaver dams are locked tight with ice, the streams thin ribbons of dark water between banks of white. The birds have fled, save for the hardiest species like the gray jays and the ravens; the moose and deer have retreated to the thickets, and the coyotes and foxes are already searching out the season's victims, those killed off by too much cold and too little to eat.

Food is where you find it in winter, and the spruce grouse finds it in the branches of the conifers it lives among. From first snow to final thaw, the grouse feeds almost exclusively on the buds and needles of spruce and other softwoods—a waxy, high-cellulose, nutrient-poor diet that requires much digestion, so much so that the grouse's intestinal tract enlarges considerably each winter to squeeze the last bit of nourishment from the food. The bird moves from tree to tree on feet that have sprouted snowshoes, elongated toe scales that grow in a fringe, spreading the grouse's weight and allowing it to walk rather than flounder.

For most of the region's winter residents, the season's biggest danger is not cold, but starvation. A moose may actually become too warm, even on a subzero day, if it is forced into prolonged movement, so thoroughly insulated from the cold is it.

Fresh snow envelopes Mt. Abraham in Vermont's Green Mountains—a brutally harsh environment in the winter for any animal.

The undercoat is thick and woolly, trapping a layer of air, a theme repeated by the layer of hollow guard hairs, each of which acts like a thermos bottle to seal in body warmth.

But if there is not enough fuel for the internal fires, then all the insulation in the world is worthless. If heavy snows continue through most of the winter, deer are unable to move freely, and the traditional "yards," where they gather become overbrowsed. The youngest and weakest go first, but none escape the debilitating effects.

What is perhaps most remarkable, then, about the mountain winter, is the fact that so many wild animals actually breed at this time of year. For some, it is a time of courtship; for others, incredibly, the moment of birth.

Rolling across the hollows and valleys, the insistent hoots of great horned owls are a fixture of winter nights, as the pairs reinforce old bonds and mark their territories with sound. By February the owls will have usurped an old hawk or crow nest and laid their clutch of eggs; by March the chicks have hatched, usually into weather conditions that would kill them in moments if they were exposed to it. But the adults carefully shield them from the elements for weeks, feeding them as they grow through the dregs of winter.

The night woods ring with the songs of procreation in winter, especially after the season pivots on the solstice and begins its long climb back toward summer. On still, moonlit nights, coyotes howl and yip with abandon—usually not the clichéd, Hollywoodesque *ow-ow-oooooo!*, but a much stranger wail, much weirder, much wilder. Many people do not even realize they are listening to a coyote—or to a red fox, when it yowls for a mate on a frigid February night.

Wild canines mate in late winter, then bear their young about two months later. Other mammals take a different approach, relegating the business of mating to fall, when they are in better physical condition for the trials of pursuit and courtship battles. These include the mustelids, or weasels, including long-tailed weasels, martens and river otters. The fisher, one of the largest weasels, mates within days of her litter's birth, but the new embryos, rather than growing, stop developing almost immediately. They remain in a state of suspension as minute clusters of cells for the next ten months, only finally implanting on the uterus wall about 30 days before birth, which usually comes in March or April.

Known as delayed implantation, this reproductive technique is rather common among northern mammals, and it offers a number of advantages. As noted, courtship can occur during the easy time of the year, when movement isn't hampered by snow and cold; this way, too, a female gets a jump on the spring, bearing her young early so they are growing up in a season when the world is awash in young—and unwary—prey animals. This is especially important with predators, like mustelids, whose young have a long development period. Baby fishers do not even open their eyes until they are nearly 7 weeks old, and are not fully weaned until they reach four months of age.

One northern animal takes delayed implantation to perhaps its greatest extreme. The black bear mates in midsummer, not long after the female has booted her previous litter of cubs (now a year and a half old) out on their own. Here again the embryos stop developing after a few cell divisions and become quiescent. But unlike weasels, which remain active all winter, female bears den up in early winter—perhaps choosing a rock den, a hollow tree or a blowdown. Bears are not true hibernators like bats or woodchucks, but their metabolic rate does slow by about half, and they become sleepy and lethargic.

In early winter, the embryos attach themselves to the uterine wall and begin to develop. About 6 or 8 weeks later—

usually sometime in late January or February, depending on latitude—the somnolent female gives birth, scarcely aware of the act. The newborn cubs, covered with a thin sheen of black fur and looking like tailless rats, weigh less than 12 ounces and are, in proportion to the size of their mother, among the smallest mammalian babies. They find their way to the female's nipples despite being blind, deaf and unable to smell. Research has shown that they react only to warmth—and the nipples are the warmest part of the mother's body.

Through the remainder of the winter, the cubs nurse on high-fat milk and grow with only the periodic, drowsy attentions of their mother. When she finally rouses and the family emerges from the den two months later, the cubs weigh about 5 pounds— bright-eyed, active furballs that bear almost no resemblance to the tiny infants just 8 weeks before, with a head start on the season of growth that lies ahead of them.

APPENDIX

Northern Lights

The Northeast's greatest natural spectacle is also its most unpredictable—and that adds to the sweetness of the moment when the night lights up with the aurora borealis, leaving a human observer at once humbled and elevated by the shimmering sky.

The aurora is the visible result of the collision of invisible forces. The sun's thermonuclear maelstrom flings an endless stream of highly charged atomic particles into space, billowing out in what is known as the "solar wind." It takes anywhere from one to three days for the particles to reach Earth, where they collide with the planet's magnetic field, which loops up and out from the poles in a magnetosphere encasing the globe.

The solar wind stretches the magnetic field on the "downwind" side away from the sun, pulling it into the far reaches of the solar system. Like a cosmic rubber band, the field may snap, crashing back toward Earth and slamming the charged particles into the atmosphere, where many funnel into the field openings near the poles. In the violence of this collision, the particles emit electromagnetic waves of their own, which resonate with the planet's magnetic lines. As the electrons hit gas molecules in the upper atmosphere, they transfer their energy to them, and the gases in turn release the energy as light, much as happens in a neon tube.

The cause may be physics, but the result is pure magic. In the upper atmosphere 100 or more miles up, oxygen atoms glow reddish, while 60 miles from the surface, they shimmer with the characteristic greenish-white of the classic aurora; nitrogen atoms provide blues, purples and pinks, depending on their charge. The aurora may glow faintly across the horizon like a false daybreak (hence the name aurora, which Galileo took from the Roman goddess of dawn), or it may sear across the zenith in fast-moving curtains.

The aurora can be one of the most awe-inspiring sights in nature, if only because of the scale; photographs from satellites and the space shuttle show the bands of color standing up through the almost invisible upper atmosphere like celestial fences, reaching out into the blackness. Some bands may stretch for thousands of miles, and be hundreds thick. For all their size, the auroral bands can move with breathtaking speed. During an especially active display, the curtains may flow and ripple across the northern sky, while pulses shoot unpredictably through them, then fade for a time only to come flaming back to brilliance in a matter of seconds. It is almost frightening to think of the vast size of the sheets—and no wonder that, for the natives of many northern lands, the aurora was a thing of great mystery and portent.

While the aurora is an almost nightly feature in the Arctic skies above 60 degrees of latitude, in New England and New York its appearance is tied closely to the roughly eleven-year cycle of sun spots and solar flares. When a flare erupts on the surface of the sun, firing incredible quanities of particles and radiation into space, the streams hit the Earth's magnetic field and excite the aurora in spectacular ways, producing dramatic displays that can be seen far south of its usual area. The peaks in the cycle are known as solar maximums, and the year or so prior to one is generally the most active for flares, and thus for auroral displays. The peak that occurred in 1989, for example, was preceded by intense solar storms and auroras that could be seen as far south as Central America.

Still, flares may happen in the otherwise placid intervals between solar maximums, and naturalists in the Northeast should get in the habit of checking the northern sky for suspicious glows. News reports usually mention major flares because of their effects on communication; watch for the northern lights one to three nights later. Auroras may also be caused by solar coronal holes, a phenomenon that builds to a peak several years following a maximum. Even better for aurora-watchers, nothern lights caused by a long-lasting coronal hole may reappear twenty-seven days later when the sun has completed one full rotation, bringing the disturbance around toward Earth again.

You can call the Space Environment Services Center in Boulder, Colorado, at (303) 497-3235, for a taped message that includes word of solar flares and the current "Boulder K Index," a reading on disturbance of the Earth's magnetic field. If the reading is four or higher, watch for an aurora.

Auroras that are visible south of Canada are most likely in the weeks before and after the spring and autumn equinoxes, when the Earth's shifting axis is aimed toward the sun, snagging the greatest quantities of charged particles. Moonless nights (or nights after the moon has set) are best, and midnight seems to be the optimal hour.

RARE BIRD HOTLINES, STATE FALL FOLIAGE UPDATES
AND MAPLE SUGARING INFORMATION

RARE BIRD HOTLINES

Connecticut
(203) 254–3665

Maine
(207) 781–2332
(evenings and weekends)

Massachusetts (Boston area)
(617) 259–8805

New Hampshire
(603) 224–9900
(evenings and weekends)

New York
(212) 832–6523
(New York City and Long Island)
(716) 896–1271 (Buffalo area)
(716) 461–9593 (Rochester area)

Vermont
(802) 457–2779
(evenings and weekends)

FALL FOLIAGE UPDATES

Massachusetts
(800) 343–9072 (out of state)
(800) 632–8038 (in state)

New Hampshire
(800) 258–3608 (out of state)
(603) 224–3608 or
(603) 224-3609 (in state)

New York
(800) CALL NYS
(weekly foliage and events update)

Vermont
(802) 828–3239

MAPLE SUGARING INFORMATION

Massachusetts Department of Food
  and Agriculture
100 Cambridge St.
Boston, MA 02202
(Ask for the brochure on maple
sugaring in the Pioneer Valley.)

Maine Department of Agriculture
(207) 289–3491
(Ask for information on Maine
Maple Sunday each March, when
sugarhouses statewide open their
doors to the public.)

Maine Publicity Bureau
97 Winthrop St.
Hallowell, ME 04347
(207) 289–2423

New Hampshire Maple Producers
  Association
28 Peabody Row
Londonderry, NH 03053
(603) 432–8427
(Ask for the listing of sugarhouses
open to the public.)

New York State Department of
   Agriculture and Markets
1 Winners Circle
Albany, NY 12235
(800) 554–4501
(518) 457–3880
(in local calling area)

Vermont Department of Agriculture, Food and Markets
116 State St.
Montpelier, VT 95620–2901
(802) 828–2416
(Ask for the listing of sugarhouses
open to the public.)

WHALE-WATCH AND PELAGIC BIRDING TRIP OPERATORS

CONNECTICUT
Captain John's Sport Fishing
    Center, Inc.
15 First St.
Waterford, CT 06385
(203) 443–7259
(Day-long whale-watching tours off Montauk Point.)

MAINE
(* denotes puffin-watch operators who share proceeds with the National Audubon Society to support Project Puffin.)

Acadian Whale Watcher
Capt. Greg Curry
Bar Harbor, ME 04609
(207) 288–9794
(Twice-daily whale-watch cruises.)

Bluenose Ferry
Marine Atlantic
P.O. Box 250
North Sydney, Nova Scotia
Canada B2A 3M3
Toll-free in the United States:
(800) 341 7981
Toll-free in Maine: (800) 432–7344
(Six-hour trip—each way—connects Bar Harbor, Maine, with Yarmouth, Nova Scotia. Good variety of pelagic birds including storm-petrels, shearwaters and gannets, as well as possibility of marine mammals. Same-day round trips are available.)

Capt. Richard Brindle
Indian
P.O. Box 2672
Kennebunkport, ME 04046
(207) 967–5912 or 985–7857
(Whale-watch cruises.)

Albert Bunker
Dorothy Diane
Mantinicus Island, ME 04851
(207) 366–3737
(Puffin cruises.)

Bold Coast Charter Co.
Barbara Frost
Cutler, ME 04626
(207) 259–4484
(Puffin cruises.)

*Cap'n Fish Tours
Boothbay Harbor, ME 04538
(207) 633–3244
(Puffin cruises.)

Frenchman Bay Co.
Friendship III Whale Watch
P.O. Box 153
Bar Harbor, ME 04609
(207) 288–3322
(Four-hour whale-watch cruises.)

*Hardy III Tours
New Harbor, ME 04554
(207) 677–2026
(Puffin cruises.)

Butch Huntley
Seafarer
Lubec, ME 04652
(207) 733–5584
(Puffin cruises.)

Capt. Dan Libby
Odyssey
634 Cape Rd.
Standish, ME 04084
(Whale-watch cruises.)

Lively Lady Enterprises
Capn's Lady
Vinalhaven Island, ME 04863
(207) 863–4461
(Puffin cruises.)

Maine Audubon Society
(207) 781–2330
(Periodic puffin cruises.)

*Maine Whalewatch
Rockland, ME 04841
(207) 276–5803
(Full-day whale-watches, puffin and seabird cruises from Northeast Harbor and Rockland. Led by College of the Atlantic naturalists.)

Capts. Barna and John Norton
Jonesport, ME 04649
(207) 497–5933
(Day trips to Machias Seal Island to observe puffins, arctic terns, murres, razorbills.)

Offshore Passenger & Freight
Mary Donna
Rockland, ME 04841
(207) 366–3700
(Puffin cruises.)

Capt. Rick Savage
Poor Richard
P.O. Box 321
Northeast Harbor, ME 04662
(207) 276–3785 (days), (207) 244–7057 (evenings and weekends).
(Whale, bird and seal cruises.)

Capt. Wayne Showalter
Elizabeth II, Nautilus
P.O. Box 2777
Kennebunkport, ME 04046
(207) 967–5595 or (207) 967-0707
(Five- to six-hour whale-watch cruises).

MASSACHUSETTS
Trips leaving from Boston area piers:
A.C. Cruise Line
(617) 426–8419 or (800) 422–8419
(Whale-watch cruises.)

Bay State Cruise Co.
Long Wharf and Commonwealth Pier, Boston
(617) 723–7800
(Whale-watch cruises.)

Boston Harbor Cruises
Long Wharf, Boston
(617) 227–4321
(Whale-watch cruises.)

Boston Harbor Whale Watch
Rowes Wharf, Boston
(617) 345–9866
(Whale-watch cruises with on-board naturalist.)

New England Aquarium
Central Wharf, Boston
(617) 973–5277 (recorded information) or (617) 973–5281 (reservations).
(Whale-watch cruises.)

Other Massachusetts cruises:
Cape Ann Whale Watch
P.O. Box 345
Gloucester, MA 01930
(508) 283–5110 or (800) 877–5110
(Research-oriented whale-watch.)

Cape Cod Cruises
(508) 747–2400 (Trips from Plymouth)
(800) 225–4000 (Trips from Provincetown)
(Whale-watch cruises with onboard naturalist.)

Captain Bill's Whale Watching
415 Main St.
Gloucester, MA 01930
(508) 283–6995 or (800) 33–WHALE
(eastern Massachusetts only)
(Whale-watch with on-board naturalist.)

New England Whale Watch
54 Merrimack St.
Newburyport, MA 01950
(508) 465–7165 or (800) 848–1111
(New England only)
(Whale-watch cruises.)

Seven Seas Whale Watching
Seven Seas Wharf
Gloucester, MA 01930
(508) 283–1776 or (800) 238–1776
(Whale-watch cruises.)

Yankee Whale Watch
75 Essex Ave.
Gloucester, MA 01930
(508) 283–0313 or (800) WHAL-ING
(Whale-watch cruises with research scientists.)

NEW HAMPSHIRE
Isle of Shoals Steamship Co.
P.O. Box 311
315 Market St.
Portsmouth, NH 03801
(603) 431–5500
(Whale and seabird cruise to Jeffrey's Ledge.)

N.H. Seacoast Cruises
M/V Granite State
P.O. Box 232
Rye, NH 03870
(603) 964–5545 or (603) 382–6743
(Six-hour whale-watch to Isle of Shoals area.)

NEW YORK
Okeanos Ocean Research
   Foundation
216 E. Montauk Hwy.
P.O. Box 776
Hampton Bays, NY 11946
(516) 728–4522
(Four-and-a-half-hour whale-watch and seabird trips leaving Viking Dock, Montauk.)

RHODE ISLAND
Lady Francis and M/V Gail Frances
Galilee, Narragansett
(401) 783–4988
(Charter for whale-watch trips.)

ADDRESSES FOR PLACES AND ORGANIZATIONS LISTED IN TEXT

NATIONAL PARKS, FORESTS AND SEASHORES

Acadia National Park
P.O. Box 177
Bar Harbor, ME 04609
(207) 288–3338

Cape Cod National Seashore
South Wellfleet, MA 02663
(508) 349–3785

Fire Island National Seashore
120 Laurel St.
Patchogue, NY 11772
(516) 289–4810

Gateway National Recreation Area
(including Jamaica Bay Wildlife
Refuge)
Floyd Bennett Field
Building 69
Brooklyn, NY 11234
(212) 338–3338

Green Mountain National Forest
P.O. Box 519, 151 West St.
Rutland, VT 05702
(802) 773–0300

White Mountain National Forest
P.O. Box 638
Laconia, NH 03247
(603) 528–8721

NATIONAL WILDLIFE REFUGES

Block Island NWR, RI
(See Ninigret NWR Complex)

Rachel Carson NWR
RR2 Box 751
Route 9 East
Wells, ME 04090
(207) 646–9226

Great Meadows NWR
Weir Hill Rd.
Sudbury, MA 01776
(617) 443–4661

Iroquois NWR
P.O. Box 517
Alabama, NY 14003
(716) 948–5445

Stewart B. McKinney NWR, CT
(See Ninigret NWR Complex)

Missiquoi NWR
P.O. Box 163
Swanton, VT 05488–0163
(802) 868–4781

Monomoy NWR
Morris Island
Chatham, MA 02633
(508) 945–0594

Montezuma NWR
3395 Routes 5/20 East
Seneca Falls, NY 13148
(315) 568–5987

Moosehorn NWR
Box 1077
Calais, ME 04619
(207) 454–3521

Ninigret NWR Complex
P.O. Box 307
Shoreline Plaza, Route 1A
Charlestown, RI 02813
(401) 364–9124
(Including Ninigret, Trustom Pond,
Block Island and Sachuest Point
NWRs, Rhode Island, and Salt
Meadow and Stewart B. McKinney
NWRs, Connecticut)

Parker River NWR
North Blvd., Plum Island
Newburyport, MA 01950
(508) 465–5753

Petit Manan NWR
P.O. Box 279
Milbridge, ME 04658
(207) 546–2124

Sachuest Point NWR, RI
(See Ninigret NWR Complex)

Salt Meadow NWR, CT
(See Ninigret NWR Complex)

Trustom Pond NWR, RI
(See Ninigret NWR Complex)

STATE PARKS, REFUGES AND RESERVATIONS

Adirondack Park Interpretive
 Centers
Newcomb Center
(518) 582–2000

Paul Smiths Center
P.O. Box 3000
Paul Smiths, NY 12970
(518) 327–3000

Baxter State Park
64 Balsam Dr.
Millinocket, ME 04462
(207) 723–5140

Hammonasset Beach State Park
Madison, CT 06443
(203) 245–2785

Lighthouse Point Park
2 Lighthouse Rd.
New Haven, CT 06515
(203) 787–8005

Mt. Tom State Reservation
Reservation Rd.
Holyoke, MA 01040
(413) 527–4805

Old Fort Niagara
Box 169
Youngstown, NY 14174
(716) 745–7611

Quabbin Park Visitors Center
Quabbin Administration Building
485 Ware Rd.
Belchertown, MA 01007
(413) 323–7221

Salisbury Beach State Reservation
Route 1A
Salisbury, MA 01952
(508) 462–4481

Salmon River Fish Hatchery
County Route 22
Altmar, NY 13302

Selkirk Shores State Park
Pulaski, NY 13142
(315) 298–5737

Sherwood Island State Park
Westport, CT 06880
(203) 226–6983

Wachusett Mountain State
    Reservation
P.O. Box 248
Princeton, MA 01541
(508) 464–2987

PRIVATE ORGANIZATIONS

Adirondack Mountain Club
Box 867
Lake Placid, NY 12946
(518) 523–3441

Audubon Society of
    New Hampshire
P.O. Box 528B, 3 Silk Farm Rd.
Concord, NH 03302
(603) 224–9909

Braddock Bay Raptor Research
432 Manitou Beach Rd.
Hilton, NY 14468
(716) 392–5685

Derby Hill Bird Observatory
Sage Creek Rd.
Mexico, NY 13114
(315) 963–8291 (in season only)

Green Mountain Audubon Nature
    Center
RD1 Box 189
Richmond, VT 05447
(802) 434–3068

Maine Audubon Society
118 Route 1
Falmouth, ME 04105
(207) 781–2330

Massachusetts Audubon Society
South Great Rd.
Lincoln, MA 01773
(617) 259–9500

NATIONAL AUDUBON SOCIETY AND AUDUBON SANCTUARIES

National Audubon Society
700 Broadway
New York, NY 10003

National Audubon—Vermont
    Office
Fiddler's Green, Box 9
Waitsfield, VT 05673
(802) 496–5727

Constitution Island Marsh
    Sanctuary
RFD#2, Route 9D
Garrison, NY 10524
(914) 265–3119

Northeast Audubon Center
RR1, Box 171
Sharon, CT 06069
(203) 364–0520

THE NATURE CONSERVANCY (REGIONAL, FIELD AND CHAPTER OFFICES)

Eastern Regional Office and
  Massachusetts Field Office
201 Devonshire St., 5th Floor
Boston, MA 02110
(617) 542–1908

Connecticut Chapter
55 High St.
Middletown, CT 06457
(203) 344–0716

Maine Chapter
122 Main St.
Topsham, ME 04086
(207) 729–5181

New Hampshire Field Office
2 1/2 Beacon St., Suite 6
Concord, NH 03301
(603) 224–5853

New York Field Office and Eastern
  New York Chapter
1736 Western Ave.
Albany, NY 12203
(518) 869–6959

New York chapter offices:
Adirondack Nature Conservancy
P.O. Box 188
Elizabethtown, NY 12932
(518) 873–2610

Central and Western New York
  chapters
315 Alexander St., Suite 301
Rochester, NY 14604
(716) 546–8030

Long Island Chapter
250 Lawrence Hill Rd.
Cold Spring Harbor, NY 11724
(516) 367–3225

Lower Hudson Chapter
223 Katonah Ave.
Katonah, NY 10536
(914) 232–9431

South Fork/Shelter Island Chapter
P.O. Box 2694
Sag Harbor, NY 11963
(516) 725–2936

Rhode Island Field Office
240 Hope St.
Providence, RI 02906
(401) 331–7110

Vermont Field Office
27 State St.
Montpelier, VT 05602–2934
(802) 229–4425

OTHER ENVIRONMENTAL ORGANIZATIONS

Project Puffin
National Audubon Society
HC 60, Box 102-P
Medomak, ME 04551

Scarborough Marsh Nature Center
c/o Maine Audubon Society
118 Route 1
Falmouth, ME 04105
(207) 781–2330

Stony Brook Nature Center and
 Sanctuary (Massachusetts
 Audubon Society)
North St.
Norfolk, MA 02056
(508) 528–3140

Wachusett Meadow Wildlife Sanctuary (Massachusetts Audubon
 Society)
114 Goodnow Rd.
Princeton, MA 01541
(508) 464–2712

West Quoddy Biological Research
 Station
P.O. Box 9
Lubec, ME 04652
(207) 733–8895

STATE DEPARTMENTS OF CONSERVATION, PARKS OR WILDLIFE

Connecticut Bureau of Parks and
 Recreation
165 Capitol Ave.
Hartford, CT 06106
(203) 566–2304

Connecticut Department of
 Environmental Protection
165 Capitol Ave.
Hartford, CT 06106
(203) 566–8121

Maine Bureau of Parks and
 Recreation
State House Station 22
Augusta, ME 04333
(207) 289–3821

Maine Department of Inland
 Fisheries and Wildlife
284 State St., Station 41
Augusta, ME 04333
(207) 289–3303

Maine Department of Marine
 Resources
State House Station 22
Augusta, ME 04333
(207) 289–6582

Massachusetts Division of Forests
 and Parks
100 Cambridge St.
Boston, MA 02202
(617) 727–3180

Massachusetts Trustees of
 Reservations
572 Essex St.
Beverly, MA 01915
(508) 921–1944

New Hampshire State Parks
P.O. Box 856
Concord, NH 03302

New Hampshire Fish and Game
 Department
2 Hazen Dr.
Concord, NH 03301
(603) 271–3211

New York State Parks
Empire State Plaza
Albany, NY 12238
(518) 474–0456

New York State Department of
Environmental Conservation
50 Wolf Rd.
Albany, NY 12233
(518) 457–3720

Rhode Island Department of
Environmental Management
Division of Parks and Recreation
2321 Hartford Ave.
Johnston, RI 02919

Vermont Department of Forests,
Parks and Recreation
103 S. Main St.
Waterbury, VT 05676
(802) 244–8711

Vermont Fish and Wildlife
Department
103 S. Main St.
Waterbury, VT 05676
(802) 244–7331

OTHER IMPORTANT ADDRESSES

*For U.S. Geologic Survey topo-
graphic maps:*
Eastern Mapping Center
U.S. Geologic Survey
12201 Sunrise Valley Dr.
Reston, VA 22042

For DeLorme atlases:
DeLorme Mapping Co.
P.O. Box 298
Freeport, ME 04032
(800) 227–1656

ADDITIONAL NATURE CENTERS, REFUGES AND
NATURAL HISTORY MUSEUMS

(Material for this listing was excerpted, with permission, from *Directory of Natural Science Centers,* published by the Natural Science for Youth Foundation, and *Northeast Field Guide to Environmental Education,* published by Antioch New England Graduate School.)

CONNECTICUT

Ansonia Nature and Recreation
Center
10 Deerfield Rd.
Ansonia, CT 06401
(203) 736–9360

Birdcraft Museum (Connecticut
Audubon Society)
314 Unquwa Rd.
Fairfield, CT 06430
(203) 259–6305

Bruce Museum
1 Museum Dr.
Greenwich, CT 06830
(203) 869–0376

Bushy Hill Nature Center
Box 557, Bushy Hill Rd.
Ivoryton, CT 06442
(203) 767–0848

Connecticut State Museum of
Natural History
75 N. Eagleville Rd., U-23
Storrs, CT 06269
(203) 486–4460

Darien Nature Center
P.O. Box 1603
Darien, CT 06820
(203) 655–7459

Denison Pequotsepos Nature
Center
Pequotsepos Rd.
Mystic, CT 06355
(203) 536–1216

Dinosaur State Park
West St.
Rocky Hill, CT 06067
(203) 529–8423

Fairfield Nature Center (Connecticut Audubon Society)
2325 Burr St.
Fairfield, CT 06430
(203) 259–6305

Goodwin Conservation Center
Hampton, 23 Potter Rd.
North Windham, CT 06256
(203) 455–9534

Guilford Salt Meadows Sanctuary
(National Audubon Society)
22 Quonnipaug Ln.
Guilford, CT 06437
(203) 457–1316

Holland Brook Nature Center (Connecticut Audubon Society)
1361 Main St.
Glastonbury, CT 06033
(203) 633–8402

Hungerford Outdoor Education
  Center
30 High St.
New Britain, CT 06051
(203) 255–3020

Kellogg Environmental Center
500 Hawthorne Ave.
Derby, CT 06418
(203) 734–2513

Miles Wildlife Sanctuary (National
  Audubon Society)
RR1 Box 295
West Cornwall Rd.
Sharon, CT 06069
(203) 364–5302

Mystic Marinelife Aquarium
55 Coogan Blvd.
Mystic, CT 06355
(203) 536–9631

National Environmental Education
  Center
613 Riversville Rd.
Greenwich, CT 06831
(203) 869–5272

Nature Center for Environmental
  Activities
10 Woodside Ln.
Westport, CT 06880
(203) 227–7253

New Canaan Nature Center
144 Oenoke Ridge
New Canaan, CT 06840
(203) 966–9577

Northeast Audubon Center
RR1 Box 171
Sharon, CT 06069
(203) 364–0520

Northwest Park and Nature Center
145 Lang Rd.
Windsor, CT 06095
(203) 285–1886

Peabody Museum of
  Natural History
170 Whitney Ave.
New Haven, CT 06511
(203) 432-4771

Eliot Pratt Education Center
163 Papermill Rd.
New Milford, CT 06776
(203) 355–3137

Roaring Brook Nature Center
70 Gracey Rd.
Canton, CT 06019
(203) 693–0263

Science Museum of Connecticut
950 Trout Brook Dr.
West Hartford, CT 06119
(203) 236–2961

Thames Science Center
Gallows Ln.
New London, CT 06320
(203) 442–0391

West Rock Nature Center
Wintergreen Ave.
New Haven, CT 06515
(203) 787–8016

Wethersfield Nature Center
30 Greenfield St.
Wethersfield, CT 06109
(203) 529–8611

White Memorial Conservation
    Center
80 Whitehall Rd.
Litchfield, CT 06759
(203) 567–0857

Woodcock Nature Center
50 Deer Run Rd.
Wilton, CT 06897
(203) 762–7280

MAINE

Augusta Nature Education Center
4 Brooklawn Ave.
Augusta, ME 04330
(207) 622–7227

Gray Visitors Center
Gray, ME 04039
(207) 657–4977

Children's Museum of Maine
746 Steven's Ave.
Portland, ME 04103
(207) 797–5484

Maine Department of
    Marine Resources Aquarium
McKown Point
West Boothbay Harbor, ME 04575
(207) 633–5572

Mount Desert Oceanarium
Clark Point Rd., Box 696
Southwest Harbor, ME 04679
(207) 244–7330

Natural History Museum of the
    College of the Atlantic
105 Eden St.
Bar Harbor, ME 04609
(207) 288–5015

Thorncrag Bird Sanctuary
P.O. Box 3172
Lewiston, ME 04243
(207) 782–5238

Todd Wildlife Sanctuary (National
    Audubon Society)
Keene Neck Rd.
Medomak, ME 04551
(207) 529–5148

Wells National Estuarine
    Research Reserve
RR2 Box 806
Wells, ME 04090
(207) 646–1555

MASSACHUSETTS

Arcadia Nature Center and Wild-
    life Sanctuary (Massachusetts
    Audubon Society)
127 Coombs Rd.
Easthampton, MA 01027
(413) 584–3009

The Berkshire Museum
39 South St.
Pittsfield, MA 01201
(413) 443–7171

Berkshire Wildlife Sanctuaries
    (Massachusetts Audubon Society)
472 W. Mountain Rd.
Lenox, MA 01240
(413) 637–0320
(Includes Pleasant Valley and
Canoe Meadows)

Blue Hills Trailside Museum
1904 Canton Ave.
Milton, MA 02186
(617) 333–0690

Broadmoor Wildlife Sanctuary
    (Massachusetts Audubon Society)
280 Eliot St.
Natick, MA 01760
(508) 655–2296

Buck Hill Conservation Center
RR1 Box 265
McCormick, MA 01562
(508) 885–2595

Cape Cod Museum of Natural History
896 Main St., Route 6-A
Brewster, MA 02631
(508) 896–3867

Caratunk Wildlife Refuge
301 Brown Ave.
Seekonk, MA 02771
(508) 761–8230

Felix Neck Wildlife Sanctuary
    (Massachusetts Audubon Society)
Box 494
Vineyard Haven, MA 02568
(508) 627–4850

Fisher Museum at Harvard Forest
Route 32
Petersham, MA 01366
(508) 724–3302

Garden in the Woods
Hemenway Rd.
Framingham, MA 01701
(508) 877–7630

Green Briar Nature Center
6 Discovery Hill Rd.
East Sandwich, MA 02537
(508) 888–6870

Ipswich River Wildlife Sanctuary
87 Perkins Row
Topsfield, MA 01983
(508) 887–9264

Laughing Brook Education Center
    and Wildlife Sanctuary
789 Main St.
Hampden, MA 01036
(413) 566–8034

Lloyd Center for Environmental
    Studies
430 Potomska Rd.
South Dartmouth, MA 02748
(508) 990–0505

Manomet Bird Observatory
Box 936
Manomet, MA 02345
(508) 224–6521

Maria Mitchell Science Museum
2 Vestal St.
Nantucket, MA 02554
(508) 228–9198

Moose Hill Wildlife Sanctuary
293 Moose Hill St.
Sharon, MA 02067
(617) 784–5691

National Marine Fisheries Service
    Aquarium
Water and Albatross Sts.
Woods Hole, MA 02543
(508) 548–7684

New Alchemy Institute
237 Hatchville Rd.
East Falmouth, MA 02536
(508) 564–6301

New England Aquarium
Central Wharf
Boston, MA 02110
(617) 973–5200

New England Science Center
222 Harrington Way
Worcester, MA 01604
(508) 791–9211

Northfield Mountain Recreation
    and Environmental Center
RR2 Box 117
Northfield, MA 01360
(413) 659–3714

Pratt Museum of Natural History
Amherst College
Amherst, MA 01002
(413) 542–2165

South Shore Natural Science Center
Jacobs Ln., P.O. Box 429
Norwell, MA 02061
(617) 659–2559

South Shore Wildlife Sanctuaries
    (Massachucetts Audubon Society)
2000 Main St.
Marshfield, MA 02050
(617) 837–9400

Springfield Science Museum
236 State St.
Springfield, MA 01103
(413) 733–1194

The Trustees of Reservations
572 Essex St.
Beverly, MA 01915
(508) 921–1944
(Owns 71 properties of natural or
historic value, including Bartholomew's Cobble, all open to public)

Wellfleet Bay Wildlife Sanctuary
(Massachusetts Audubon Society)
P.O. Box 236, Off West Rd.
South Wellfleet, MA 02663
(508) 349–2615

NEW HAMPSHIRE
Beaver Brook
117 Ridge Rd.
Hollis, NH 03049
(603) 465–7787

Bretzfelder Memorial Park
Prospect St.
Bethlehem, NH 03574
(603) 869–2683

Harris Center for Conservation
    Education
King's Hwy.
Hancock, NH 03449
(603) 525–4073

Little Nature Museum
59 Boyce Rd.
Weare, NH 03281
(603) 529–7180

Paradise Point Nature Center (New
    Hampshire Audubon Society)
North Shore Rd.
East Hebron, NH 03232
(603) 744–3516

Pinkham Notch Center
Appalachian Mountain Club
Pinkham Notch
Gorham, NH 03581
(603) 466–2721

Seacoast Science Center
Kingman Farm
Durham, NH 03824
(603) 749–7565

Science Center of New Hampshire
    at Squam Lake
Box 173
Holderness, NH 03245
(603) 968–7194

Stonedam Island Wildlife Reserve
Lakes Regional Conservation Trust
Box 1097
Meredith, NH 03253
(603) 279–7278

Tin Mountain Conservation Center
P.O. Box 1170
Conway, NH 03818
(603) 447–6991

NEW YORK
Alley Pond Environmental Center
228-06 Northern Blvd.
Douglastown, NY 11363-1890
(718) 229–4000

Aquarium of Niagara Falls
701 Whirlpool St.
Niagara Falls, NY 14301
(716) 285–3575

Beaver Lake Nature Center
E. Mud Lake Rd.
Baldwinsville, NY 13027
(315) 638–2519

Beaver Meadow Audubon Center
1610 Welch Rd.
North Java, NY 14113–9713
(716) 457–3228

Brooklyn Botanic Garden
1000 Washington Ave.
Brooklyn, NY 11225
(718) 622–4433

Brooklyn Children's Museum
145 Brooklyn Ave.
Brooklyn, NY 11231
(718) 735–4400

Buttercup Farm Sanctuary
   (National Audubon Society)
Route 82
Stanfordville, NY 12581
(914) 868–1361

Cayuga Nature Center
1420 Taughannock Blvd.
Ithaca, NY 14850
(607) 273–6260

Clay Pit Ponds State Park Reserve
83 Nielsen Ave.
Staten Island, NY 10309
(718) 967–1976

Cold Spring Harbor Fish Hatchery
   and Aquarium
P.O. Box 535, Route 25A
Cold Spring Harbor, NY 11724
(516) 692–6768

Cornell Laboratory of Ornithology
159 Sapsucker Woods Rd.
Ithaca, NY 14850
(607) 254–2420

Cummings Nature Center
   (Rochester Museum and
   Science Center)
6472 Gulick Rd.
Naples, NY 14512
(716) 374–6160

Environmental Centers of Setauket-
   Smithtown
Box 257
62 Eckernkamp Dr.
Smithtown, NY 11788
(516) 979–6344

Finch Hollow Nature Center
1428 Oakdale Rd.
Johnson City, NY 13790
(607) 729–4231

Five Rivers Environmental
   Education Center
Game Farm Rd.
Delmar, NY 12054
(518) 453–1896

Frost Valley Environmental
Education Center
Box 97
Oliverea, NY 12462
(914) 985–2291

Garvies Point Museum and
Preserve
Barry Dr.
Glen Cove, NY 11542
(516) 671–0300

Great Neck Outdoor Education
Center
345 Lakeville Rd.
Great Neck, NY 11020
(516) 773–1463

Greenburg Nature Center
Dromore Rd.
Scarsdale, NY 10583
(914) 723–3470

Hicksville Gregory Museum
Heitz Place
Hicksville, NY 11801
(516) 822–7505

Hoyt Farm Park-Preserve
New Hwy.
Commack, NY 11725
(516) 543–7804

George Landis Arboretum
Box 186, Lape Rd.
Esperance, NY 12066
(518) 875–6935

Mendon Ponds Visitors' Center
Clover and Pond Rds.
Honeoye Falls, NY 14472
(716) 334–3780

Minna Anthony Common Nature
Center
Wellesley Island State Park
RD1 Box W437
Alexandria Bay, NY 13607
(315) 482–2479

Museum of the Hudson Highlands
The Blvd.
Cornwall-on-Hudson, NY 12520
(914) 534–7781

Pember Museum of Natural History
and Hebron Nature Preserve
33 W. Main St.
Granville, NY 12832
(518) 642–1515

Roger Tory Peterson Nature
Center
Jamestown Audubon Society
RD5, Riverside Rd.
Jamestown, NY 14701
(716) 569–2345

Petrified Creature Museum of
Natural History
RD2, Route 20
Richfield Springs, NY 13439
(315) 858-2868

Wilson M. Powell Wildlife
Sanctuary
Alan Devoe Bird Club
P.O. Box 20
Chatham, NY 12037

Prospect Park Environmental Center
The Tennis House, Prospect Park
Brooklyn, NY 11215
(718) 788–8500

Queens Botanical Garden
43–50 Main St.
Flushing, NY 11355
(718) 886–3800

Rensselaer County Junior Museum
282 Fifth Ave.
Troy, NY 12182
(518) 235–2120

Rockland Lake Nature Center
Palisades Interstate Park Commission
Bear Mountain, NY 10911
(914) 268–2503

Rogers Environmental Education
    Center
P.O. Box 716, Route 80
West Sherburne, NY 13460–0716
(607) 674–4017

Theodore Roosevelt Sanctuary
    (National Audubon Society)
134 Cove Rd.
Oyster Bay, NY 11771
(516) 922–3200

Rye Nature Center
873 Boston Post Rd.
P.O. Box 435
Rye, NY 10580
(914) 967–1549

Sands Point Preserve
95 Middleneck Rd.
Port Washington, NY 11050
(516) 883–1610

Schoellkopf Geological Museum
Niagara Frontier State Parks
Prospect Park Niagara Reservation
Niagara Falls, NY 14303

Scully Sanctuary (National
    Audubon Society)
306 South Bay Ave.
Islip, NY 11751
(516) 277–4289

Seneca Park Zoo
2222 St. Paul St.
Rochester, NY 14621–1097
(716) 266–6846

Stony Kill Farm Environmental
    Education Center
Route 9D
Wappingers Falls, NY 12590
(914) 831–8780

Tackapausha Museum and Preserve
Washington Ave.
Seaford, NY 11783
(516) 785–2802

Tanglewood Community Nature
    Center
Box 117, West Hill Rd.
Elmira, NY 14902
(607) 732–6060

Teatown Lake Reservation
Spring Valley Rd.
Ossining, NY 10562
(914) 762–2912

Tifft Nature Preserve
1200 Fuhrmann Blvd.
Buffalo, NY 14203
(716) 896–5200

Trailside Museums and Zoo
PIPC Administration Building
Bear Mountain, NY 10911–0427
(914) 786-2701

Utica Zoo
Steele Hill Rd.
Utica, NY 13501
(315) 738–0472

Waterman Conservation Education
  Center
Box 288, Hilton Rd.
Apalachin, NY 13732
(607) 625–2221

RHODE ISLAND
Audubon Society of Rhode Island
12 Sanderson Rd.
Smithfield, RI 02917
(401) 231–6446

Kimball Wildlife Refuge (Audubon
  Society of Rhode Island)
Watchaug Pond, P.O. Box 908
Charlestown, RI 02813

Norman Bird Sanctuary
583 Third Beach Rd.
Middletown, RI 02840
(401) 846–2577

Parker Woodland Wildlife Refuge
(Audubon Society of Rhode Island)
Maple Valley Rd.
Coventry, RI 02827
(401) 397–4474

Roger Williams Park Museum of
  Natural History
Roger Williams Park
Providence, RI 02905
(401) 785–9451

Ruecker Wildlife Refuge (Audubon
  Society of Rhode Island)
Sapowet Ave.
Tiverton, RI 02878

VERMONT
Discovery Museum
51 Park St.
Essex Junction, VT 05452
(802) 878–8687

Fairbanks Museum and
  Planetarium
Main and Prospect Sts.
St. Johnsbury, VT 05819
(802) 748–2372

Merck Forest and Farmland Center
P.O. Box 86, Route 315
Rupert, VT 05768
(802) 394–7836

Montshire Museum
P.O. Box 770
Norwich, VT 05055
(802) 649–2200

Vermont Institute of Natural
  Science
P.O. Box 86, Churchill Rd.
Woodstock, VT 05091
(802) 457–2779

CONNECTICUT
Barkhamsted
Edwin Way Teale Trail Wood
Greenwich-Stamford
Hartford
Litchfield Hills
Lakeville-Sharon
New Haven
New London
Old Lyme-Saybrook
Oxford
Quinnipiac Valley
Salmon River
Storrs
Stratford-Milford
Westport
Woodbury-Roxbury

MAINE
Augusta
Bangor-Bucksport
Bath-Phippsburg-Georgetown
Biddeford-Kennebunkport
Calais
Dover-Foxcroft
Eastport
Farmington
Greater Portland
Lewiston-Auburn
Monhegan Island
Moose Island-Jonesport
Mount Desert Island
Misery Township
Orono-Old Town
Pemaquid-Damariscotta
Presque Isle
Schoodic Point
Sweden
Thomaston-Rockland
Waterville
York County

MASSACHUSETTS
Andover
Athol
Buzzards Bay
Cape Ann
Cape Cod
Central Berkshire
Cobble Mountain
Concord
Greater Boston
Greenfield
Marshfield
Martha's Vineyard
Mid-Cape Cod
Nantucket
New Bedford
Newburyport
Northampton
Northern Berkshire
Plymouth
Quabbin
Quincy
Stellwagen Bank
Springfield
Taunton-Middleboro
Tuckernuck Islands
Uxbridge, MA-RI
Westminster
Worcester

NEW HAMPSHIRE
Baker Valley
Coastal New Hampshire
Concord
Errol-Umbagog
Hanover, NH - Norwich, VT
Keene
Laconia-New Hampton
Lake Sunapee
Lee-Durham
Nashua-Hollis
North Conway
Peterborough-Hancock
Pittsburg

NEW YORK
Albany County
Beaver Meadow
Binghamton
Brooklyn
Bronx-Westchester Region
Buffalo, NY-ON
Captree
Catskill-Coxsackie
Central Cayuga County
Central Suffolk County
Chatham
Clinton
Conesus-Hemlock-Honeoye Lakes
Cortland
Dunkirk-Fredonia
Dutchess County
Eastern Orange County
Elizabethtown
Elmira
Fort Plain
Geneva
Hamburg-East Aurora
Herkimer
Hudson Falls
Ithaca
Jamestown
Johnstown-Gloversville
Letchworth-Silver Lake
Massena, NY - Cornwall, ON

Mohonk Lake-Ashokan Reservoir
Montauk
Montezuma
Monticello
Northern Nassau County
Oak Orchard Swamp
Old Forge
Oneida
Oneonta
Orient
Oswego-Fulton
Owego
Pawling (Hidden Valley), NY-CT
Peekskill
Plattsburg
Putnam County
Queens
Quogue-Watermill
Rochester
Rockland County
Rome
Salem
St. Bonaventure
Saranac Lake
Saratoga Spa State Park
Schenectady
Scio
Sherburne
Skaneateles
Smithtown, Long Island
Southern Nassau County
Southern Rensselaer County
Staten Island
Syracuse
Troy
Watertown
Watkins Glen

RHODE ISLAND
Block Island
Newport County, RI-MA
South Kingston

VERMONT
Bennington
Brattleboro
Burlington
Champlain Islands-St. Albans
Craftsbury-Greensboro
Ferrisburg
Hinesburg
Island Pond
Middlebury
Plainfield
Rutland
Saxton's River
Springfield
Winhall
Woodstock

SELECTED BIBLIOGRAPHY

Backcountry Publications (various authors). *Fifty Hikes in ...* series. Woodstock, Vermont.

Bent, Arthur Cleveland. *Life Histories of North American Birds of Prey,* Part 2. New York: Dover Publications, 1961.

Billings, Gene. *Birds of Prey in Connecticut.* Gene Billings, 1990.

Bonney, Richard E. Jr. "Iron Heads" (Research and Review), *Living Bird Quarterly,* Vol. 5 (Summer 1986) 19.

Clark, William S., and Brian K. Wheeler. *Hawks.* Boston: Houghton Mifflin Co., 1987.

"The Changing Seasons," *American Birds* Vols. 37–46 (January/February 1983–Fall 1992).

Cobb, Boughton. *A Field Guide to the Ferns and Their Related Families.* Boston: Houghton Mifflin Co., 1963.

Conat, Roger and Joseph T. Collins. *Reptiles and Amphibians of Eastern and Central North America,* Third Edition. Boston: Houghton Mifflin Co., 1991.

DeBlieu, Jan. *Meant to Be Wild.* Golden, CO: Fulcrum Publishing, 1991.

DiNunzio, Michael G. *Adirondack Wildguide: A Natural History of the Adirondack Park.* Elizabethtown, NY: Adirondack Conservancy and Adirondack Council, 1984.

"Directory of Pelagic Birding Trips in North America." *Winging It,* Vol. 4, No. 1, January 1992.

Drennan, Susan Roney. *Where to Find Birds in New York State.* Syracuse: NY; Syracuse University Press, 1981.

Dunne, Pete, David Sibley and Clay Sutton. *Hawks in Flight.* Boston: Houghton Mifflin Co., 1988.

Ellison, Walter G. *A Guide to Bird Finding in Vermont.* Woodstock, VT: Vermont Institute of Natural Science, 1983.

Erlich, Paul, David S. Dobkin and Darryl Wheye. *The Birder's Handbook.* New York: Simon & Schuster, 1988.

Gosner, Kenneth L. *A Field Guide to the Atlantic Seashore.* Boston: Houghton Mifflin Co., 1978.

Green Mountain Club. *Guide Book of the Long Trail,* 24th edition. Montpelier, Vermont, 1990.

Green Mountain Club. *Hiker's Guide to Vermont,* third edition. Montpelier, Vermont, 1990.

Hale, Sue and Jeff Schwartz, editors. *The Northeast Field Guide to Environmental Education.* Keene, New Hampshire: Antioch New England Graduate School, 1991.

Hamilton, W.J., and J.O. Whitaker. *Mammals of the Eastern United States.* Ithaca, NY: Cornell University Press, 1979.

Harrison, Peter. *Seabirds: An Identification Guide.* Boston: Houghton Mifflin Co., 1983.

Hawk Migration Studies, *Hawk Migration Association of North America.* Vols. 12–17 (1987–1992).

Hayman, Peter, John Marchant and Tony Prater. *Shorebirds: An Identification Guide.* Boston: Houghton Mifflin Co., 1986.

Heintzelman, Donald S. *A Guide to Hawk Watching in North America.* University Park, PA: Pennsylvania State University Press, 1979.

Hill, Ruth Ann. *Maine Forever.* Topsham, ME: Maine Chapter, The Nature Conservancy, 1989.

Hogan, Barbara. "Please, Watch Your Step," *The Conservationist* (May/June 1992) 50–53.

Hulbert, Philip, Daniel Zielinski and Eileen Stegemann. "The Salmon of New York," *The Conservationist* (November/December 1989) 24–31.

Johnsgard, Paul A. *A Guide to North American Waterfowl*. Bloomington, IN: Indiana University Press, 1979.

────── . *Hawks, Eagles and Falcons of North America*. Washington: Smithsonian Institution Press, 1990.

Katona, Steven K., Valerie Rough and David T. Richardson. *A Field Guide to the Whales, Porpoises and Seals of the Gulf of Maine and Eastern Canada*, Third Edition. New York: Charles Scribner's Sons, 1983.

Kaufman, Kenn. *Advanced Birding*. Boston: Houghton Mifflin Co., 1990.

Kricher, John C., and Gordon Morrison. *Eastern Forests*. Boston: Houghton Mifflin Co., 1988.

Kulik, Stephen, Pete Salmansohn, Matthew Schmidt and Heidi Welch. *The Audubon Society Field Guide to the Natural Places of the Northeast: Coastal*. New York: Pantheon Books, 1984.

────── . *The Audubon Society Field Guide to the Natural Places of the Northeast: Inland*. New York: Pantheon Books, 1984.

Long, M.E. "Secrets of Animal Navigation," *National Geographic*, Vol. 179 (June 1991) 70-99.

Madge, Steve and Hilary Burn. W*aterfowl*. Boston: Houghton Mifflin Co., 1988.

Mahan, John and Ann Mahan. "Capture the Aurora," *Outdoor Photographer*, Vol. 9 (March 1993) 50–76.

McClane, A.J. *McClane's Field Guide to Freshwater Fishes of North America*. New York: Holt, Rinehart and Winston, 1974.

────── . *McClane's Field Guide to Saltwater Fishes of North America*. New York: Holt, Rinehart and Winston, 1974.

McIntyre, Judith W. "Moonlight Cantata," *Natural History* (May 1992) 56–57.

McMartin, Barbara. *Discover the Adirondack High Peaks*. Woodstock, Vermont: Backcountry Publications, 1989.

Murie, Olaus J. *A Field Guide to Animal Tracks.* Boston: Houghton Mifflin Co. 1974.

Nadareski, Christopher A., and Barbara Allen Loucks. "Watching the Wanderer," *The Conservationist* (September/October 1992) 34–43.

National Geographic Society. *Field Guide to the Birds of North America.* Washington, D.C., 1983.

Nelson, Bryan. *Seabirds: The Biology and Ecology.* London: Hamlyn Publishing Group, 1979.

Newcomb, Lawrence. *Newcomb's Wildflower Guide.* Boston: Little, Brown and Co., 1977.

Nicholson, Thomas D. "The Northern Lights Head South," *Natural History* (November 1989) 104–108.

"The 92nd Christmas Bird Count." *American Birds,* Vol. 44, No. 4.

Nowak, Ronald M. *Walker's Mammals of the World,* Fifth Edition. Baltimore, MD: John Hopkins University Press, 1991.

Nye, Peter. "A Second Chance for Our National Symbol," *The Conservationist* (July/August 1990) 16–23.

——— . "Winter Eagles," *The Conservationist* (January/February 1992) 2–7.

——— . "Return of a Native," *Natural History* (May 1992) 54–55.

Page, Lawrence M., and Brooks M. Burr. *Freshwater Fishes.* Boston: Houghton Mifflin Co., 1991.

Pasachoff, Jay M., and Donald H. Menzel. *Stars and Planets.* Boston: Houghton Mifflin Co., 1992.

Peattie, Donald Culross. *A Natural History of Trees of Eastern and Central North America.* Boston: Houghton Mifflin Co., 1948.

Peterson, Roger T. *A Field Guide to the Birds of Eastern and Central North America,* fourth edition. Boston: Houghton Mifflin Co., 1980.

Peterson, Roger T. *A Field Guide to Bird Songs of Eastern and Central North America* (recording), second edition. Ithaca, New York: Cornell University Laboratory of Ornithology, 1983

Peterson, Roger T., and Margaret McKenny. *A Field Guide to Wildflowers of Northeastern and Northcentral North America*. Boston: Houghton Mifflin Co., 1968.

Petrides, George A. *Eastern Trees*. Boston: Houghton Mifflin Co., 1988.

Pettingill, Olin Sewall. *A Guide to Bird Finding East of the Mississippi*. New York: Oxford University Press, 1977.

Pierson, Elizabeth Cary, and Jan Erik Pierson. *A Birder's Guide to the Coast of Maine*. Camden, ME: Down East Books, 1981.

Rezendes, Paul. *Tracking and the Art of Seeing*. Charlotte, VT: Camden House Publishing, 1992.

Riley, Laura and William Riley. *Guide to the National Wildlife Refuges*. New York: Anchor Press, 1979.

Rudnicky, James L. "The New York Botanical Garden Forest—An Urban Natural Area in the Bronx," *The Conservationist* (May/June 1989) 46–49.

Saunders, D. Andrew. *Adirondack Mammals*. State University of New York College of Environmental Science and Forestry.

Touvell, Dick and Owen D. Winters, editors. *Directory of Natural Science Centers*. Rosewell, Georgia: Natural Science for Youth Foundation, 1990.

Turner, John. "Preserving the Plains at Edgewood," *The Conservationist* (May/June 1990) 20–25.

Tyning, Thomas F. *A Guide to Amphibians and Reptiles*. Boston: Little, Brown, 1990.

Ursin, Michael J. *A Guide to Fishes of the Temperate Atlantic Coast*. New York: E.P. Dutton, 1977.

Walcott, Charles. "The Mystery of Jersey Hill and Other Stories," *Birdscope*, Vol. 4 (Spring/Summer 1990) 1–3.

Walton, Richard K. *Bird Finding in New England*. Boston: David R. Godine, Publisher, Inc., 1988.

Welty, Joel C. *The Life of Birds*. Philadelphia: W.B. Saunders, 1982.

INDEX

NOTE: Boldfaced entries denote directions.

ABOUT THE AUTHOR

Photo: Rick Walters

Scott Weidensaul is the author of more than a dozen books on natural history, including *American Wildlife, A Kid's First Book of Bird-watching and The Birder's Miscellany*. For thirteen years, he wrote and illustrated an award-winning newspaper column on the outdoors, and he is currently outdoor editor for the Harrisburg, Pennsylvania *Patriot-News*. A bird bander and avid naturalist, he is also a widely published photographer and artist. He lives near Schuylkill Haven, in the mountains of eastern Pennsylvania.